Drugs and Society

Drugs and Society

U.S. Public Policy

Edited by
Jefferson M. Fish

ROWMAN & LITTLEFIELD PUBLISHERS, INC.
Lanham • Boulder • New York • Toronto • Oxford

ROWMAN & LITTLEFIELD PUBLISHERS, INC.

Published in the United States of America
by Rowman & Littlefield Publishers, Inc.
A wholly owned subsidiary of The Rowman & Littlefield Publishing Group, Inc.
4501 Forbes Boulevard, Suite 200, Lanham, Maryland 20706
www.rowmanlittlefield.com

PO Box 317
Oxford
OX2 9RU, UK

British Library Cataloguing in Publication Information Available

Library of Congress Cataloging-in-Publication Data

Drugs and society : U.S. public policy / edited by Jefferson M. Fish
    p. cm.
    Includes bibliographical references and index.
    ISBN 0-7425-4244-0 (cloth : alk. paper) — ISBN 0-7425-4245-9 (pbk. : alk. paper)
    1. Drug abuse—Government policy—United States. 2. Narcotics, Control of—United
States. 3. Narcotics and crime—United States. 4. Substance abuse—Prevention—United
States. 5. Drug legalization—United States. I. Fish, Jefferson M.
    HV5835.D813 2005
    362.29'1561'0973—dc22   2005005099

Printed in the United States of America

∞™ The paper used in this publication meets the minimum requirements of American
National Standard for Information Sciences—Permanence of Paper for Printed Library
Materials, ANSI/NISO Z39.48-1992.

To the people and government of the Netherlands, who have demonstrated
that a rational and effective drug policy is possible here and now

Contents

Foreword

As a parent, husband, entrepreneur, athlete, adventurer, and former governor of New Mexico, I believe that people should refrain from drinking alcohol, smoking cigarettes, and doing drugs. They should also limit their intake of caffeine and sugar. I believe that eating a balanced diet and getting moderate exercise have enormous health benefits.

Public policy should promote healthy lifestyles—but not by coercion. A major reason I ran for governor of New Mexico was my conviction that leaders should question our nation's counterproductive War on Drugs and offer alternatives. The black market in adulterated illegal drugs; the mass incarceration of drug addicts, drug mules, and other minor offenders; the confiscation of property; and the loss of constitutional rights—all cause more damage than the drugs themselves.

Conventional wisdom says that even mentioning "legalization" equals political suicide. But when I spoke out during my second term as governor of New Mexico, even many drug war supporters agreed it was time for rational public discussion. I learned that decades of "just saying no" could be changed with logic, facts, and reason. I worked hard to educate people in the state on drug reform, taking every opportunity to speak to groups statewide. I started a gigantic debate that I view as hugely successful. Based on my experience, I would encourage people who want to improve our drug policy to get informed and talk to others. Start your own debate with friends and family.

The drug problem has a solution. We should end drug prohibition. It did not work with alcohol, and it's not working with drugs. As a society, we should adopt public policies that promote the reduction of death, disease, crime, and corruption. Drug policy should put more resources into education and more money into treatment for those who want it. Half the money spent by law enforcement, the courts, and the prisons is drug-prohibition related. As a result, we are arresting 1.6 million people a year, with drugs being more readily available, more potent, and cheaper than ever before. It is time to change public policy. To do the same thing over and over again expecting different results is the definition of insanity.

Marijuana should be legalized. Harder-drug use should be viewed as a health problem rather than a criminal justice problem. When I say that marijuana should be legal, it will never be legal to smoke marijuana, become impaired, and get behind the wheel of a car. It will never be legal to sell marijuana to children. Legalization comes with control, regulation, and taxation, similar to the controls placed on alcohol. I believe that 90 percent of the drug problem in this country today is prohibition related, not use related. Changing our policy would not discount the problems with abuse but would make them our focus. We need policies aimed at reducing the abuse of drugs, and we have learned that punishing drug use will not get us there.

Drugs and Society is just the kind of book we need to help Americans understand how we got into the current morass, what went wrong, and how we can fix it. Jefferson Fish has brought together leading thinkers from the social sciences, law, and public policy to present the issues and offer solutions in one compact, readable volume. The book shows us that the mistake we made during alcohol prohibition—creating a huge black market, crime, and corruption—is the same mistake we have been making for decades with our drug policy. When we changed our alcohol policy from prohibition to regulation, matters got much better, and that can happen if we do the same thing with drug prohibition.

We need to think carefully about what to do instead of filling up our prisons with drug addicts. We have the highest incarceration rate in the world, and the money we spend on locking people up is taken away from education and health. People who are educated, healthy, and self-supporting do not need to escape from their misery via drug abuse. This book presents a lot of thought-provoking information. Not all drugs are the same. If we made marijuana legal for adults and regulated and taxed it—the way we do for alcohol and cigarettes—we could use that money for prevention, education, and treatment. But that does not mean we would have to have the same policy for heroin as for marijuana. *Drugs and Society* helps us to distinguish between different substances and think about policy alternatives.

We need to protect individual freedom and keep the government out of people's private lives. Even when people make bad choices, they should be left alone, as long as they do not harm others. When given good information, most people will make wise choices. That is why truthful drug education—as opposed to scare tactics that backfire when people find out they have been misled—is so important.

We need to think more about promoting healthy behavior instead of punishing unhealthy behavior. I believe that taking on challenges—both personal and physical—makes us stronger. That is why I think that a public health approach to drug policy makes more sense than a criminal justice approach. That is why I took the risk of challenging the conventional wisdom on drug policy. And that is why, after returning to private life, I climbed Mount Everest.

This is no time for pessimism. We can make change happen. By working together, we *can* change our drug policy.

—Gary E. Johnson

Preface

American drug policy is a mess.

For decades, we have been spending tens of billions of dollars per year and incarcerating hundreds of thousands of individuals, with few positive results to show for the economic and social costs.

When a policy does not work, there are two options — do more of the same or try something different. We have spent more and more money, locked up more and more people, and — as we discovered with the prohibition of alcohol — the cure is worse than the disease. It is time to think seriously about doing something different.

Prominent critics of all political persuasions have been calling for a change of course. Their unity at a time of deep political rifts calls attention to an underlying theme of freedom versus social control that cuts across party lines and political philosophies. Stated simply, civil-liberties liberals and libertarian conservatives believe that the government has no business interfering with adults who use psychoactive substances in private. In contrast, social liberals want to save people from drugs (lock them up for their own good and prevent them from influencing others) and are allied with social conservatives who want to punish people for using drugs (lock them up because they are bad people).

If locking them up does not work, and we want to do something different, then it would be a good idea to think through the issues before taking action; that is what this book is about. In discussing alternative policies, *Drugs and Society* considers ways of limiting or ending the involvement of the criminal-justice system in people's use of psychoactive substances. For at least some substances at some dosage levels in some quantities, as well as for substance-related paraphernalia, the government should simply leave responsible adults alone. This book examines, from multiple perspectives, a variety of proposals for achieving this end and discusses their likely consequences.

Drugs and Society is organized in three parts: Part I—Historical Background, Part II—Conceptual Background, and Part III—Policy Considerations. Parts I and II provide a historical, methodological, and philosophical foundation for considering the drug policy issues and options dealt with in Part III. The latter begins with a discussion of substantive issues that need to be considered before drafting legislation and with an examination of actual laws that have been proposed. The last four chapters examine a variety of more general suggestions and models. These include both rights-based and public health proposals and vary from rather limited plans to quite comprehensive ones.

Drugs and Society is written for students and concerned citizens, as well as for health professionals, social scientists, legislators, judges, lawyers, and others involved with law enforcement and criminal justice. It aims at helping individuals to work out their own positions on drug policy by deciding for themselves which evidence or arguments they find most compelling.

In order for the book to provide adequate breadth of coverage, I have included chapters by leading scholars and practitioners from a wide variety of fields. These include economics, history, law (a law professor, policy analysts, and practicing attorneys, as well as scholars in two other fields who also hold law degrees), philosophy, political science, psychology, and sociology.

As part of the first chapter, I have attempted to summarize some of the central points of each subsequent one, as well as to indicate how the various chapters fit into the overall organization of the book. In addition, I have, in a few instances, discussed, reacted to, or amplified ideas raised by the authors in ways that differ from or go beyond the authors' presentations. In those instances where I have introduced my own commentary, I have tried to make clear that I was doing so.

Editing such a wide-ranging volume has been a fascinating intellectual experience, but it also revealed a minor technical difficulty—each discipline has its own stylistic practices, especially with regard to text-related notes and the listing of references. Because any given chapter will most likely be cited, and its references consulted, primarily by those in the author's (or authors') field, I made the editorial decision to allow authors to follow their own disciplines' stylistic practices. In apologizing to readers for this lack of editorial standardization, I take heart in Oscar Wilde's observation, "Consistency is the last refuge of the unimaginative," but hasten to add that consistency remains a virtue of the internal logic of each chapter.

It has been a privilege to edit this book and to work with dedicated colleagues from a variety of fields to bring the project to fruition. I want to take this opportunity to express to them my gratitude and admiration not only for their professional competence but for their personal courage in working for long overdue, but belligerently resisted, policy changes. Their chapters are what the First Amendment is all about. Their contributions are good citizenship in action.

* * * * *

The author of a book usually devotes some space to thanking those whose assistance made the work a better one, but this is an edited book, so the contributions of chapter authors *are* the book. Hence, I must begin by expressing once again my gratitude to them for joining me in this project. They are all extremely busy people, and they put up with my frequent inquiries, reminders, and feedback with remarkably good humor. My apologies go out to the many people I do not know whose competing needs must have been put on hold so that chapter authors could do their part for this book.

Research reductions in my teaching load at St. John's University have provided me with some badly needed time to work on this and other contemporaneous projects, and my research assistants, Emma Cruz and Harrald Magny, were also of help.

I have benefited from the advice of others at all stages of the project, and most of their names appear below under various rubrics; however, responsibility for the book's overall organization and conception, for better or worse, remains with me. As an editor, I have deliberately included chapters that disagree with one another, or with me, or which formulate issues differently from the way I would. The point of this book is to encourage debate about drug policy alternatives, and I have tried to do so between its covers as well.

I am a member of the Board of Directors of Partnership for Responsible Drug Information (PRDI), an organization aimed at encouraging informed discussion of drug policy issues. (I should mention that PRDI does not sponsor legalization or any other specific drug policy—its purpose is to stimulate thought, analysis, and consideration of all alternatives. Its slogan could well be, "Just say 'know'.") I would like to thank two other members of the board of directors who contributed chapters to this book: Mary M. Cleveland and Stanley Neustadter.

I am grateful to those friends and colleagues from various disciplines who made helpful suggestions, commented on my parts of the book or on the entire manuscript, or reviewed versions of one or more chapters, including Charles Adler, Mary M. Cleveland, Robert Ghiradella, Jeremy Haritos, Bart Majoor, Dolores Newton, David Sprintzen, and Lynn Zimmer. (Charles Adler and Mary M. Cleveland are also members of the board of directors of PRDI.)

Finally, I would like to thank Christopher Anzalone, my editor at Rowman & Littlefield Publishers, for his encouragement of this project.

It was difficult for me not to dedicate this book to my wife, Dolores Newton. Her support and encouragement have, as always, made the burden lighter and the journey more interesting; she remains my beloved and lifelong traveling companion.

1

Rethinking U.S. Drug Policy

Jefferson M. Fish

Increasing numbers of people have become convinced that the policy of drug prohibition has failed, just as alcohol prohibition failed in the last century. The question is now, as it was then, What to do? It is an important question, deserving serious consideration from multiple perspectives so that informed people can take remedial action.

Trenchant critiques of American drug policy have accumulated over the last few decades, and those who want to dip into the literature might begin with *Licit and Illicit Drugs* by Edward Brecher and the Editors of Consumer Reports (1972) or Ethan Nadelmann's article, "Drug Prohibition in the United States" in *Science* (1989). In the 1990s, Steven Duke and Albert Gross's *America's Longest War* (1994) and Dan Baum's *Smoke and Mirrors* (1996) showed how the United States, by ever more vigorously pursuing a counterproductive policy, has managed to create for itself an unprecedented drug, crime, corruption, civil-liberties, AIDS, and foreign policy disaster.

This book attempts to give readers some historical and theoretical background for coming to grips with drug policy issues, then presents a variety of alternatives to our current policy.

There are two main approaches to rethinking drug policy, which reflect differing American values, and they are both represented in this book. One is the public health, or harm-reduction, or cost-benefit approach, which implements the American value of pragmatism. It looks at the social science and biomedical evidence regarding the effects of each drug, attempts to weigh the positive and negative consequences of various courses of action, and proposes policies with the best overall mix of outcomes. Public health approaches to drug policy emphasize harm reduction (e.g., preventing the spread of disease, maintaining the health of drug users, and guaranteeing drug purity) and controlling in various ways the quantities available for individual purchase, dosage levels, and other aspects of drugs and their use, as well as drug advertising. Public health strategies often involve taxing currently illicit substances (as well as alcohol and tobacco)—possibly in rough relation to their harmfulness (Grinspoon 1990)—and usually dedicate tax revenues to the treatment and prevention of drug-related problems. Such strategies aim to minimize the negative effects of psychoactive substances while holding regulation to a level that will keep the black market as small as possible.

The other—libertarian or rights-based—approach to legalizing drugs can be seen to implement the American value of individualism. It views the private behavior of adults as none of the government's business and aims to maximize individual freedom. Whether the issue is consensual heterosexual or homosexual activity, masturbation, contraception, abortion, suicide, or using psychoactive substances, the position of libertarians is the same—people should be free to do in private whatever they want with their own bodies, as long as they do not injure others in some quite direct way.

Libertarians argue that along with freedom comes responsibility for the consequences of one's actions. The great majority of those who use currently illegal substances recreationally can do so with no ill effects; and they should be allowed to do so in peace. The small minority who use those substances in ways that others view as self-destructive should also be allowed to do so as long as they do not injure others—and if they do, they should be punished for their crimes just like anyone else.

Opponents of drug prohibition have long recognized that the great majority of social ills attributed to drugs are actually the result of the War on Drugs—and specifically of the colossal black market created by prohibitionist policy.

The black market causes crime by driving drug prices through the roof so that some miserable and socially marginalized consumers, who seek solace in illicit substances, steal or prostitute themselves to finance purchases. Drug prohibition brings crime into existence by criminalizing otherwise normal market transactions. The black market created by prohibition produces bystander deaths from turf battles and kills drug users with unpredictable dosage levels, impurities, and AIDS and other diseases spread through clandestine drug-taking practices.

By allocating limited resources to fight the War on Drugs, government increases crime in several other ways. Violent crime and property crime increase because resources are diverted from combating them to jailing drug offenders; those who commit crimes of violence are returned to the streets early to make room in overcrowded prisons for drug offenders serving mandatory minimum sentences. In addition, while putting a rapist or murderer in jail decreases the number of rapes and murders and makes society safer, putting a drug dealer in jail has the opposite effect. Because of the black market, jailed drug dealers are simply replaced by others who fill their shoes, thereby increasing the total number of such people. And when drug dealers get out of prison, after years of training to develop their worst potential, they return to poor neighborhoods to make them even more unsafe (Blumstein 1993, 1995).

Profits from the War on Drugs are used to fund terrorism in many parts of the world. The more "successful" the War on Drugs is in making the drug trade a dangerous business, the greater the profits are from increased prices and the more drug money goes to support terrorist organizations. Furthermore, at a time of conflicting demands for limited government resources, the tens of billions of dollars devoted to the War on Drugs divert significant funds from the fight against terrorism (Fish 2002).

Because smugglers need to pack as much illicit substance into as small a space as possible, the black market pushes people to use higher, therefore more dangerous, dosage levels. Just as Prohibition promoted a transition from safe low-dosage alcohol (beer) to high-dosage alcohol (whiskey) of unpredictable safety, drug prohibition has promoted a transition from low-dosage coca (coca tea or the original Coca Cola) to powdered cocaine to crack. Because marijuana is bulky and aromatic, it is easy to detect and, therefore, to seize. This drives the black market price of marijuana up relative to that of cocaine and heroin, creating an economic incentive for more people to use "hard drugs" over "soft drugs."

Black market money corrupts American lawyers, judges, police, and politicians; overseas, it has distorted and undermined entire economies and corrupted and destabilized entire governments. The black market responds to severe, adult criminal penalties by recruiting poor children at high wages. This results in increased drug experimentation and abuse among children (from sampling their product), youth crime, dangerous schools, and deaths of children working for or caught in the crossfire of the black market. Drug prohibition spreads AIDS because clean needles are not freely available. And the ever-expanding black market created by drug prohibition leads to ever more draconian attempts to control it. These controls have led to the "drug exception to the Bill of Rights," in which all basic rights and freedoms, from private property to life itself (in erroneous drug raids), have been suspended in a self-defeating war on drugs. Ubiquitously and inevitably, as the War on Drugs has escalated, the black market has grown in size, power, and corrosiveness—leading for calls to further intensify the war and making matters ever worse.

Advocates of both public health and libertarian approaches recognize that the black market–generating effects of prohibition must be reversed by a black market–destroying strategy of legalization. But they deal with the issue in different ways.

Public health approaches emphasize a regulated market, building on and adapting to each substance the kinds of strategies used to control tobacco and alcohol. Libertarian approaches advocate a free market (for adults), requiring only guarantees of purity and truth in labeling and advertising—and they advocate a free market in tobacco, alcohol, and prescription drugs as well. Libertarians believe that the free market, individual preferences, liability lawsuits, and other nongovernmental social pressures will control drug use at least as well as a regulated market, with the added benefit of keeping government out of areas of personal preference. Advocates of public health approaches remain skeptical to varying degrees and in varying ways about the adequacy of an unfettered free market as an alternative to the prohibition of psychoactive substances.

The end of Prohibition did not lead to a single, uniform legalization of alcohol. Rather, states and local governments became the laboratories for policy experimentation envisioned by the Constitution—and some areas of the country remain dry to this day. Similarly, one likely scenario for the end of drug prohibition—terminating the federal government's oppressive role— would encourage a diversity of approaches, implementing different mixes of public health and libertarian rationales, as different parts of the country attempt to develop the forms of legalization (or continued restrictions) that suit them best.

Drug prohibition has caused many deaths from drug overdoses and drug impurities, from turf battles and other drug-related crime, and by spreading AIDS. It has ruined the lives or harmed the careers of numerous people, whose only crime was the crime of pleasure, or curiosity, or yielding to peer pressure. It has ravaged the communities of our inner cities and of Third World countries, undermined our democratic institutions, wreaked havoc with our foreign policy, and uncorked a gusher of funding for terrorism.

Drug prohibition has encouraged the expression of repugnant forms of social scapegoating by cloaking base deeds in the garments of moral outrage. The temperance movement, which led to alcohol prohibition, provided a handy way for Protestants to attack immigrant Catholic groups (the Irish and whiskey, Italians and wine). And drug prohibition has repeatedly legitimized racist attacks on minority groups by demonizing them—from Chinese opium smokers to African American crack users. At the individual level, drug hysteria has made it seem normal, even praiseworthy, to jail recreational drug users, confiscate their property, and destroy their lives. Meanwhile, the similarly popular destruction of problem drug users amounts to a state-enforced policy of kicking people while they are down.

For decades, the federal government—the president, Congress, and the courts—state governments, both political parties, and a wide array of extragovernmental forces have combined to stifle the expression of a simple truth: *drug prohibition, and its instrument of oppression, the War on Drugs, makes the drug problem worse rather than better by creating a gigantic black market. America has the world's worst drug problem because America has the world's worst drug policy.*

* * * * *

This book aims at providing individuals with the information necessary to think through drug policy issues so that they can evaluate alternative proposals and work out their own positions on this important topic.

The nine chapters that follow are organized into three parts. The two chapters in Part I, "Historical Background," give a sense of how U.S. policy regarding opium and alcohol developed over time, and provide pointed lessons for contemplating future options. The two chapters in Part II, "Conceptual Background," discuss methodological and philosophical issues relevant to making policy decisions. The five chapters in Part III, "Policy Considerations," deal with conceptual and practical issues involved in rewriting our laws and offer a variety of policy options. While these are by no means exhaustive, they illustrate the kinds of proposals currently under discussion in policy circles and the reasoning that goes into them.

In chapter 2, Jerry Mandel examines the origins of the War on Drugs at the start of the twentieth century. He rejects as myth the notion that social ills made both a national and international crackdown necessary. Instead, opening with a discussion of opium prohibition in the Philippines in the early years of the twentieth century, he portrays widespread opium smoking and concomitant vast fiscal benefits to merchants and government, wherever there were large Chinese populations. Those who did not benefit from it generally accepted opium smoking. It was the demand for prohibition by influential American Protestant missionaries, pressuring and gaining appointment to key positions representing the U.S. government, that overcame opposition from both American and some key Asian policy makers. This movement grew out of the missionaries' lack of success in China, where they had encountered widespread opium use and hatred of them, and conflated the two. The War on Drugs then spread both domestically in the United States and, as our foreign policy export, throughout Asia and to the rest of the world, setting in motion the self-made disaster we live with today.

In chapter 3, Harry G. Levine and Craig Reinarman examine alcohol prohibition in the United States and its implications for drug policy. For example, as regards public health effects, before Prohibition, Americans got twice as much of their alcohol from beer as from hard liquor; after Prohibition, that proportion was gradually restored. During Prohibition, however, drinkers got two to three times as much of their alcohol from hard liquor as from beer. Not only were the dosage levels higher, but many people died or were injured from contaminated alcohol or other unregulated substances sold as alcohol. And, we all are familiar with the massive scale of crime and corruption caused by Prohibition. Levine and Reinarman argue that post-Prohibition government regulation of alcohol has worked well and can serve as a model for the way other substances can be regulated following the end of drug prohibition. Not only does regulation work as well as prohibition in reducing consumption, but it raises tax revenue instead of costing huge amounts for law enforcement.

In examining various drug policy issues for which the alcohol experience can serve as a model, Levine and Reinarman suggest the kinds of public health measures that might be undertaken as alternatives. In addition, they point to a growing international consensus that cannabis should be removed from the list of prohibited substances. They make clear, however, that drug prohibition is a worldwide policy and that international treaties, especially the United Nations Single Convention of 1961, will have to be taken into account in implementing new policies.

One unfortunate theme running through chapters 2 and 3 is that America's prohibitionist wars on alcohol and drugs have, from the beginning, been driven largely by religious attempts to eliminate sin rather than by reasoned economic, public health, or public-policy analyses. The refusal to base policy on evidence and logic has, for more than a century, repeatedly led to unwanted and costly social consequences.

In chapter 4, I discuss five fallacies that often appear unacknowledged in discussions of drug policy—selection bias, ignoring base rates, using reified concepts, not considering probabilistic predictions, and not considering cost-benefit analyses. These methodological errors are well known to social and behavioral scientists but not necessarily to the public at large. The chapter explains the fallacies and shows how they are often used to justify faulty conclusions with unfortunate social consequences.

In chapter 5, Douglas Husak explores the philosophical bases of the two main rationales for drug policy reform—the public health, or harm-reduction, or cost-benefit approach, and the rights-based, or libertarian, approach. While Husak makes clear his preference for the rights-based approach to legalization, he presents a thorough explication of both approaches.

A strength of the public health approach is that, by devising a different policy for each substance based on scientific knowledge, it should be possible to minimize health and social problems. A weakness of the public health approach is that its very pragmatism leaves it open to the vagaries of political and social trends since the means for minimizing harm vary over time, as do judgments about what constitutes a problem and how serious a problem is. Furthermore, in times of economic adversity, political upheaval, or ethnic conflict, the label of "public health" could be used as a pretext for scapegoating minority groups—as "public safety" and "mental health" are now being used to justify the mistreatment of social deviants.

A strength of the rights-based approach is that, by guaranteeing the rights of individual adults, those who make unpopular choices would have a better chance of being protected, even when the political climate was hostile. I thought it might be useful to include a list of rights—most of which are enshrined in the Constitution—that have been ignored on a massive scale in what has come to be known as "the drug exception to the Bill of Rights." I should mention, though—to paraphrase the Ninth Amendment—that the enumeration in the following list of certain rights shall not be construed to deny or disparage others retained by the people that are infringed by drug prohibition:

- The right to freedom of speech (e.g., for physicians to recommend marijuana or other controlled substances)
- The right to freedom of religion (e.g., for Native American peyote rituals)
- The right to privacy (e.g., so that one's liquor cabinet and medicine cabinet are not the government's business, no matter what intoxicating substances they contain)
- The right to control over one's own body (e.g., to take adequate pain medication or other psychoactive substances)
- The right to equal protection under the law (e.g., so that penalties for crack cocaine, used by inner-city blacks, are not many times more severe than those for powdered cocaine, used by suburban whites)
- The right to protection against illegal searches and seizures (e.g., so that neither the government nor employers can investigate the contents of one's bladder)
- The right not to be deprived of life, liberty, or property without due process (e.g., not to be harmed, jailed, or have one's property destroyed in drug sweeps; not to be jailed because the government misclassifies the properties of psychoactive substances; not to be jailed because the government defines "selling drugs" to include sharing a marijuana cigarette with another person at a party)

- The right not to be deprived of one's property without just compensation (e.g., having one's house confiscated if drugs are found in it)
- The right not to be forced to incriminate oneself (e.g., by mandatory breath or blood samples)
- The right not to suffer cruel and unusual punishment (e.g., a life sentence for possession of a single marijuana cigarette, as under "three strikes and you're out" laws)
- The right not to be tried twice for the same crime (e.g., trying people in a federal court who have already been found not guilty of drug charges in a state court, and vice versa)

A weakness of the rights-based approach is that the policy that gives individuals the most freedom to choose might not wind up with as good a mix of outcomes for society as a whole as the more limited freedom of public health approaches would produce.

Finally, chapter 5 examines claims that drug use is immoral and finds them to be unsupported assertions, thus an inadequate basis for drug policy. We must ask ourselves whether it is the legacy of our industrial society, founded on the work ethic and Puritanism, that people who indulge in aimless pleasure are viewed as immoral simply because they are not spending their time producing and consuming economically significant quantities of goods and services.

With the initial chapters in Parts I and II as background, the reader should have a well-founded basis for evaluating the merits of the varied approaches to drug policy discussed in Part III.

In chapter 6, Richard M. Evans and Stanley Neustadter examine the concept of legalization. They discuss a variety of approaches to changing current policy, from de jure and de facto decriminalization, to limitation of access (through prescriptions, licensing, or restrictions on places where substances can be used), to regulation and taxation, to complete legalization (where currently illicit substances would be no different from any other commodity).

At this point, I would like to digress to react to an interesting point that the authors make along the way. It is that alcohol prohibition—even though it was codified in a constitutional amendment—was actually much weaker than drug prohibition since possession of small amounts of alcohol for personal use was never a crime. In other words, Prohibition was an example of what we would now call decriminalization.

One might ask why it is, then, that even though there was a constitutional amendment, Prohibition fell so rapidly once its counterproductive, black market–creating aspect became evident? Clearly, it was not because alcohol is not dangerous. From what was known at the time, it appeared to be the most dangerous psychoactive substance. Only once we became aware of tobacco's initially less obvious but ultimately more devastating health effects did we realize that a more dangerous substance existed.

Rather, the answer seems to be that too many people used alcohol. Thus, even under a regime of decriminalization, it was not politically sustainable to direct governmental power against so large a proportion of the population. (The lack of funds available for enforcement during the Great Depression was also a significant factor in the demise of Prohibition.) In order for prohibition to "work," the target needs to be a smaller minority so that a significant majority of the population can cloak its scapegoating in the garments of moral outrage. In other words, cocaine and heroin are useful substances to demonize because relatively few people want to use them. (This is because their negative effects are easy to see. For example, people can smoke while working, or drink during a lunch break; but cocaine and heroin are not "worker friendly" substances—using them has not been found to be career enhancing.) Because relatively few people want to use them, however, the government cannot build up a "prison industrial complex" with a war against only "hard drugs."

Marijuana is a more problematic substance because well over a third of adolescents and adults have used it, which is plenty to mobilize a huge criminal justice bureaucracy but beginning to approach the numbers that made alcohol prohibition untenable. If only marijuana—and no other substances—were legalized, then the War on Drugs would shrink dramatically, prisons would close, and many drug warriors and criminal justice bureaucrats would be looking for jobs.

We now know that tobacco is the most dangerous substance, even more dangerous than alcohol. This is because it is responsible for many more deaths—both direct (i.e., more lung cancer than cirrhosis of the liver) and indirect (i.e., more people killed by second-hand smoke than by drunk drivers). Since a much greater proportion of smokers than of drinkers are heavy users and have difficulty stopping, the more devastating effects of smoking are harder to avoid. Thus, if any substance should be prohibited because of its disastrous effects on society, it is tobacco.

Unfortunately, as we have seen from the case of alcohol, it would be a dreadful idea to make tobacco illegal. The magnitude and viciousness of the black market that would develop, and the "breathtaking" speed of its appearance, would make the current drug war disaster pale by comparison. The only argument in favor of making tobacco illegal is that to do so would create so colossal a calamity so quickly that the entire regime of drug prohibition might collapse along with it. No matter how strongly one is opposed to drug prohibition, however, nothing could justify putting the country through so pointless a social catastrophe. (This ends the digression.)

In their chapter, Evans and Neustadter review a range of legislative options, based on actual bills that have been presented to state legislatures. These legislative models roughly correspond to a range of public health policy options and include bills legalizing only marijuana, as well as omnibus/all drugs bills.

International treaties and federal laws would supersede new state laws, even if enacted, but the repeal of drug prohibition in a number of states would increase the enforcement burden on the federal government—a tactic that was used successfully by the movement to repeal alcohol prohibition. In addition, passing state laws for one or another form of legalization would be a dramatic sign to politicians around the country of a significant shift in voter opinion. (Perhaps the success in many states of medical marijuana referenda is a harbinger of such a change.)

After reviewing the range of current bills, the chapter goes on to present a series of policy issues that must be considered in drafting legalization legislation. These issues, which include the definition of "drugs," the allocation of federal/state prerogatives, setting the level of taxation, liability waivers, the degree of government involvement in legalized markets, prescription drugs, designer drugs, home growers, licensing users, parent-child transfers of drugs, drug testing, and the fate of large numbers of people imprisoned for activities that will cease to be criminal, require careful thought. Many of them are discussed elsewhere in this book.

The last four chapters present a variety of approaches to drug policy reform. The chapters are arranged in an approximate sequence from the most limited (change the government's classification of licit and illicit substances—and, by implication, any penalties associated with them—to reflect scientific evidence of dangerousness) to the most sweeping (make virtually all widely used substances available but subject to regulations aimed at minimizing the dangers of misuse). These differing proposals include public health, rights-based, and mixed stated and/or implied rationales for the various, sometimes overlapping, policies. Furthermore, the disciplinary backgrounds of the authors and the kinds of evidence and modes of argument they use to support their suggestions come from constitutional law, economics, philosophy, political science, and psychology. Thus, these last four chapters invite readers, in formulating their own thinking, to consider and reflect on the proposals, and to compare them to one another or choose elements from several.

In chapter 7, Robert S. Gable condenses findings from a wide range of experimental studies to classify sixteen psychoactive substances—legal, prescription, and illegal—on the two key dimensions of acute toxicity and dependence potential. His presentation makes it easy to see that the penalties for using the various substances bear little relationship to their dangerousness on these dimensions.

I would like to react briefly to the clear implication of this chapter that any prohibitionist penalties that do exist should be roughly proportional to the dangerousness of the substances involved. The fact that this is not the case and that repeated efforts to achieve this kind of appropriateness have been consistently rebuffed over the years makes one wonder about the motivation of government policy makers. As I see it, the fact that prohibitionism has been used as a way of legitimizing the mistreatment of minority groups points to the dark side of our irrational classification of substances.

In chapter 8, I discuss fourteen proposals, short of legalizing cocaine and heroin, that would significantly reverse the damage caused by drug prohibition. These suggestions are based on both public health and rights-based rationales. In addition, I discuss three general proposals concerning the ways in which reform takes place, which are aimed at fostering a more rational and humane drug policy.

In chapter 9, Mary M. Cleveland provides an economic perspective on drug policy, illustrated by a series of informative tables and figures. She contrasts prohibitionist assumptions with alternative assumptions about drug use and abuse and the policy options associated with them, and she provides compelling evidence for the alternative assumptions. Cleveland presents federal drug-use statistics, which confirm what readers can recognize in patterns of alcohol use, that there are a small proportion of abusers, a larger proportion of regular users, and a substantial majority of occasional users. Combining this information with knowledge about patterns of use of different substances, she proposes three very different policies for marijuana, cocaine, and heroin. Implicit throughout her chapter is the idea of using economic tools to construct a public health policy that offers the best chance of minimizing drug abuse among troubled youth.

In chapter 10, Steven B. Duke and Albert C. Gross advocate legalizing virtually all widely used substances so as to avoid the greater costs of prohibition, but they propose a variety of forms of regulation to minimize the dangers of drug abuse. These include restricting the places where drugs can be used, preventing juvenile access, encouraging employee-assistance programs, licensing the refining, production, and distribution of psychoactive substances, and banning their advertising.

The chapters in Part III provide both a clear sense of the issues involved in drug policy reform and an instructive variety of current proposals. They are based on both public health and rights-based rationales and should help readers formulate their own ideas. By stimulating critical thinking and informed debate, it is hoped that this book will contribute to reforming America's drug policy.

* * * * *

While *Drugs and Society* concerns American drug policy, appendix 1A by Douglas A. McVay compares the results of our prohibitionist policy to those obtained by the public health approach of the Netherlands. The numbers speak for themselves and explain why the policies of European and other developed countries (Canada, Australia) are moving increasingly in the public health direction.

REFERENCES

Baum, D. 1996. *Smoke and mirrors: The War on Drugs and the politics of failure.* Boston: Little, Brown.

Blumstein, A. 1993. Making rationality relevant—the American Society of Criminology 1992 presidential address. *Criminology* 31(1):1–16.

———. 1995. Crime and punishment in the United States over 20 years: A failure of deterrence and incapacitation? In *Integrating crime prevention strategies: Propensity and opportunity.* Edited by P. H. Wikstrom, R. V. Clarke, and J. McCord, 123–40. Stockholm, Sweden: Swedish National Council for Crime Prevention.

Brecher, E. 1972. *Licit and illicit drugs: The Consumers Union report on narcotics, stimulants, depressants, inhalants, hallucinogens, and marijuana—including caffeine, nicotine, and alcohol.* Boston: Little, Brown.

Duke, S. B., and A. C. Gross. 1993. *America's longest war: Rethinking our tragic crusade against drugs.* New York: Putnam.

Fish, J. M. 2002. Divert drug-bust money to war on terrorism. *New York Newsday,* January 2, A25.

Grinspoon, L. 1990. The harmfulness tax: A proposal for regulation and taxation of drugs. *North Carolina Journal of International Law and Commercial Regulation* 15(3):505–10.

Nadelmann, E. 1989. Drug prohibition in the United States: Costs, consequences, and alternatives. *Science* 245:939–47.

Appendix 1A: The United States and the Netherlands

Douglas A. McVay

The contrast is sharp between the United States and the Netherlands in both drug policy and policy outcomes.

As the Trimbos Institute noted in its report to the European Monitoring Centre for Drugs and Drug Addiction (EMCDDA) in the "Report to the EMCDDA by the Reitox National Focal Point, the Netherlands Drug Situation 2002," drug policy in the Netherlands has four major objectives: (1) prevention of drug use and treatment and rehabilitation of addicts, (2) reduction of harm to drug users, (3) diminishing public nuisance caused by drug users (i.e., disturbance of public order and safety in neighborhoods), and (4) combating the production and trafficking of drugs.[1]

Dutch drug policy gives priority to a public health approach. In some cases, this has resulted in a certain degree of tolerance and nonprosecution, instead of strict law enforcement. In 2001 the Trimbos Institute noted, "In the Netherlands, cannabis use is not legalised, only tolerated by the authorities. According to the Opium Act, possession of marijuana for personal use is a crime. However, the law distinguishes between drugs, to ensure a separation of markets; substances are classified as 'hemp' [cannabis products] and 'drugs of unacceptable risk' [other drugs]."[2]

The Dutch public health approach extends to the schools, where a comprehensive health-education program for children and adolescents offers accurate, useful, and age-appropriate information on a range of topics. These include sex education as well as drug education. As a result, not only is drug use lower among Dutch youth, but so are the rates of sexually transmitted diseases (including AIDS), abortion, and teen pregnancy.

Thanks to Emma Cruz for her assistance in preparing this appendix.

On the other hand, "In the United States, whose legislation serves as a model for international drug control agreements and which claims the leadership of the global antidrug fight, the war 'on drugs' is one of the main reasons for a rapid and dramatic increase of the prison population that started in the mid-1980s."[3]

Official U.S. policy does not support harm reduction. Indeed, John Walters, the U.S. drug czar during the administration of George W. Bush, is quoted by the *Washington Post* as saying of harm reduction, "The very name is a lie."[4]

U.S. policy regarding marijuana also differs from that of the Netherlands. The news service Reuters reported on July 19, 2004, that "officials at the National Institutes of Health and at the White House are hoping to shift some of the focus in research and enforcement from 'hard' drugs such as cocaine and heroin to marijuana." According to Reuters, "'Most people have been led to believe that marijuana is a soft drug, not a drug that causes serious problems,' John Walters, head of the White House Office of National Drug Control Policy, said in an interview."[5]

The difference in policy outcomes is even more striking: The U.S. drug war is, by practically any measure, a failure, while the Netherlands does a better job at controlling problem drug use and the harms resulting therefrom (as does most of the rest of the European Union).

For example, the Netherlands Ministry of Health, Welfare, and Sport noted in 1999, "The prevalence figures for cocaine use in the Netherlands do not differ greatly from those for other European countries. However, the discrepancy with the United States is very large. The percentage of the general population who have used cocaine at some point is 10.5 percent in the US, five times higher than in the Netherlands. The percentage who have used cocaine in the past month is 0.7 percent in the US, compared with 0.2 percent in the Netherlands."[6]

The EMCDDA in its 2003 annual report noted, "Cannabis lifetime experience and recent use are higher in the United States than in any EU country. Cocaine lifetime experience is also higher in the United States than in any EU country, and recent use is higher than in most countries, except Spain (2.6 percent) and the United Kingdom (2.0 percent)."[7]

Table 1A.1 illustrates the different outcomes associated with the two countries' differing policies.

For more information on U.S. and international drug policies, see Drug War Facts on the Web at www.drugwarfacts.org or Common Sense for Drug Policy at www.csdp.org (both accessed March 14, 2005).

More information about the Netherlands' drug policies is also available from EMCDDA at www.emcdda.eu.int or from the Netherlands Ministry of Justice at www.minjust.nl (both accessed March 14, 2005).

Table 1A.1

Social Indicator	Comparison Year	United States	Netherlands
Lifetime prevalence of marijuana use (ages 12+)	2001	36.9%[a]	17.0%[b]
Past-month prevalence of marijuana use (ages 12+)	2001	5.4%[a]	3.0%[b]
Lifetime prevalence of heroin use (ages 12+)	2001	1.4%[a]	0.4%[b]
Incarceration rate per 100,000 population	2002	701[c]	100[c]
Per capita spending on criminal justice system (in euros)	1998	379[d]	223[d]
Homicide rate per 100,000 population	(average) 1999–2001	5.56[e]	1.51[e]
AIDS rate per 100,000 population	2002	14.1[f]	0.29[g]
Rate of legal abortions per 1,000 women (ages 15–44)	1996	22.9[h]	6.5[h]
Rate of pregnancies per 1,000 women (ages 15–19)	1996	84.6[i]	12.2[i]

[a] U.S. Department of Health and Human Services (HHS), *Summary of National Findings,* Vol. I of *Substance Abuse and Mental Health Services Administration, National Household Survey on Drug Abuse* (Washington, D.C.: HHS, August 2002), 109, table H.1.

[b] Trimbos Institute, "Report to the EMCDDA by the Reitox National Focal Point, the Netherlands Drug Situation 2002" (Lisboa, Portugal: European Monitoring Centre for Drugs and Drug Addiction, November 2002), 28, table 2.1.

[c] Walmsley, Roy, "World Prison Population List," 5th ed. (London: Research, Development and Statistics Directorate of the Home Office, December 2003), 3, table 2.

[d] Frans van Dijk and Jaap de Waard, "Legal Infrastructure of the Netherlands in International Perspective: Crime Control" (Netherlands: Ministry of Justice, June 2000), 9, table S.13.

[e] Barclay, Gordon, Cynthia Tavares, Sally Kenny, Arsalaan Siddique, and Emma Wilby, "International comparisons of criminal justice statistics 2001," Issue 12/03 (London: Home Office Research, Development and Statistics Directorate, October 2003), 10, table 1.1.

[f] Centers for Disease Control and Prevention, *HIV/AIDS Surveillance Report 2002* 14: 6.

[g] European Centre for the Epidemiological Monitoring of AIDS. HIV/AIDS Surveillance in Europe. Mid-year report 2003. Saint-Maurice: Institut de veille sanitaire, 2003. No. 69.

[h] Henshaw, S. K., S. Singh, and T. Haas, "Recent Trends in Abortion Rates Worldwide," *International Family Planning Perspectives* 25(1) (1999): 44–48.

[i] Singh, S., and J. E. Darroch, "Adolescent Pregnancy and Childbearing: Levels and Trends in Developed Countries," *Family Planning Perspectives* 32 (2000): 14–23.

NOTES

1. European Monitoring Centre for Drugs and Drug Addiction, *Annual Report 2003: The State of the Drugs Problem in the European Union and Norway* (Lisboa, Portugal: EMCDDA, 2003).

2. EMCDDA, *Decriminalisation in Europe? Recent Developments in Legal Approaches to Drug Use* (Lisboa, Portugal: EMCDDA, November 2001).

3. Observatoire Geopolitique des Drogues, *Trends for 1998/1999: The Globalization of the Trafficking Economy* (Paris: OGD, April 2000).

4. DeNeen L. Brown, "With Injection Sites, Canadian Drug Policy Seeks a Fix," *Washington Post*, August 2, 2003, A1.

5. Maggie Fox, "Stronger Pot May Lead to Reefer Madness," Reuters, July 19, 2004.

6. Ministry of Health, Welfare, and Sport, *Drug Policy in the Netherlands: Progress Report Sept. 1997–Sept. 1999* (The Hague: Ministry of Health, Welfare and Sport, November 1999).

7. EMCDDA, *Annual Report 2003*.

I

HISTORICAL BACKGROUND

2

Protestant Missionaries: Creators of the International War on Drugs

Jerry Mandel

OPIUM PROHIBITION ARRIVES SUDDENLY, NOT BECAUSE OF A WORSENING DRUG PROBLEM

The War on Drugs did not emerge, as the mainstream historians' paradigm would have it, as self-defense, society's response to a steady, long-standing, continuously growing drug problem that finally required a firm response. Rather, drug prohibition was an act of will, a sudden takeover, a power grab, with no new or growing drug problem to justify it, a bolt from the blue, from outer space. One day the drug problem is irrelevant: all use takes place in a context of legitimacy; drugs are a trade and a pleasure and highly taxed. The next day, under prohibition, drugs are a crime, an underground business; narcotics police are a constant worry, and drugs are a drain on the treasury.

There are two different histories of drugs — one of peace and prosperity, the other a raging war on drugs. One begins when the other dies. To see this, however, requires denoting the moment of transition, which differs from place to place. Once that moment is found, the contrast from one day to the next, from peace to war, is enormous: like night and day, a switch turned off and on. The War on Drugs has defining characteristics, which makes it easy to determine the setting of the switch. It requires a *law* and its *enforcement*, it has to be *more than just local*, and it requires *continuity*.

Just when the switch was turned is crucial. Only if you get to that moment is the before-after contrast clear. Drug historians in the United States usually consider the Harrison Act of 1914 the seminal drug law in the United States. The Harrison Act banned opiates (such as heroin) and cocaine — the same two classes of drugs that have most plagued the United States in almost every year since then. The legendary U.S. narcotics czar from 1930 to 1962, Harry Anslinger, saw history that way:

> In 1914, when the Harrison Act was passed, narcotic trafficking in America was largely in the hands of the Chinese. Opium . . . was the most popular, addictive drug in use. Only later did the so-called "white drugs"—morphine and heroin . . . and cocaine [—]. . . replace opium in popularity.[1]

Anslinger was not known for his logic or his accurate interpretation of history, and here he is off by about five years.

Reports from many cities across the United States show opium being replaced by morphine, cocaine, and heroin, and Chinese addicts being replaced by white and black drug users, as early as 1909. The reason: a law.

> Since . . . the law prohibiting the importation of the drug for smoking went into effect, the price of opium has doubled several times.[2]

San Francisco's newspapers in May 1909 record "the first man caught smuggling opium into the U.S. since the operation of the restrictive law."[3] By the end of 1910, federal agents were working with San Francisco's police and special agents of the mayor, and "as a result of the crusade the price of opium 'pills' . . . increased . . . [i.e., doubled after] secret service men swooped down."[4] In 1911, California's State Board of Pharmacy agents escalated their enforcement of recent drug legislation. Twenty-nine opium dens in Sacramento's Chinatown were raided and 150 prisoners were taken, including fifteen white men.[5] The biggest raid by agents within the United States was in San Francisco late in 1911. The first night, 125 men raided sixty-two opium dens in Chinatown—"break down the doors of dens with axes and sledge hammers." The agents discovered a new style of drug dealing, according to the head of the Bureau of Pharmacy: "messenger boys in Chinatown and the adjacent districts were purveying morphine and cocaine in the streets."[6]

By 1912–1913, reports of morphine, cocaine, and heroin becoming new styles of drug use were reported in many places across the United States.

- *El Paso* (June 1912): "Opiates used to mean opium, when it came to the habit we had our army of smokers. Two things happened in coincidence. The importation of opium was prohibited. The clumsy, expensive habit became almost impossible. . . . At the same time a new stepping stone towards the hypodermic needle appeared. It was 'flake'—powdered cocaine."[7]
- *Cleveland and Toledo* (December 1912): "Heroin is being used extensively by means of 'snuffing,' in the tenderloin district of large cities."[8]

- *Boston* (1912): The New England Watch and Ward Society arrested nineteen cocaine users and knew of seven who had "died in the agonies of the drug deliriums"; (December 1913): A physician told the Society for the Study of Alcohol and Other Narcotics that a new drug, heroin, was sweeping through Boston, making hundreds of new victims "the last few months . . . [at] 'sniffing parties'."[9]
- *Chicago* (March 1913): "A new habit-forming drug has suddenly come to public notice . . . youthful cases of heroin addiction."[10]
- *Lansing* (June 1913): Lansing detectives "found several boys in gangs . . . confirmed cocaine and heroine snuffers."[11]
- *New York* (June 1913): "scores of young men in . . . the Bronx were addicted to the heroin habit . . . [They would] sneak into hallways . . . and sniff it up their noses."[12]
- *Philadelphia* (1911–15): "About 1912 the dissipated and vicious began the use of heroin. . . . About 1910–1911 there was a restriction placed on the importation and sale of crude opium; it naturally became very expensive an could only be obtained in small quantities by those who could afford it at all. Prior to this time the opium pipe was the great source of pleasure to the denizens of the 'tenderloin'."[13]

So, the date of passage of the Harrison Act does not mark the start of the War on Drugs in the United States. Rather, the years immediately before it indicate a great change in the character of drug use in the United States following the Opium Exclusion Act of 1909. Prior to that date, there were few drug arrests in the United States (relative to what came after), and the bulk of these were of opium smokers or traffickers, overwhelmingly Chinese. So, to see the United States, at least, at the cusp, when the societal drug policy changes from tolerance to prohibition, the comparison must be pre– versus post– February 1909, when Congress brought the War on Drugs to the United States.

In 1909, the recreational drug of choice, by far, in the United States was opium; a large majority of opium smokers were Chinese Americans—quiet, hard working, law abiding. Chinese, wherever they migrated in large numbers, had a yen for opium smoking that few in any other civilization had. A huge worldwide network catered to the Chinese taste for opium smoking. At the far, far reaches of the Celestial Empire were the Chinese in the United States. They smoked opium, too, from the same Asian market as Chinese from around the world. Opium smoking had been a popular style of drug use among the Chinese in the United States for roughly half a century. Since the late 1870s, though, there were local and state laws that technically prohibited some aspect of opium smoking, but none were actively enforced over the years. Take away these intermittent, local, anti-Chinese crusades, and the

norm at the start of the twentieth century in the United States was no enforcement of opium-smoking laws, which meant no enforcement of laws prohibiting the use of any recreational drug. One day, suddenly, the United States
declared war on drugs . . . again. This time, though, the war stuck.

If February 1909, with the passage of the Opium Exclusion Act, marks the
cusp of the U.S. War on Drugs, and if before that date there was no significant drug problem—nothing essentially any worse than the previous half-
century[14]—how did we get from one side of the cusp to the other? If it was
not a new and growing drug problem, what was it?

THE U.S. WAR ON DRUGS WAS CREATED BY
PROTESTANT MISSIONARIES OUTSIDE THE UNITED
STATES IN RESPONSE TO CHINESE DRUG USE OVERSEAS

At the start of the War on Drugs, a small band of Protestant missionaries in
China initiated, wrote, and were the key publicists and lobbyists for the piv-
otal drug-prohibition legislation in the United States and throughout the
world. In every case, at key moments in the initial years of the International
War on Drugs, the Protestant missionaries easily enlisted key officials of the
U.S. government (and, in their greatest coup, China's empress dowager herself) to further opium prohibition. The Opium Exclusion Act of 1909 was a
direct result of that essentially Asian-based and China-focused Protestant
missionary movement. They conceived the law, suggested it to top officials
in the U.S. government, and probably played a lead role in writing the law
and herding the bill through Congress onto the president's desk in near
record time. Whatever notice the bill might have gotten in the media, the
time from its introduction until its passage was too swift for any criticism or
dissent to arise.

For those Asian-based prohibitionist Protestant missionaries, the Opium Exclusion Act was their third major legal triumph in four years. The *U.S.* War on
Drugs was not the central part of the *international* war on drugs. The missionaries' makeover of world drug policy began in 1903. From 1905 to 1909, missionaries were primarily responsible for national drug laws in the Philippines,
China, and the United States and largely responsible for China's ban on opium
smoking. (The Empress Dowager's Anti-Opium Edict of September 20, 1906,
was, I'd argue, the major act initiating the international war on drugs.) Additionally, in 1909, the First International Opium Commission was created, again
by a missionary, to foster prohibition everywhere, a clear progenitor of the narcotics bodies of the League of Nations and today's United Nations' narcotics
bodies.

This chapter details only the first of these four events—Philippine prohibition. Here, Protestant missionaries derailed a traditional opium policy and created a new [Philippines] Opium Committee, which was to suggest an opium policy for that country. Their report contained two different views, two different styles of thinking. Most of the report focused on what the committee found in research visits to eight Pacific countries in which opium was legal and popular: Chinese opium smokers paid enough in taxes that they paid for a substantial part of government. These field reports described opium throughout much of Asia during the last moments it would be legal. The other view in the committee report appeared as either missionary bromides assailing the evils of opium, or—without any connection to the research data they had collected—a recommended policy of opium prohibition. Both perspectives were in full view—the present, to which no one objected except the missionaries, and a future prohibition that everyone dreaded, except the missionaries.

After detailing the Opium Committee's contradictions, the context—the later two prohibition laws and the International Opium Commission—will be revisited, and I will trace the connection between the initiators and prime movers—Protestant missionaries almost to the man—of each of the four events. Finally, I'll address why. The Protestant missionaries were blind with anger at the Chinese, who had frustrated all attempts of several generations of missionaries to convert them to Christianity. Blaming opium for their personal and collective failures was classic scapegoating.[15] The U.S. government warrants credit for facilitating the missionaries, although at the cusp, the moment peace with drugs turned into a War on Drugs, many high up in government (including a future president) totally disapproved of opium prohibition and the missionaries' attempts to make it policy. I'm not sure who the key political figure was or how he got his power, but at a certain moment, a decision was made that rippled throughout the U.S. government, putting it in the service of the Protestant missionaries on the opium question. Is that a coup d'état?

DRUGS IN THE PHILIPPINES: PEACE WITHOUT POLICY OR GOVERNMENT PROFITS, 1898–1903

When the United States took over the Philippines in 1898, no one in government seemed to have any particular animus against drugs or reason for any drug policy. First, it took time to figure out what opium policy was in the Philippines. During the first years of its occupation of the Philippines, the United States lacked a consistent opium policy of benefit to anyone. Free enterprise seemed to reign, with mixed results.

The traditional system of farming out the opium concession to the highest bidder was scrapped just *before* the U.S. occupation because

> The Philippine Revolution, beginning in 1896, caused serious damage to the opium business . . . where revolutionary activities were strongest. . . . [T]here was no security for Chinese property, and so many Chinese fled to Manila that the provincial contractor was forced into default for lack of customers. . . . Elsewhere, it was a case of difficulty in moving the opium. . . . [F]rom 1896 to the end of Spanish rule in 1898 contracts went begging for bidders.[16]

There were also complaints that those running the opium farms were corrupt price gougers.

The moment before the Philippine insurrection, "Philippine Chinese tax monopolists . . . paid 576,000 pesos to the insular treasury" for the opium contract for fiscal year 1896–1897.[17] As the monopoly went into free fall, a private entrepreneur, Don Carlo Palanca, emerged to oversee the distribution of opium among the 40,000 Chinese Filipinos. He could be a strong-arm monopolist, but then again, the trade was more palatable to the Chinese consumers than under the previous monopoly.[18]

Early on, missionary antidrug crusaders saw the Philippines as an opening. "In 1899, an American in China who headed the missionaries' Anti-Opium League, Rev. Hampden Du Bose, apprised the American government of the increasing consumption of opium in the Philippines" in a letter transmitted to the president. Du Bose's letter "did not evoke any immediate change in American policy" and, after going through the departments of state, war, and treasury, "came to rest with the collector of customs in the islands . . . [who] recommended a return to the Spanish farming out system." Opium smoking in the Philippines was confined to Chinese, and "to price it beyond the reach of the poorer Chinese would merely cause smuggling, an art at which the Chinese were adept . . . facilitated by the extent and irregularities of the Philippine coastline." Additionally, the collector concluded, "'farming out [alone] . . . will entirely relieve the Government from . . . maintaining an expensive . . . Department to prevent the smuggling of opium'." However, the secretary of treasury in Washington, D.C., "disliking the monopoly feature of the farming out system . . . rejected the suggestions of the collector . . . [as] 'foreign to our administration of the revenue'." This, and a decision freeing Chinese to import opium into the Philippines, resulted in "a threefold increase in the amount of opium imported legally into the Philippines, and a corresponding increase in import revenue" from opium.[19] So, from the outset, U.S. colonial policy in the Philippines was driven by ideology (free enterprise at key times) rather than ongoing practice (tax heavily but tolerate).

PROTESTANT MISSIONARIES TORPEDO A TRADITIONAL
REVENUE-RAISING OPIUM SUPPLY SYSTEM

In early 1903, Philippines Governor William H. Taft and the Philippine Commission proposed resurrecting the pre-1897 Spanish system. The bill to contract out the opium monopoly was two weeks before a third and final reading before the Philippine Commission when Manila's Protestant missionaries reacted against it. On May 31, 1903, Rev. Homer Stuntz (Methodist presiding elder in Manila, cohead of the Methodist Episcopal Mission, and president of the Evangelical Union) telegrammed Wilbur Crafts, president of the International Reform Bureau (a missionary lobby for prohibition) in Washington, D.C.:

> Highest bidder opium monopoly bill pending . . . opposed by evangelical union Chinese chamber of commerce will greatly stimulate consumption focus public sentiment on president secretary of war bill . . . bad morals and worse politics.[20]

On June 11, four days before

> the opium monopoly franchise was to be fastened on the Philippines for three years . . . the Bureau appealed to a few hundred leaders for a telegraphic vote against opium "revenue" and for opium prohibition. The result was a snow of telegrams on June 13 and 15 . . . [and a] cablegram sent to Manila by the War Department. "Hold opium bill further investigation, many protests."[21]

President Roosevelt "demanded a full report from the War Department. Secretary Root thereupon ordered the postponement of the third reading of the bill pending . . . a report from the Philippines Commission . . . on the opium problem in the islands" and how other Asian lands treated it.[22]

Missionaries Co-opt Manila's Chinese Community

The whirlwind campaign against the resumption of the opium monopoly was unique in that a large contingent of Chinese worked with the missionaries. Reverend Stuntz was lavish in his praise:

> 1903, the Chinese Chamber of Commerce engaged a lawyer, and set about it to defeat the bill [before the Philippines Commission]. . . . [T]he Chinese Chamber of Commerce stood by us in the entire fight, helping by their sympathy, and . . . money. . . . [T]hey prepared and circulated a petition asking that the proposed [Monopoly] Bill be withdrawn . . . [which was] signed by seven thousand in Manila . . . [although it was] only in circulation a few days.[23]

Could the lions have lain down with the lambs? Others had markedly different views of the relation between American missionaries and Chinese merchants in the Philippines. One noted "very different motives. The Evangelical Alliance disapprove *in toto* of the sale and use of opium. . . . [T]he Chinese object to any restriction being put on the sale of cheap opium."[24] Another testified, "Chinese opium merchants feared that the system would put them out of business, and Chinese consumers feared . . . a rise in the price of the drug."[25] An American lobbyist whom the Chinese merchants had hired tried to smooth over any disagreements ("his clients would prefer prohibition to the contract system as the former could more easily be evaded"),[26] and another commentator condemned the Chinese merchants, the missionaries, and opium in general:

> The [Philippine] Commission . . . [has] two . . . elements of opposition. . . the Chinese merchants who would like to poison the whole community. They want opium for everybody—and they sell the opium. The other . . . the Philippine Evangelical Union [the American evangelical missionary bodies] . . . wants opium prohibited altogether . . . which would doubtless result in a clandestine, unregulated business in the highest degree mischievous and demoralizing.[27]

So, Stuntz created the illusion that missionaries and Chinese merchants were one on opium policy and sold this idea to the U.S. government in Washington, D.C., and to Manila's Chinese—at least for long enough to scrap the proposed opium monopoly and start a process to generate an alternative policy.

PHILIPPINE CIVIL GOVERNMENT SURRENDERS OPIUM POLICY TO A HIGHER POWER IN WASHINGTON, D.C.

Governor Taft, the Philippine Commission, and others had trouble accepting the alternative forced on them by Washington higher-ups. "Gov. Taft . . . [who] courageously championed the theory of regulation . . . declared . . . the opium habit as practiced by all the Chinese was less pernicious than was whisky drinking, and mercilessly exposed the corrupt combination of Chinese dealers who were circulating falsely signed protests."[28] In a letter to the secretary of war, Taft and the commission "criticized the missionary opponents of the [proposed opium monopoly bill] as prohibitionists on principle who were therefore unable to properly understand the far eastern opium situation."[29] Even the "Chinese consul in Manila suggested [to Taft] that the system in use by the British in the Straits Settlement . . . be tried [in the Philippines] . . . [and that] the right to sell opium and run places for smoking [be] let to one or more persons, so as to keep it under control."[30] But, a month or so after the orders from Washington, all hope of convincing their superiors to refute the missionaries waned. Taft and the commissioners fell silent. (Behind the scenes, sabotage has to be inferred mainly from what was not done, although in a short while, prohibition prevailed.)

Early in August 1903, Taft and the commission appointed a three-man Opium Committee "to visit countries where opium is used and ascertain the methods of regulation and control." The appointees were an army major, a local physician, and Charles Brent, Episcopal bishop of the Philippines. (Given Brent's preeminence in subsequent prohibitionist campaigns and the absence of the other two committee members in any subsequent or previously published article or action against drugs, I assume, as others have, that Brent was the primary figure who set the report's tone and conclusions.)

THE (PHILIPPINE) OPIUM COMMITTEE REPORT: RESEARCH AT THE CUSP

The Opium Committee was a result of Protestant missionary concerns and actions, and it is thus no surprise that it concluded that opium prohibition was the best policy. The Opium Committee's report was submitted to the Philippine Commission on June 15, 1904 (a year to the day after the secretary of war's telegram vetoed Governor Taft's opium monopoly proposal). The Philippine Commission sat on the report for fourteen months before approving and sending it up the chain of command to the War Department, where "time . . . [was] taken . . . in the correction of typographical and other errors contained in it."[31] Even in its final version, the report is a mess. The outline wanders; paragraphs or thoughts pop in and out unexpectedly.

The quality of the report itself and the logic of the arguments made are not what distinguish the report. It suffices that the conclusions recommend prohibition after all that research. Bishop Brent often referred to his approach as scientific. There's that image. That image was presented, without any substantive rebuttal so far as I can tell, as support for Philippine opium prohibition in 1905, before the report itself had been published by the U.S. government. Prohibition would be the law of the land, as the report recommended, after a brief three-year transition period. The report provides, for better or worse, the best written arguments at the time for Philippine opium prohibition.

On the Cusp 1—The Past: Final View of a World at Peace with Drugs

The report itself, when it was finally released, was actually two reports, two warring ways of conceiving of problems and government policies. The bulk of the final report of 1906 discusses of the opium situations in eight Asian countries. Both the country-by-country analyses by the committee and the notes of interviews or places visited seem outright refutations of the wisdom of opium prohibition.

In each separate country the committee visited (with the exception of Japan, which had near-zero Chinese residents and, therefore, essentially no opium smokers), the government profited handsomely by selling opium, overwhelmingly to resident Chinese smokers.

- *Formosa:* "The government . . . decided . . . the best way to treat the opium smokers is leniently . . . not to act directly against their wishes. The purpose of the opium monopoly is both to derive a revenue and to reduce gradually the number of smokers. . . . The revenue from opium [to the Government Opium Monopoly] . . . is now considerable [3,000,000 yen in 1902]" (64–65, 27).
- *China:* "The Chinese government, at Shanghai at any rate, does nothing more than place a somewhat heavy duty and tax on opium"(30). "Opium culture occupies more and more land. The use of the drug is spreading. The old edicts against its use have fallen into desuetude, and the home and foreign supply together are not now equal to the demand" (33).
- *Hong Kong:* "Farming is the system . . . and a considerable part of the income of the colony is obtained from this source"(35).
- *Saigon:* "63,184 kilos of Yunnan opium and 86,440 kilos of Benares [Indian] opium were imported into Indo-China in 1892. . . . [P]resent government monopoly [opium sales are] . . . nine and one-half millions to sixteen millions of piasters per annum"(15, 95). "Nearly every adult male native is said to use it" (36).
- *Straits Settlement:* "The opium system . . . is that of the farm. . . . [R]evenue from opium alone for the last three years [excluding license fees] amounted to $3,732,000 annually; for the current term [1904–1907], the annual rental is $5,580,000"(36).
- *Burma:* "An effort was made about a dozen years ago to prohibit the use of opium . . . but the effort was not successful, for opium was smuggled in from all sides. . . . [T]he government abandoned prohibition, seeing that it was doing no good" (37).
- *Java:* "Opium smoking among the [273,000] Chinese . . . [is] between 40 and 50 percent" (44). "The concession of monopolies to private persons . . . when in vogue . . . [brought in] 19,000,000 guilders for the whole of the Dutch Indies," and a new system placing control in the hands of the government increased sales and profits to the state (45–46).

- *Philippines:* "From 1843 to 1898 the farming system was in vogue . . . its purpose being to raise revenue" (49).

In the world at peace with opium smoking, the government tried to make it as pleasant as possible and made substantial revenues in return. A sin tax was never so easy to impose and collect.

Periodic opium prohibition, however, turned out to be disasters and had to be abandoned (in Burma, Formosa, Hawaii, and Hong Kong[32]). Special opium inspectors (early narcotics agents), in particular, were singled out by witnesses as a bad mistake, warranting immediate correction.[33] A medical missionary in China, the first secretary of the Anti-Opium League,[34] and Formosan authorities recommended against immediate opium prohibition in impassioned terms. (The advice of Formosa's authorities resonated because of the similarity in the situations of the Philippines and Formosa, both islands having recently been conquered by the up-and-coming new powers of the Pacific, Japan and the United States).[35]

How could anyone conclude that the above evidence was a call for prohibition?

On the Cusp 2—The Philippine Opium Committee Report: Bishop Brent and the Betrayal and Dismissal of the Chinese in Manila

At committee hearings in Shanghai, a high Chinese official had this exchange with the committee chairman (not, I believe, Brent):

> Mr. Li: I would suggest that the [Philippine] government get hold of their leading Chinese and in consultation with them make rules that will be best for the regulation of the matter.
>
> Chairman: The government has already consulted with the leading Chinese of the islands. Two ideas were advanced by them: one, total prohibition, and the other, government monopoly.
>
> Mr. Li: The Chinese should be consulted. . . . [T]hey understand the inner workings of the Chinese mind.

The committee chairman obviously had trouble hearing the Chinese, for in the rush to derail proposals for resurrecting the Philippine opium monopoly, the Chinese Filipino community *opposed* both policies the chairman said they advanced. The Chinese Filipino merchants actually favored a looser market system, which would bring less expensive drugs, with the trade in the hands of local Chinese merchants, not in the hands of a government monopoly.[36]

Bishop Brent may have been especially hard of hearing when it came to Chinese Filipinos. When Brent was the Protestant missionary appointed to give moral compass to the (Philippine) Opium Committee, he was a new-comer to Asia and the drug issue. He came from Boston in 1902 to head the Philippine Islands (Episcopal) Missionary District, bringing $100,000 he had just raised to build a cathedral in Manila. His partner in the Methodist Episcopal Union, which was central to derailing Governor Taft's opium monopoly proposals, Reverend Stuntz, had qualms about several aspects of Brent's initial work. "There are no religious services for Filipinos held in the Settlement House. Bishop Brent has not yet seen his way to beginning definite religious work in that part of the city." Rather, Brent says, "The most important section of our work at present, and . . . for some time to come, is among Americans and other English-speaking people."[37] Ergo, Brent had very little experience with non-Americans in the Philippines because of background and choice.

The final committee hearings (early 1904) were back in Manila. The Chinese Chamber of Commerce, asked by the Opium Committee "to give aid, by expressing its mind, declined to do so except under conditions such as no government committee could accept."[38] The Protestant missionaries and the Chinese Filipino business leaders, supposedly linked in derailing proposals for an opium monopoly in mid-1903, could not, by early 1904, define the ground rules for a dialogue on a matter of great concern to both. They would not even talk to each other. The missionaries would make the policy by themselves based on what they imagined to be the Chinese experience.

On the Cusp 3—First View of the Future War on Drugs: Bishop Brent's Shameless Arguments for a Future of Prohibition

Bishop Brent bases his case for opium prohibition on the best arguments he could find from the testimony he had heard and witnessed. He makes four points, using tortured logic and stretching examples to a fantastic degree. In seeing his case unfold, ask yourself, Would I trust a man like Bishop Brent to fly an airplane? In other words, Brent's thought patterns, how he puts two and two together, are off the charts.

Throughout the Opium Committee Report, there are periodic inserts of prohibitionist ideological content, the type one would expect from a high missionary.[39] The first point of the conclusion is just a reiteration of the evils of opium. Second, to soften criticism or convince others of its wisdom, the Opium Committee, to make the report seem more like a study than a recital of the party line, rejects *immediate* prohibition as too painful, even lethal, to the smokers.

Manifest as is the impossibility of adopting absolute and immediate prohibition in the Philippine Islands, we may now proceed to discuss the policy which shall be the most suitable and . . . practical.[40]

Third, Brent proposes "progressive prohibition," or delayed prohibition, until some time after the law is passed—three years for the Philippines. He manages to come up with two examples from the countries studied by the Opium Committee of how to ameliorate the pain from, and insure the success of, a three-year transition period—Japanese policy in their Formosan colony showed that other world powers delayed prohibition as a step to absolute prohibition; and the Dutch colony of Java illustrated how government monopoly can control usage. If these were the best examples, Brent's case was rickety, for Formosa and Java were the two largest user-friendly national opium distribution schemes studied by the committee and possibly in the world. The Japanese and Dutch hoped to be in the opium trade for the long haul and the most revenue. But in a world at peace with drugs, it was hard for the committee to find examples of other government policies analogous to prohibition.

In the Formosan example, Brent equates the three-year transition period he advocates for the Philippines to a thirty-year projection of a vague future in Formosa. The colonialists who ran the Formosan system said, according to the report, "their purpose was and is the complete extirpation of the vice at the earliest moment possible—in perhaps thirty years."[41] Thirty years! More realistically, the Japanese director of the Formosan Monopoly Bureau testified, prohibition would increase smuggling, eradicate a custom over a century old, lead the people to violate the law and obtain opium under any circumstances, increase the number of prisoners, and entail costs, such as for more customs and police officers, that could not be satisfactorily met.[42] In hearings on Formosa, the only witness (a Catholic father), reported to have been asked if it was possible "with the present system . . . to eradicate the [opium] vice within thirty years," was pessimistic. "Neither in thirty nor in fifty years," he answered, "will opium smokers disappear with the present system."[43]

In the Javanese example, Brent stakes a claim that his progressive prohibition for the Philippines is sensitive to claims that capitalists are the benefactors of the opium trade. Instead of farming out opium to local businessmen, the committee lauds "a system of absolute government control, entrusting to this moral entity all the responsibility involved in the gradual suppression of the vice . . . eliminating all private interests which tend to swell the sale . . . following the practice observed in Java."[44] The example cited, however, was the most modern, user-friendly opium supply system in the world. Does the following seem like the rapid path to opium prohibition?

The Dutch Government in 1900 erected in Batavia a magnificent opium factory . . . [which] cost 1,250,000 guilders, for . . . supplying opium . . . where the drug is consumed . . . the most complete of its kind among all those . . . visited. It has all the departments necessary for its operation . . . [from the] laboratory, which examines the quality of the dross . . . to keep a strict vigilance over smuggling, to the sawmill which turns out the lumber . . . in the . . . boxes for packing. . . . [E]mployed in the factory are 600 natives and 50 Dutchmen. . . . The government manufactures also a special kind of opium . . . "tiké" . . . opium and the leaves of the awar-awar, intended for sale to opium smokers . . . too poor to buy the better class of drug. The prepared opium is sold in metallic tubes of different sizes . . . 100, 50, 25, 12 1/2, 5, 2, 1 and 1/2.[45]

The examples cited by the Opium Committee to be emulated in the Philippines during a transition period (the "progressive" in progressive prohibition) were obviously impossible to implement for a small population of opium smokers, in a brief three-year span, when there were no existing production and packaging facilities to build upon. Bishop Brent and partners were proposing "absolute prohibition" in disguise. The proposals were not really to ease the pain of eventual prohibition to the Chinese Filipinos but to avoid criticism of the inhumane consequences of opium prohibition when it arrived. It's the difference between being a humanitarian and a charlatan.

The fourth and final point was the easiest to conceive of and describe—"as soon as practicable . . . absolute prohibition." Brent deemed three years practicable. There was no ongoing precedent for opium prohibition anywhere in the nations the committee studied.

THE EXISTENCE OF THE OPIUM COMMITTEE REPORT, NOT ITS DATA OR IDEAS, IS USED TO JUSTIFY OPIUM PROHIBITION

Although the (Philippine) Opium Committee Report was the rationale for opium prohibition, in one sense it had no immediate impact. It was not officially published until twenty-one months after it was submitted in mid-1904, possibly backstage payback by Taft and the Philippine Commission for derailing their recommendations in 1903. By the time the Senate printed the report, its reason for being—to advise the Philippine government on policy alternatives—was passé, for its recommendations were already law. It was as if opium prohibition had been decided upon, probably when higher-ups, in June 1903, vetoed the proposed opium monopoly of Governor Taft and the Philippine Commission. As I read it, the higher-ups told them to shut up and toe the party line—opium prohibition. From that perspective, the Opium Committee and its report justified a previously made decision and served as an official position paper for any who wished to follow, or were called upon to support, the opium prohibition policy initiated by the United States in the Pacific. It did not matter what it contained, or if anyone read it, or if the arguments were sound and convincing, so long as it could be asserted that an official government commission supported prohibition. Image trumped content. So weak was the Opium Committee Report that it probably served the cause of opium prohibition more because it was buried and kept out of public discussion rather than a debated topic of everyday mass concern.

TAKING OPIUM PROHIBITION TO
THE NEXT STAGE, 1906–1909

Missionaries in China Print and Distribute the (Philippine) Opium Committee Report in Chinese Translation and English

In mid-1905, before the Philippine Commission had approved the Opium Committee Report, its "final" report was published in several consecutive issues[46] of the most respected English-language newspaper in China, the weekly *North China Herald* (*NCH*) out of Shanghai. The report was obtained for Reverend Du Bose by Sen. John Morgan from the U.S. War Department and brought to the attention of the *NCH,* most probably by Du Bose.[47] He was so enamored with the report that his Anti-Opium League printed and distributed ten thousand copies of the report in English and eight thousand in Chinese translation.[48] Possibly Du Bose hoped to influence Philippine policy; possibly he hoped to bolster the prestige of the Opium Committee and its report; possibly he just wanted to stir Chinese interest in opium prohibition and show that with the United States as a new power in the Pacific, any Chinese who dreamed of resurrecting an opium war would not be bereft of powerful allies. Whatever the reasons, the reprint of the Opium Committee Report took up more space in the *NCH* than all other articles about drugs published between 1904 and September 20, 1906.

Missionaries Conceive of, Lobby for, and Write China's 1906 Anti-Opium Edict: The Dynasty Enters Tailspin as Prohibition Triggers Insurrection and Violent Repression

On September 20, 1906, the aged ruler of China, the empress dowager, issued an Anti-Opium Edict, setting ten years as the period of transition from being the world's leading consumer of smoking opium to prohibiting opium. In the *NCH* issue for the week after it announced the edict, Du Bose claimed that he and other missionaries were responsible for initiating, lobbying, petitioning, and actually writing the Anti-Opium Edict.[49] The empress dowager pro-claimed, and out came the words of Du Bose and peers.

Prohibiting opium in China in 1906 would be a Herculean task, harder even than in the failed opium war sixty-five years previously. In 1906, the number of Chinese opium smokers was substantially greater than twenty-five or fifty years before, and the proportion of the opium smoked in China that had been grown and processed within China had greatly increased in recent years and was estimated at 80 percent. A conservative estimate for China would be ten million opium smokers (3 percent of the population), predominantly male adults (just under 10 percent of that section of the population). Millions of Chinese were gainfully and happily employed in the trade, from growing to processing, to transporting, to retail selling. Just as in neighboring countries with substantial Chinese émigré populations, on the Chinese mainland numerous governments at all levels made substantial revenues from the opium trade. Opium was a major part of the national economy and was the single most important part of the economy in several of the eighteen Chinese provinces (Yunnan and Szechuan, certainly). Opium was the very soul of those vast regions in which the poppy was the dominant visual component during the long season it was in blossom, when huge valleys sparkled. The dominant occupation of those provinces involved opium, over much of the year, involving men and women and older children at several tasks.[50]

In China, opium prohibition would turn people's lives, as well as governments, upside down. In China, opium prohibition wiped out the livelihoods of close to half of the population as well as half the government revenues in some rural provinces and coastal cities. Opium prohibition meant revolution, a revolution in an empire that was already proving incapable of stopping insurgency throughout the realm, a revolution in an already revolutionary situation.

Du Bose's feat was extraordinary. He intruded himself (and by reason of their cohesiveness in pursuit of a single goal, the Protestant missionaries) into the heart of Chinese politics. Du Bose, almost silently, got hold of drug policies in a society with a record number of recreational drug users, who spent more time and money on a recreational drug than ever before. Du Bose stood opium policy on its head forever. And, he virtually sneaked off that stage as unnoticed as when he had transformed it, as soon as the shooting war began. The time between Du Bose's first proposal of his idea to a Chinese official and the empress dowager's issuing the Anti-Opium Edict was four months.

Bishop Brent Conceives and Runs the First International Opium Commission, 1906–1909

Also in May 1906, Bishop Brent shifted his attention to a larger stage than the Philippines. He proposed to the president that the United States call an international drug meeting, inviting the Pacific powers to discuss ways of combating opium, especially in helping China with her problem (this four months before the empress dowager proclaimed prohibition to be the law of the land). By 1906, Brent, like Du Bose, seemed highly skilled at getting his proposals considered at the top levels of key departments and by the president as well as the empress dowager. Brent's proposal seemed to glide through the executive branch of the federal government, right to the convening of the First International Opium Commission in Shanghai in February 1909. Nine nations gathered and selected Brent (the head of a three-man U.S. delegation) to preside over its four-day meeting. In many ways, it was the start of an international drug-prohibitionist body endorsed by the United Nations as, between world wars, the League of Nations endorsed it. With no public debate, with no electoral mandate, it presumed a world interest, shared by all nations in eliminating drugs used recreationally (apart from alcohol). Trickle-down prohibition.

U.S. Delegates to the International Opium Commission Conceive of and Steamroll Congress to Pass the First National Drug Prohibition Law in the United States, 1909

Shortly before the commission convened in Shanghai, Brent (and another of the appointed U.S. delegates) requested that Congress approve legislation to demonstrate, to the Chinese especially, that the United States was serious about opium prohibition. In near record time, with hardly any discussion, let alone debate, just weeks after a new Congress was installed, it approved what Brent and Hamilton Wright had suggested, the Opium Exclusion Act. The president signed the act immediately, just before the First International Opium Commission convened. The Opium Exclusion Act banned the importation of opium prepared for smoking, which effectively banned opium smoking in the United States—it was the start of the U.S. War on Drugs, apart from its policy in its Pacific colony.

* * * * *

So, at the beginning, in four spurts, Protestant missionaries played a key role in opium prohibition from conception to legislative enactment. Du Bose provided the ideas and words for the empress dowager in 1906 in the truly cataclysmic Chinese war on opium smoking, and Bishop Brent, following his role in enacting opium prohibition in the Philippines in 1906, was the prime mover in generating an international war on drugs and the first national drug-prohibition law in the United States (both at the start of 1909).

It's hard to imagine an international war on drugs beginning without the Protestant missionaries.

Reasons for Missionary Hatred of Opium

Why create a war on drugs, let alone an international war on drugs? It was not capitalists' idea—they made fortunes from the opium trade. Government administrators didn't dream it up—the opium trade was the largest contributor to civil coffers. In the beginning, Protestant missionaries provided the initiating and moving force; their target was opium smoking, and the smokers were always, almost everywhere, overwhelmingly Chinese.

What did the missionaries have against the Chinese? The Chinese had rejected the missionaries resoundingly since at least the Tientsin Treaty of 1858 (allowing missionaries to enter the Chinese interior and protecting them).[51] The missionaries got swallowed up in China. It was too vast, too populous, too different. Worst of all, the missionaries were simultaneously harassed and ignored. Certainly the cause could not, the missionaries believed, be anything they thought or said or their manner of presentation, for all was done for God. The statistics suggest that the missionaries made about one convert per missionary per year. The Chinese rejected and disdained what the missionaries had given their lives to—lonely, frustrating, unhealthy lives.

A dean of inland China Protestant missionaries expressed his frustration in the late 1800s:

> When we look back to eighty years of missionary labor [in China] . . . our brows must be covered with shame and our hearts filled with sorrow. After eighty years of missionary labor we are thankful for thirty-two thousand communicants; after eighty years of commercial labor there are one hundred and fifty millions of the Chinese who are either personally smokers of the opium or sufferers from the opium vice of husband or wife, father or mother, or some relative. . . . Ah! We have given China something beside the gospel, something that is doing more harm in a week than the united efforts of all our Christian missionaries are doing good in a year. . . . [T]he opium traffic is the sum of all villainies. It debauches more families than drink; it makes more slaves directly than the slave trade.[52]

Just a few years after this screed was released, conditions for missionaries in China would get worse than ever.

> During the brief four months at the height of the uprising [the Boxer Rebellion of 1900] . . . at least 32,000 Chinese Christians were slain. More than 185 Protestant missionaries and members of their families [over 5 percent of the total in China], and 47 Roman Catholic clerics and nuns were killed . . . the greatest single tragedy in the history of Christian evangelism.[53]

Opium is the scapegoat to explain away the failure of the missionaries and their message in China. In their most private, contemplative times, the Chi-

nese chose to smoke opium. Opium, in China, was the religion of the masses. The missionaries were jealous of opium and punished its users. In creating a war on drugs, they distracted attention from their utter failures as missionaries. Opium prohibition was missionary revenge.

Events after 1909 proved that you did not have to be a missionary to love the War on Drugs, but if it were not for the Protestant missionaries in Asia just before then, I cannot see where a war on drugs would come from. The U.S. government only became an active force for drug prohibition after it had a bureaucracy—legislators, narcotics agents, prosecutors, judges, prison guards, drug-treatment agencies, and so forth—that benefited from it and emerged *after* and *as a result of* drug prohibition. In the beginning, the U.S. government merely facilitated the Protestant missionaries who acted as if they occupied a space between heaven and Washington, D.C. What was special about the U.S. government as opposed to Great Britain's was the absence in the United States of a vested interest in the opium trade. The missionary prohibitionists had been urging drug prohibition for decades, but always the British government bureaucracy fought them off. When the United States emerged as a world power, what tipped the balance regarding opium policy was that the missionaries had an open playing field. So, in a sense, it was a coalition of Protestant missionaries and the U.S. government that brought permanent prohibition to the world, but the missionaries were clearly the initiators, the creators, of the International War on Drugs.

NOTES

1. Harry Anslinger and Will Oursler, *The Murderers* (New York: Avon Book Division, 1961).

2. "Conspiracy to Smuggle Opium into This Port," *San Francisco Call*, May 6, 1909, 1.

3. "Opium Smuggler Caught with Goods," *San Francisco Call*, May 25, 1909, 1. That smuggler, San Francisco saloon keeper Joseph Alexander, seems also to have been the first drug snitch for the federal government, for a few weeks later, customs inspectors seized "hop" in a raid in Chinatown (and without a warrant). "Inspectors Seize Contraband 'Hop'," *San Francisco Call*, June 22, 1909, 5.

4. "Grand Jury to Delve into the Bullion Theft," *San Francisco Call*, December 20, 1910, 3.

5. "Strikers Aid in Opium Den Raids," *San Francisco Call*, October 16, 1911. Many other cities experienced raids by California state drug enforcement officers in 1911.

6. "Raids on Joints Net 200 'Dope' Victims—WHITE WOMEN IN DENS," *San Francisco Examiner* November 26, 1911, 73.

7. D. R. McCreesh, "Hop and Dope Fiends Fast Being Recruited from Better Families," *El Paso World*, June 15, 1912, 10–11.

8. John Phillips, "Prevalence of the Heroin Habit," *JAMA* 59(24) (December 14, 1912): 2146–47.

9. J. Frank Chase, *The Dope Evil: From a Reformer's Point of View* (Boston: New England Watch and Ward Society, 1912), and "Says Drug Habit Grips the Nation," *New York Times*, December 5, 1913.

10. Anonymous, "Health," *Survey* 29 (March 22, 1913): 861.

11. Harry Behrendt (Lansing police chief), "The Cause of Vice and Prostitution" (presented to the International Association of Chiefs of Police Hearings, 20th Annual Convention, June 1913; reprinted New York: Arno Press, 1971).

12. "Caught Using Heroin—Forbidden Drug Was Taken Habitually by Bronx Boys," *New York Times*, June 2, 1913.

13. Joseph McIver and George Price, "Drug Addiction: Analysis of 147 Cases at the Philadelphia General Hospital," *JAMA* 66 (February 12, 1916): 476–80. Also see Clifford Farr, "Relative Frequency of the Morphia and Heroine Habits," *New York Medical Journal* 101 (April 1, 1915): 892–94, and "Use of Heroin Spreading Rapidly among Drug Fiends," *Pacific Pharmacist* 7(8) (December 1913): 210–11.

14. As a result of the Chinese Exclusion Act of the 1880s, the number of Chinese in the United States was considerably lower in the early 1900s than it had been twenty years earlier, so I assume the number of Chinese opium smokers had actually gone down in the decades immediately preceding the prohibition of the importation of opium for smoking.

15. Getting the empress dowager to declare a war on opium within China was an incredible coup, which at first glance weakens the notion that the War on Drugs at its origin was anti-Chinese. If the empress dowager's motives for making war on opium could be understood, I suspect she shared a fundamental similarity with the missionaries. She, too, hated the Chinese people for their near total rejection of her for generations. Why else would the she, nearing the end of her long life, declare war on the national pastime of China? The dowager, herself, was an opium smoker still. Under her reign, the Manchu Dynasty was falling apart after four hundred years. She needed an excuse.

16. Edgar Wickberg, *Chinese in Philippine Life, 1850–1898* (New Haven: Yale University Press, 1965), 119.

17. Wong Kwok-Chu, *Chinese in the Philippine Economy, 1898–1941* (Manila: Ateneo de Manila University Press, 1999), 24, 30. Also see Wickberg, *Chinese in Philippine Life*.

18. W. E. Johnson, Commissioner of *The New Voice*, Manila, June 23, 1900, quoted in Dr. and Mrs. Wilbur Crafts and Misses Mary and Margaret Leitch, *Protection of Native Races against Intoxicants and Opium* (New York: Fleming Revell Co., 1900), 208. And "Opium in Philippines," *Washington Post*, June 10, 1903, 2.

19. Arnold Taylor, "American Confrontation with Opium Traffic in the Philippines," *Pacific Historical Review* 36 (August 1967): 307–24. Opium import statistics in the Philippines, as in the United States throughout the late nineteenth and early

twentieth centuries, were influenced by many vagaries. Importation always soared when there was the perception of an imminent crackdown or tariff hike on opium, then tapered off as the opium reserve got smoked away. In "a cholera epidemic of 1902 . . . opiates were administered medically," which partly accounted for the rise in imports (Richard Davenport-Hines, *Pursuit of Oblivion* [New York: W. W. Norton & Company, 2002], 203).

20. Dr. and Mrs. Wilbur Crafts and Misses Mary and Margaret Leitch, *Intoxicants and Opium in all Lands and Times*, 6th rev. ed. of *Protection of Native Races Against Intoxicants and Opium* (Washington, D.C.: International Reform Bureau, 1904), 259–60.

21. The Crafts and Leitches, *Intoxicants and Opium in all Lands and Times*. Taylor, "American Confrontation with Opium Traffic in the Philippines," 313–14, reports that Wilbur Crafts' IRB "sent out 2,000 petitions printed on telegraphic blanks to influential people throughout the country, most of whom signed and returned them to the president."

22. Taylor, "American Confrontation with Opium Traffic in the Philippines," 315.

23. Homer Stuntz, *The Philippines and the Far East* (Cincinnati: Jennings & Pye (and) Eaton & Mains, 1904), 277. The Philippine Commission, reflecting in 1906 on events three years earlier, likewise found "the sinews of war . . . against the proposed legislation were furnished mainly by opium dealers, and the cablegrams which were sent to the US for . . . arousing the moral sentiment . . . against the law, were paid for by the importers and dealers in opium in Manila" (*Philippine Commission Annual Report, 1906* 7[1]: 60).

24. "Opium in the Philippines," *Indian Medical Gazette* 38 (December 1903): 406. The author notes that the *Boston Medical and Surgical Journal* believed that "the wily celestial" had tricked the missionaries into an alliance.

25. Taylor, "American Confrontation with Opium Traffic in the Philippines," 315.

26. Taylor, "American Confrontation with Opium Traffic in the Philippines," 315.

27. "Opium in the Philippines," *Washington Post* (from the *New York Mail and Express*, undated), July 11, 1903, 6.

28. "Opium in the Philippines," *Washington Post*, July 16, 1903, 4.

29. The quote is from Taylor, "American Confrontation with Opium Traffic in the Philippines," 317. It is unclear if the comments summarized by Taylor were the words of Taft or of Taft referring to the views of the Philippine Commission. Taylor's source is "Taft to Root," July 13, 1903, *BIA* (Bureau of Insular Affairs), 1023–25, 1046.

30. "Opium in the Philippines," *Washington Post* (from the *Philadelphia Press*, undated), July 14, 1903, 6.

31. U.S. Senate, "Use of Opium and Traffic Therein." *Message from the President of the United States, Transmitting the Report of the Committee Appointed by the Philippine Commission to Investigate . . . Opium,* March 12, 1906, 59th Cong., 1st sess., S. Doc. 265 (Washington, D.C.: GPO, 1906).

32. U.S. Senate, *Use of Opium and Traffic Therein.* The failure of opium in Hawaii is cited by Dr. Sluggett: after the law, "opium . . . was smuggled in; and the law was sometimes made use of by unscrupulous persons as a means of blackmailing Chinese" (87); its failure in Hong Kong is cited by Ho Su Cho, a merchant: "Many years ago, an attempt was made to forbid the use of opium, but it was unsuccessful" (90); and

its failure in Burma is cited by its commissioner of finance: an attempt to limit opium smoking to registered users revealed that it was "absolutely impossible to prevent unregistered opium smoking and caused such a great extension of smuggling that we decided to change" (120–21). A municipal magistrate in Rangoon testified, "our registers are worse than useless . . . very easily dodged" (119); the U.S. consul said of Formosa, "A prohibitive policy would cause constant friction between the authorities and the Chinese. . . . [It] would drive from the island the element [better-class Chinese] which the authorities wished to retain. . . . Smugglers would swarm the coast, prepared to risk arrest . . . [for] large profits. It was then decided . . . to permit the smoking of opium by the Chinese under certain conditions" (206).

33. U.S. Senate, *Use of Opium and Traffic Therein*. For the negative effects of special opium police in Java, see the interview with de Jongh, the opium excise inspector in Java (124–27); for the negative effects in Formosa, see the interview with Goto, the vice governor of Formosa (66).

34. U.S. Senate, *Use of Opium and Traffic Therein*, 88, Interview XX with Mrs. Fearon. "Absolute prohibition . . . would entail extreme suffering among the victims of the opium habit. . . . [It is] impossible . . . [for many to] break off immediately without . . . causing distress and even death." For similar views by the former managing partner of Singapore's opium farm, see p. 97.

35. "[T]he suffering caused by immediate [opium] prohibition would have been great, and, moreover, such action would have been unintelligible to Chinese consumers, among whom the use of opium has become a traditional custom. In view of the sensitive condition of the islanders . . . who had only just been chastised into submission, the government felt that a prohibitive measure would be construed as oppressive and would tend to excite disturbance. Added to this, the smuggling problem made drastic measures seem impracticable" (U.S. Senate, *Use of Opium and Traffic Therein,* 26).

36. U.S. Senate, *Use of Opium and Traffic Therein,* 81, Interview XVI with Messrs. Yu, Yeng, Chao, Li, and Su, all "leading Chinese Merchants of Shanghai . . . holding Taotai rank." The "actual" desires of the Chinese merchants is from Taylor, "American Confrontation with Opium Traffic in the Philippines," 315.

37. See Stuntz, *The Philippines and the Far East*, 464–73, in reference to Episcopalians; see pp. 465, 467 for the quotes about Brent.

38. U.S. Senate, *Use of Opium and Traffic Therein,* 19, "Findings and Recommendations" (lead paragraph).

39. U.S. Senate, *Use of Opium and Traffic Therein,* 19. Some of the suspected moralistic add-ons by Brent to the Opium Committee report are "[Opium] is one of the gravest, if not the gravest, moral problems of the Orient" (20); "[U.S. treaties with China in 1880 and 1903 are] due to a recognition that the use of opium is an evil for which no financial gain can compensate and which America will not allow her citizens to encourage even passively" (21); in China "(1) . . . the user of opium commonly increases his dose; (2) . . . he is worthless and unfit for work when deprived of his customary dose; . . . (4) . . . excessive use of opium is in all ways deleterious, leading to unthrift and occasionally to arson and other crimes, but generally to crimes against self. . . . Nevertheless, the sales of wives and children are frequently made in order to secure opium" (33).

40. U.S. Senate, *Use of Opium and Traffic Therein*, 51.

41. U.S. Senate, *Use of Opium and Traffic Therein*, 26.

42. U.S. Senate, *Use of Opium and Traffic Therein*, 73.

43. U.S. Senate, *Use of Opium and Traffic Therein*, 72

44. U.S. Senate, *Use of Opium and Traffic Therein*, 46–47.

45. U.S. Senate, *Use of Opium and Traffic Therein*, 45–46.

46. "Opium in the Orient: Report of the Philippine Commission," *North China Herald* 75 (April 14, 20, 28, 1905): 88–89, 104–6, 133–36, 193–95, 211–12.

47. "Opium in the Orient," 88.

48. Hampden Du Bose, "The Philippines Report on Opium," *North China Herald* 79 (May 18, 1906): 379.

49. Hampden Du Bose, "Correspondence—The Opium Memorial and the Imperial Edict," *North China Herald* 80 (September 28, 1906): 777–78): "On May 25 . . . [the] Viceroy of Nanking, offered, if a Memorial on opium in proper form and signed by the Protestant missionaries of all nationalities labouring in China were sent to him, that he would forward the same to the throne." After it was sent out in July "to all the Mission stations . . . twelve hundred missionaries signed the Memorial . . . [which was then] sent from Soochow [where Du Bose resided] on August 13 to the Viceroy; . . . [S]ignatures were from seventeen provinces and represented seven nationalities. His Excellency promptly forwarded the same through the Foreign Office to the Emperor. On . . . September 20, His Majesty . . . issued an [antiopium] edict. . . . The wording of the edict was quite similar to that of the Memorial." Deliberation of a new and radically different opium policy, which in the 1830s took years and involved a sharp debate among the emperor's top advisers (the Censorate), seemed nonexistent in the 103 days between the time the viceroy of Nanking offered his advice on how to reach the throne until the imperial antidrug edict.

50. The description of men, women, and children working in concert over many months in different roles regarding opium growth and processing is not based on Chinese sources but on reports from India. I assume that practices in growing, harvesting, and postharvesting processing procedures and their impact on local populations were similar where opium was the mainstay of a vast territory.

51. The 1858 Treaty of Tientsin, which allowed missionaries access to inland China, essentially brought the opium war of the early 1840s to a close. The special status accorded missionaries has nothing to do with that war and probably everything to do with the fact that the British relied on missionary translators.

52. J. Hudson Taylor, address at the Centenary Conference of Protestant Missions of the World, London 1888, reprinted with permission in the Crafts and Leitches' *Protection of Native Races*, 107–8. Taylor, the superintendent of the China Inland Mission, stated in 1900 that the 1888 address "expresses his present views."

53. Nat Brandt, *Massacre in Shansi* (Syracuse, N.Y.: Syracuse University Press, 1994), xiii. To get a good sense of the impact of the murders on the missionaries and their supporters, see Marshall Broomhall, ed., *Martyred Missionaries of the China Inland Mission . . . Perils and Sufferings of Some Who Escaped* (London: Morgand & Scott, 1901).

3

Alcohol Prohibition and Drug Prohibition: Lessons from Alcohol Policy for Drug Policy

Harry G. Levine and Craig Reinarman

Since the mid-1980s, growing numbers of Americans have come to recognize the harshness, expense, and ineffectiveness of U.S. drug prohibition, and they have advocated alternative approaches, including harm reduction, drug decriminalization, and even outright drug legalization. They have also looked for lessons in America's own experiences with alcohol prohibition and how the United States turned from nationwide alcohol prohibition to various forms of local alcohol regulation.

In the first part of this chapter, we review the rise, effects, and fall of national alcohol prohibition in the United States, and we examine the rationale and organization of the system of alcohol regulation instituted after repeal. We focus on lessons from the American experience with alcohol prohibition and alcohol regulation that might be useful for understanding drug prohibition and drug regulation.

In the second part, we discuss the current worldwide system of drug prohibition. We focus on three crises, or dilemmas, that global drug prohibition now faces: the international harm-reduction movement; the growing opposition, especially in Europe, to harsh drug policies; and the unstoppable use of cannabis throughout the world.

Historical studies cannot provide simple and straightforward answers to the complex drug policy questions now confronting Americans. However, closer attention to the history of alcohol prohibition and regulation and to the character and scope of global drug prohibition can help us better understand the

---

Earlier versions of portions of this chapter have appeared in several publications. Some of the materials on prohibition and alcohol control are drawn from Levine, 1985; Levine and Reinarman, 1993, 1998. The materials on drug prohibition are drawn from Reinarman and Levine, 1997; Levine, 2002, 2003; and Reinarman 2003.

situation we face in the early twenty-first century and move toward less costly and more humane and effective drug policies.

FROM TEMPERANCE TO PROHIBITION
TO ALCOHOL CONTROL

The antialcohol (or temperance) movement was created in early-nineteenth-century America by physicians, ministers, and large employers concerned about the drunkenness of workers and servants. By the mid-1830s, temperance had become a mass movement of the middle class. Temperance was not, as is sometimes thought, the campaign of rural backwaters; rather, temperance was on the cutting edge of social reform and was closely allied with the antislavery and women's rights movements. Always very popular, the antialcohol crusade remained the largest enduring middle-class movement of the nineteenth century. (Levine 1978, 1984; Tyrell 1979; Gusfield 1986; Rumbarger 1989; Blocker 1989).

The antialcohol movement was devoted to convincing people that alcoholic drink in any form was dangerous and destructive. Throughout the nineteenth century, temperance supporters insisted that alcohol slowly but inevitably destroyed the moral character and the physical and mental health of all who drank it. Temperance supporters regarded alcohol the way people today view heroin: as an inherently addicting substance. Moderate consumption of alcohol, they maintained, naturally led to compulsive use—to addiction.

From the beginning, temperance ideology contained a powerful strand of fantasy. It held that alcohol was the major cause of nearly all social problems: unemployment, poverty, business failure, slums, insanity, crime, and violence (especially against women and children). For the very real social and economic problems of industrializing America, the antialcohol movement offered universal abstinence as the panacea.

From roughly the 1850s on, many temperance supporters endorsed the idea of prohibition. After the Civil War, the Prohibition Party, modeled on the Republican Party, championed the cause. Nineteenth-century Prohibitionists believed that only when sufficient numbers of their party members held office would prohibition be practical because only then would it be fully enforced.

In the twentieth century, a new Prohibitionist organization—the Anti-Saloon League—came to dominate the movement (Odegard 1928; Timberlake 1963; Sinclair 1964; Gusfield 1968; Kerr 1985; Rumbarger 1989). The league patterned itself on the modern corporation, hiring lawyers to write model laws and organizers to raise funds and collect political debts. The league put its considerable resources behind candidates of any party who would vote as it directed on the single issue of liquor. By expanding the numbers of elected officials beholden to it, and by writing laws for those legislators to enact, the league pushed through many local prohibition laws and some state measures. In 1913, the league finally declared itself in favor of constitutional prohibition. Increasing numbers of large corporations joined the many Protestant churches that had long supported the league. Prohibitionists mobilized the final support for prohibition during the hyperpatriotic fervor of World War I.

By December 1917, both houses of Congress had voted by the required two-thirds majority to send to the states for ratification a constitutional amendment prohibiting the manufacture, sale, transportation, import, or export of intoxicating liquor. In November 1918, Congress passed the War Prohibition Act banning the manufacture and sale of all beverages with more than 2.75 percent alcohol. On January 16, 1919, Nebraska became the thirty-sixth state to ratify the Eighteenth Amendment, which was to go into effect in one year. In October 1919, Congress overrode President Woodrow Wilson's veto to pass a strict prohibition-enforcement act known by the name of its sponsor, Andrew Volstead of Minnesota, chair of the House Judiciary Committee. The Volstead Act defined as "intoxicating liquor" any beverage containing more 0.5 percent alcohol.

At midnight on January 16, 1920, the Eighteenth Amendment took effect. The famous minister Billy Sunday celebrated by preaching a sermon to ten thousand people in which he repeated the fantasy at the heart of the temperance and prohibition crusades:

> The reign of tears is over. The slums will soon be a memory. We will turn our prisons into factories and our jails into storehouses and corncribs. Men will walk upright now, women will smile, and the children will laugh. Hell will be forever for rent. (Quoted in Kobler 1973, 12)

Prohibitionism was not, as is sometimes implied, a public health campaign to reduce mortality from cirrhosis of the liver or alcoholic admissions to state hospitals. As Joseph Gusfield (1968) has pointed out, Prohibitionists were utopian moralists; they believed that eliminating the legal manufacture and sale of alcoholic drink would solve the major social and economic problems of American society.

National Alcohol Prohibition, 1920–1933

The many literary, photographic, and cinematic images of the Prohibition era capture some of the essential features of the period. Prohibition was massively and openly violated, and alcohol was readily available in most of the

United States. New institutions and cultural practices appeared: bootleggers and speakeasies, hip flasks and bathtub gin, rum runners smuggling in liquor and prohibition agents like Elliott Ness smashing down doors. Adulterated and even poisonous alcohol was sold, and many people were locked up for violating prohibition laws. (For rich descriptions of the Prohibition era, see Allen 1931; Lyle 1960; Allsop 1961; Mertz 1970; Kobler 1973; Everest 1978; and Cashman 1981. Burnham (1968) offers perhaps the only serious scholarly case for the success of Prohibition. For the most recent evidence and discussions of its failures, see Miron and Zwiebel 1991; Morgan 1991; and Thornton 1991.)

Public opposition to Prohibition began even before the Volstead Act passed, especially among labor unions, but organized opposition remained small and fragmented until 1926. Then one organization, the Association against the Prohibition Amendment (AAPA), took over the campaign for repeal. Headed by Pierre DuPont and other powerful corporate leaders, the AAPA gathered increasing numbers of wealthy and prominent supporters, including many former Prohibitionists. Although Prohibition would have been repealed eventually, the AAPA unquestionably accelerated the process (Kyvig 1979; Levine 1985; Rumbarger 1989).

Just as World War I had provided the necessary context for rallying popular support to pass Prohibition, the Great Depression provided the necessary context for repeal. Prohibition's supporters had long argued that banning alcohol would ensure prosperity and increase law and order. In the late 1920s and early 1930s, Prohibition's opponents made exactly the same argument. Repeal, they promised, would provide jobs, stimulate the economy, increase tax revenue, and reduce the "lawlessness" stimulated by and characteristic of the illegal liquor industry.

The Depression also played a crucial role in undermining elite support for Prohibition. To some extent, alcohol prohibition had originally gained the support of large employers because they believed it would increase worker discipline and productivity and reduce other social problems. The mass violations of national prohibition in the 1920s, followed by the economic depression of the 1930s, raised a new specter: Prohibition, many came to believe, undermined respect for all law, including property law. This "lawlessness," as people then termed it, frightened many of the rich and powerful, like DuPont and John D. Rockefeller Jr., far more than problems with worker efficiency did (Leuchtenburg 1958; Kyvig 1979; Levine 1985). In addition, in the early 1930s, the threat of revolt and revolution was in the air. There were food riots in many cities; unemployed people formed militant organizations; mobs stopped trains and took over warehouses of food. Socialists and Communists held rallies of tens of thousands, angry armies of marchers camped in front of the White House, and some wealthy people had machine guns mounted on the roofs of their estates (Leuchtenburg 1958; Piven and Cloward 1971, 1977; Manchester 1974).

Those with wealth and power increasingly supported repeal, in part because they felt the need to do something to raise public morale and show that the government was in some way responsive to popular pressure in a terrible depression. In 1931, Matthew Woll, vice president of the American Federation of Labor and the sole labor member of the AAPA board, told President Herbert Hoover's National Commission on Law Observance and Enforcement (the Wickersham Commission) that workers were losing faith in the government's willingness to help them, and that Prohibition was causing them further to distrust and resent government. By 1932, a number of influential leaders and commentators had also concluded that legalizing beer would make workers feel better about government and take their minds off their troubles. Senators were told, "Beer would have a decidedly soothing tendency on the present mental attitude of the working men. . . . It would do a great deal to change their mental attitude on economic conditions." Walter Lippman argued, "Beer would be a great help in fighting off the mental depression which afflicts great multitudes" (quotes in Gordon 1943, 104). The Wickersham Commission explicitly pointed to the class resentment and lawlessness engendered by Prohibition in its report to Congress:

> Naturally . . . laboring men resent the insistence of employers who drink that their employees be kept from temptation. Thus the law may be made to appear aimed at and enforced against the insignificant while the wealthy enjoy immunity. This feeling is reinforced when it is seen that the wealthy are generally able to procure pure liquors, while those with less means may run the risk of poisoning. Moreover, searches of homes . . . have necessarily seemed to bear more upon people of moderate means than upon those of wealth or influence. (1931, 54–5)

On November 16, 1932, the Senate voted to submit the Twenty-first Amendment to the states for ratification. It would repeal the Eighteenth Amendment and return to the states the power to regulate alcohol. On March 13, 1933, a few days after he was sworn in as president, Franklin Roosevelt asked Congress to modify the Volstead Act to legalize 3.2 percent–alcohol beer to provide needed tax revenue. By April 7, beer was legal in most of the country. On December 5, 1933, Utah became the thirty-sixth state to ratify the Twenty-first Amendment. National alcohol prohibition was repealed, effective immediately.

In late 1933 and in 1934, bills creating state alcohol-control agencies sped through state legislatures. The model for most of the legislation had been written by a group of policy-oriented researchers and attorneys associated with Rockefeller and policy institutes he had created or financially supported (Levine 1985). Within two years of repeal, nearly every state had an agency to supervise the sale and distribution of alcoholic beverages, and alcohol had ceased to be a controversial and politically charged issue. The production, sale, and distribution of alcoholic beverages today is still largely governed by the alcohol-control structures designed and implemented at that time.

Effects of Prohibition on Consumption and Public Health

It has frequently been observed that drug prohibition tends to drive out the weaker and milder forms of drugs and to increase the availability and use of stronger and more dangerous drugs (see, e.g., Brecher 1972). This has been reported so often that many analysts speak of it as an "iron law" of drug prohibition that holds because milder drugs are usually bulkier, harder to hide and smuggle, and less remunerative. People involved in the illicit drug business, therefore, frequently find it in their interest to do business in the more compact and potent substances. For example, current interdiction efforts are most successful at capturing boats carrying many large bales of marijuana; therefore, many drug smugglers have turned to smuggling cocaine or heroin because it is easier and far more lucrative than smuggling marijuana (see Murphy, Waldorf, and Reinarman 1991).

This "law" of drug prohibition captures what happened during alcohol prohibition. The major effect of the Eighteenth Amendment was to dramatically reduce beer drinking (and therefore total alcohol consumption). At the same time, prohibition increased the consumption of hard liquor (especially among the middle class). The fashionableness of the martini and other mixed drinks among the middle class is in part a historical legacy of prohibition, when criminalization made hard liquor the most available form of beverage alcohol.

From 1890 to 1915, beer accounted for more of the total alcohol consumed than hard liquor. In 1915, for example, beer drinking accounted for nearly twice as much of the alcohol consumed as spirits did. C. Warburton compared alcohol consumption in the period from 1911 to 1914 with that during the Prohibition years from 1927 to 1930 and concluded that while "the per capita consumption of beer has been reduced about 70 per cent . . . the per capita consumption of wine has increased about 65 per cent . . . [and] the per capita consumption of spirits has increased about 10 per cent" (Warburton 1932, 260). This change was not permanent—after repeal, spirits consumption fell while beer consumption rose. By 1935, the alcohol consumed from beer equaled that from spirits, and by 1945, Americans were getting 50 percent more of their total alcohol from beer than from hard liquor (Levine and Reinarman 1993, 1998; Rorabaugh 1979; Miron and Zwiebel 1991).

The recent public debate about drug laws has increased interest in the effects of prohibition on public health, the economy, and social problems. These were very lively questions during the Prohibition period, but they have been largely ignored since. However, in the last two decades, alcohol researchers in a number of countries have investigated at length the relationship between total per capita alcohol consumption and specific illnesses, especially cirrhosis of the liver. The data available for the Prohibition years in the United States will always be poor because it is impossible to get accurate consumption figures for an illegal substance. However, changes over many decades in countries that have kept accurate consumption and health statistics do allow us to make some inferences about the relationship between overall alcohol consumption and liver cirrhosis. Although not all liver cirrhosis is caused by heavy drinking, much is. Furthermore, cirrhosis rates generally follow overall per capita consumption rates. These effects are mediated by dietary patterns, by type of alcoholic beverages consumed, and by when they are consumed. The level of health care people receive also affects cirrhosis death rates. In general, however, the positive relationship between alcohol consumption and cirrhosis holds: when consumption increases, liver cirrhosis increases (Bruun et al. 1975; Mäkelaä et al. 1981; Moore and Gerstein 1981; Single, Morgan, and Delint 1981).

One important way to evaluate the public health consequences of alcohol policies, then, is in terms of how they affect consumption. In 1932, Warburton pointed out that "except for the first three years, the per capita consumption of alcohol has been greater under prohibition than during the war period [1917–1919], with high taxation and restricted production and sale" (260). Both Prohibition and post-Prohibition alcohol regulation kept overall consumption down compared with the decades prior to Prohibition; indeed, post-Prohibition regulatory policies kept alcohol use sufficiently low that it was not until the end of the 1960s, thirty-five years after repeal, that per capita alcohol consumption rose to the levels of 1915 (Levine and Reinarman 1993, 1998). Whatever public health benefits prohibition achieved in terms of reducing consumption, alcohol regulation in the 1930s and early 1940s accomplished them as well. Further, this occurred despite the fact that the post-Prohibition regulatory system had little or no public health focus, and despite the fact that the liquor industry (like most other U.S. industries) gained increasing influence over the agencies that were supposed to regulate it. In short, alcohol control worked almost as well as Prohibition in limiting alcohol consumption and more effectively than pre-Prohibition policies.

It is also important to note that other nations achieved even greater reductions in per capita consumption than the United States—without the negative consequences of Prohibition. Robin Room (1988) says that in Australia, a series of alcohol-control measures instituted in the early twentieth century substantially reduced spirits consumption. More important, Australia's regulatory policies significantly reduced total alcohol consumption as well as the incidence of alcohol-related health problems, notably cirrhosis mortality and alcoholic psychosis. All of this happened under regulated sale, not prohibition.

Great Britain's experience parallels that of Australia. England reduced overall consumption by instituting fairly stringent alcohol regulation at about the same time as the United States instituted Prohibition. Moreover, as Ethan Nadelmann notes, it reduced "the negative consequences of alcohol consumption more effectively than did the United States, but it did so in a manner that raised substantial government revenues." By contrast, the U.S. government not only spent large sums attempting to enforce its prohibition laws, but it was also unable to prevent the flow of money into criminal enterprises (Nadelmann 1989b, 1102–3).

As Nadelmann puts it, "British experience [as well as the Australian experience] strongly indicates that the national prohibition of alcohol in the United States was, on balance, not successful." Prohibition of course failed to fulfill the fantasies of Prohibitionists about eliminating major social problems like poverty, unemployment, and crime. Yet, even in the less utopian terms of reducing total alcohol consumption, U.S. prohibition was no more effective than regulated sale in the 1930s and early 1940s. Prohibition, however, produced far more substantial negative side effects than did regulation.

Few other nations had local alcohol-prohibition laws, and only Finland instituted constitutional prohibition (repealing it before the United States and for many of the same reasons). Although there are, today, movements in some Nordic and English-speaking countries (Canada, Australia, New Zealand, Great Britain) focusing on the public health dangers of alcohol, these are not prohibitionist groups. In the United States, even many local prohibition laws have been replaced by regulation of some kind. Long after repeal, the consensus remains that national alcohol prohibition was bad public policy.

Alcohol Production and Distribution during Prohibition

During constitutional alcohol prohibition, consumption was shaped by the requirements of illicit production. It was much more profitable and cost-effective to make and distribute distilled spirits (gin, vodka, whiskey, or rum) than beer. Beer is mostly water—only 3 to 6 percent alcohol. Production and storage of beer require enormous tanks, many barrels, huge trucks, and a substantial investment in equipment. Hard liquor is 40 to 50 percent alcohol; it contains up to fifteen times more pure alcohol than beer. Because alcohol content was the main determinant of price, spirits were much more valuable than beer and also could be hidden and transported more easily. Furthermore, spirits could be preserved indefinitely, whereas beer spoiled very quickly. Large-scale beer bottling and refrigeration only developed in the 1930s, after repeal (Baron 1962; Kyvig 1979).

The rising supply of hard liquor came from many sources. Tens of thousands of people produced it in small, compact stills in sheds, basements, and attics and in the woods. It was also smuggled from Canada, Mexico, and Europe. Some of the largest names in distilling today entered the business or grew wealthy during the Prohibition era—notably the Bronfmans of Canada, who owned Seagrams. A considerable amount of alcohol was also diverted from purported industrial or medical uses (Baum 2003).

Wine consumption also increased during prohibition, to about 65 percent more than the pre–World War I period, according to Warburton (1932). Standard table wine contains 10 to 14 percent alcohol. Much of the wine was made for personal consumption and as a profitable side-business by immigrants from wine countries, especially Italy. After the first few years of prohibition, the California wine-grape industry experienced a boom, and vineyard prices increased substantially. California grape growers planted hearty, thick-skinned grapes that could be shipped easily and used for small-scale and home wine making. Much of the California wine-grape crop was shipped to Chicago and New York in newly developed refrigerated boxcars. The grapes were bought right off the train by wholesalers, who resold them in immigrant neighborhoods. The homemade wine was then distributed to smaller cities and towns (Muscatine, Amerine, and Thompson 1984).

Although it is true that Prohibition provided a major boost for organized crime, it is not true (although widely believed today) that gangsters and large criminal organizations supplied most Prohibition-era alcohol. In Chicago and a few other large cities, large criminal gangs indeed dominated alcohol distribution, especially by the end of the 1920s.

Most of the alcohol production and distribution, however, was on a smaller scale. In addition to homemade wines and family stills, people drove cars and trucks to Canada and returned with a load of liquor. Fishing boats and pleasure boats did the same. Spirits and wine were also prescribed by physicians and available at pharmacies. Many people certified themselves as ministers and rabbis and distributed large quantities of "sacramental wine." Alcoholic beverages were made and sold to supplement other income during hard times. Prohibition thus shaped the structure of the alcohol industry in a distinctive way: it decentralized and democratized production and distribution (Lyle 1960; Allsop 1961; Sinclair 1964; Everest 1978; Cashman 1981).

Today, as well, most people in the illicit drug business are small-scale entrepreneurs. Supporters of the drug war frequently suggest that elimination of the current large-scale producers and distributors would have a lasting effect on drug production and distribution. There is no more evidence supporting this now than there was during alcohol prohibition. Much illicit drug production today is also decentralized and democratized. There is no criminal syndicate whose elimination would stop the distribution of any currently illicit drug or even reduce the supply for very long. Today, some groups, families, and business organizations (like the so-called Medellin cocaine cartel) have grown very rich in the illicit drug business. However, just as Al Capone was quickly replaced, so have new producers taken the place of those cocaine kingpins who have been arrested. Indeed, after billions of dollars have been spent on interdiction by Customs, the Drug Enforcement Agency, and even the Armed Forces, both heroin and cocaine are more plentiful, cheaper, and purer than they were in the 1970s. Even when interdiction does affect the supply of a criminalized substance, the effects are often ironic. The partial success of the Nixon administration's "Operation Intercept," for example, gave rise to what is now a huge domestic marijuana industry (Brecher 1972) that has become ever more decentralized and democratic as armed helicopter raids have increased.

In short, whereas prohibition regimes tend to be a boon to organized crime, they also increase the number and types of people involved in illicit production and distribution (Williams 1989; Murphy, Waldorf, and Reinarman 1991). Whether production occurs in a mob syndicate or on a family marijuana patch, the result tends to be a shift toward production and sale of more concentrated forms of intoxicating substances. Recognition of such tendencies in the Prohibition era accelerated the process of repeal and informed the search for alternative regulatory systems.

Establishing an Alcohol-Control System

In 1933, at the very end of constitutional prohibition, the difficulties of creating an alcohol-control system seemed formidable. In the years before constitutional prohibition in the United States, there had been little systematic control of the alcohol industry. The Eighteenth Amendment had not eliminated the business but rather had profoundly altered its shape. By 1933, a sprawling, illegal industry for producing and distributing alcoholic beverages was in place, composed of uncountable numbers of small, independent distributors and producers and some larger ones. For fourteen years, this industry had kept the United States well supplied with alcohol. The mass patronage of this illicit industry—and the political and economic implications of such a popular display of disrespect for the law—was a major factor in convincing Rockefeller and other prominent supporters of Prohibition to reverse field and press for repeal.

During Prohibition, the liquor business was wide open. In most cities and many towns, speakeasies closed when they wished or not at all; they sold whatever they wanted, to whomever they cared to, at whatever price they chose. They decorated as they wished and had a free hand in providing food and entertainment. Producers completely controlled alcohol production, used whatever ingredients they wished, and manufactured alcohol of whatever strength they wished. Neither producers nor distributors paid any taxes (excepting payoffs to police and politicians), and they were not regulated by any government agency. During Prohibition, the liquor industry was probably the freest large industry in America.

Alcohol control, on the other hand, was premised on government intervention in every aspect of the liquor business. Controversial issues, such as whether food must be served, women admitted, music and games banned, bars and bar stools allowed, all had to be settled. The number, types, and locations of on- and off-premises outlets and their hours of sale had to be determined. Producers had to be regulated to ensure that products were safe and of a uniform alcohol content. In order to eliminate untrustworthy or disreputable persons, both producers and distributors had to be screened, licensed, and made to pay taxes. Legal drinking had to be socially organized in a way that would not be an affront to the abstaining portion of the population. Conversely, the control system could not make regulation so tight or taxes so high that drinkers would prefer to patronize illicit bootleggers or speakeasies. Americans, after all, were by then quite used to disobeying liquor laws.

Prohibitionists had always argued that the liquor business was inherently unregulatable. The onus was now on reformers to show that this was not true and that they could create structures to make the industry obey laws and yield taxes. The task, as expressed in the catchall title for alternatives to prohibition, was "liquor control" or "alcohol control" in the fullest sense of the term. In short, repeal posed an enormous problem of social engineering. Constructing alcohol control involved problems of government regulation so large and complex as to make some of the classic Progressive-era reforms—regulating meat packing, for example—seem paltry. Except for national prohibition, postrepeal alcohol regulation is probably the most striking twentieth-century example of government power used to reshape directly both an entire industry and the conditions under which its products are consumed.

The Rockefeller Report

Prior to the passage of the Eighteenth Amendment, alcohol was regulated by cities, towns, and sometimes counties. State governments were rarely involved in regulating production or distribution. Prohibition then shifted control to the federal government. Postrepeal policy, however, made state governments chiefly responsible for devising and implementing a regulatory system. States could, and often did, then allow for considerable local option and variation.

By the end of the 1920s, the AAPA had outlined some rough plans for alternatives to prohibition, but they had not been well worked out. The central principles of post-Prohibition alcohol-control systems adopted by almost every state legislature were first fully laid out in a report sponsored by Rockefeller and issued in October 1933, shortly before repeal was ratified. Rockefeller's long-time adviser, Raymond Fosdick, was the senior author. Fosdick supervised the group of attorneys and policy analysts, most of whom worked with or for the Institute of Public Administration, a Progressive-era policy institute in New York that Rockefeller had funded for a number of years. The report was issued in press releases to newspapers and magazines over several weeks. Finally, the Rockefeller Report (as it was called at the time) was released as a book, *Toward Liquor Control*, by Raymond Fosdick and Albert Scott.

Although few at the time recognized it, *Toward Liquor Control* had taken as its basic conclusions virtually all of the central recommendations made thirty years earlier by another elite-sponsored alcohol-policy group called the Committee of Fifty. The Committee of Fifty, which was generally opposed to alcohol prohibition, had produced five books on various aspects of the "alcohol problem" around the turn of the century. Fosdick and the other study members had read the Committee of Fifty's reports and quoted them on the corruption and lawlessness resulting from earlier forms of local prohibition. The Rockefeller Report echoed the Committee of Fifty's conclusion that the legitimacy of the law must be of primary concern in liquor regulation. Both reports agreed that the specific content of the law mattered less than that the laws be obeyed. Both reports argued that alcohol regulation required a flexible system that could be continually monitored and adjusted. Further, both reports advised that, if possible, government should take over the selling of alcoholic beverages (Billings 1905; Levine 1983; Rumbarger 1989).

The specific plan for alcohol control suggested by *Toward Liquor Control,* and the Rockefeller Report's most controversial proposal, was that each state take over as a public monopoly the retail sale, for off-premises consumption, of spirits, wine, and beer above 3.2 percent alcohol. As Fosdick and Scott explained, "The primary task of the [State Alcohol] Authority would be the establishment of a chain of its own retail stores for the sale of the heavier alcoholic beverages by package only." This is the source of the term "package stores" still used today for liquor outlets in many states where people buy alcohol beverages in a bottle to be consumed off premises. The state-run outlets of Canadian provinces and of Sweden, Norway, and Finland were cited as working examples of such a plan. This quickly became known as the "monopoly plan" and at the time was usually called the "Rockefeller plan."

For those states not willing to establish government liquor stores, Fosdick and Scott proposed an alternative system: regulation by license. They cited England as the best example of a working license system. A nonpartisan board appointed by the governor would have statewide authority to issue liquor licenses and regulate the industry. "Tied houses" would not be permitted; that is, no retail establishments could be owned directly by or under exclusive contract to a distiller or brewer.

Although it offered guidelines for a licensing system, *Toward Liquor Control* favored the monopoly plan. The possibility of increasing profits, they said, would encourage private businesses to sell more alcohol, to buy political influence and lax enforcement, and to violate laws. Rockefeller explained the chief advantage of government-owned liquor stores in his foreword to the book: "Only as the profit motive is eliminated is there any hope of controlling the liquor traffic in the interests of a decent society. To approach the problem from any other angle is only to tinker with it and to ensure failure." The irony of a Rockefeller warning about the dangers of the profit motive was not lost on observers in 1933. Like others at the time, Rockefeller had concluded, probably correctly, that government ownership brought greater powers than licensed businesses to regulate and control behavior and ensure obedience to the law.

For both the licensing plan and the monopoly plan, *Toward Liquor Control* outlined a detailed set of matters over which the state agency would have jurisdiction. These included the power to acquire real estate and other capital by purchase, lease, or condemnation; determine and change prices at will; establish a system of personal identification of purchasers; issue permits for and regulate the use of beer and wine for off-premises consumption and for on-premises consumption in hotels, restaurants, clubs, railway dining cars, and passenger boats; require alcohol manufacturers and importers to report on quantities produced and shipped; regulate or eliminate alcohol beverage advertising; and determine the internal design, visibility from the street, hours and days of sale, number, and location of alcohol outlets.

In January 1934, a model law based on the guidelines of *Toward Liquor Control* and written by the staff of the Institute for Public Administration was published as a supplement to the *National Municipal Review*. The *Review* was the official journal of the National Municipal League, another Progressive-era policy organization supported by the Rockefellers. The model law and other supporting documents were widely circulated to legislators throughout the country in the months following repeal. State legislators, faced with difficult political choices and having little personal expertise in the complexities of liquor regulation, turned to the authoritative and virtually unchallenged plans of the Rockefeller commission and the National Municipal League. In a letter in the Rockefeller Archives, one of the model law's authors estimated that the monopoly law was taken almost verbatim by fifteen states and that the licensing law served as the text or draft for many more (Gulick 1977; Levine 1985).

Alcohol Control in Operation

Postrepeal regulation transformed the alcohol beverage industry. Finland, the only other nation to have experimented with constitutional prohibition, had nationalized production of spirits. However, such proposals were not seriously discussed in the United States. Instead, production took the form of an oligopoly of relatively few corporations. By the end of the 1930s, about 80 percent of all distilled liquor made in the United States was manufactured by four corporations. The beer industry, although more diverse nationally because beer required quick and local distribution, was monopolized by region or area. Regulatory agencies preferred to deal with a few large corporations—they were easier to police and to make agreements with and more likely to be concerned with keeping the image of the industry clean and respectable. This pattern of monopolization was not unique of course; most major American industries—the steel, automobile, soft drink, and chemical industries, for example—were increasingly dominated by a few large corporations. (From at least the time of the National Recovery Act at the start of the New Deal, federal government policy often encouraged such concentration. The alcohol industry was exceptional only in how quickly many small producers were overtaken by a few dominant ones.)

Although production became oligopolistic, distribution was splintered and scattered. Perhaps the most important long-term innovation in post-Prohibition alcohol regulation was that it permitted the legal sale of alcohol at a wide variety of sites. Before Prohibition, the saloon had been a single, all-purpose institution—there one drank beer, wine, or spirits, and there one purchased for off-premises consumption a bottle of spirits or a bucket of beer. After repeal, alcohol control created several different types of establishments to sell alcoholic beverages. In most states, special stores were designated for selling distilled liquor and wine—often they could not sell any food at all or even cigarettes. Beer, on the other hand, was made relatively widely available in bottles and cans, with grocery stores and small markets licensed to sell it. In other words, after Prohibition, the sale of bottled alcohol was increasingly separated from the public drinking place. This encouraged the privatization of drinking. Whether alone or with others, drinking became something more commonly done at home—where, it should be noted, drinking patterns were often moderated by family norms (see Zinberg 1984). By 1941, off-premises consumption accounted for the majority of alcohol sales (Harrison and Laine 1936; Kyvig 1979, 189).

The character of public drinking was significantly altered by these regulatory changes. A new class of licenses for on-premises consumption of beer only, or of beer and wine, was established and liberally issued to restaurants and cafeterias, where eating moderated the character and effects of drinking. This separated the barroom selling distilled liquor and beer as a distinct institution. Many state alcohol-control laws made provision for a local option whereby a county government could prohibit specific kinds of liquor selling within its borders. This option has been widely exercised. As late as 1973, of the 3,073 counties in the United States, 672 prohibited sales of distilled liquor by the drink for on-premises consumption, and 545 totally prohibited sales of distilled spirits (Alcohol Beverage Control Administration 1973).

Under alcohol control, all establishments licensed for on-premises consumption of spirits were specifically restricted in ways that shaped the cultural practice of drinking. In some areas, control laws attempted to moderate the effects of drinking by encouraging food consumption. For example, spirit sales were often limited to bona fide restaurants, with laws specifying how many feet of kitchen space and how many food-preparation workers there must be. Most states established restrictions on the number of entrances and their locations (back entrances are usually prohibited); times of day and days of the week when sales may occur; permissible decorations; degree of visibility of the interior from the street; numbers and uses of other rooms; distance of the establishment from churches, schools, and other alcohol outlets; whether customers may sit at a long bar—a counter in close proximity to the source of alcohol—or whether they must sit at tables and order drinks as one orders food; and the ratio of chair seating to bar seating.

The public character of drinkers' comportment was also regulated. Many states, for example, prohibit dancing or live music except under special license. Most gambling or betting is prohibited, and other games are restricted as well. For many years, New York and other states did not allow barrooms to have pinball machines. Many states specifically ban the use of the word "saloon," others ban the use of the word "bar," and some forbid all words that indicate a drinking place. Until about 1980, most drinking establishments in California displayed only a name and a symbol: a tilted cocktail glass with a stirrer.

From a pre-Prohibition or Prohibition-era perspective, there are two surprising characteristics of postrepeal alcohol controls. First, most laws and regulations are *obeyed*. Almost all drinking places, for example, stop serving and collect glasses at the required hours, and they observe the regulations about tables, dancing, decorations, signs, entrances, and so on. By and large, this obedience has been relatively easily achieved through careful policing, coupled with the power to revoke or suspend licenses. Operating a liquor-selling business is usually quite profitable compared to other kinds of retail establishments, so owners tend to guard their licenses carefully. Unlike Prohibition, alcohol control uses the profit motive to encourage lawful business practices. Minimum-age drinking laws constitute the one obvious exception to this regulatory success; they are also one of the few remaining forms of prohibition. Second, postrepeal alcohol regulation is usually *not* perceived as especially restrictive by customers. The many layers of laws and regulations are rarely noticed; most drinkers take them completely for granted.

A third, less surprising characteristic of postrepeal alcohol control is that policy has not been aimed specifically at maximizing what earlier reformers had called "temperance"—meaning, above all, reducing habitual drunkenness or repeated heavy drinking. In his preface to *Toward Liquor Control*, Rockefeller maintained that such problems could not be effectively addressed by liquor regulation and that they would have to be taken up by other agencies as part of broader educational and health efforts. Since repeal, these tasks have been adopted by a number of independent and government groups, notably Alcoholics Anonymous and the National Council on Alcoholism, various state and local alcoholism agencies, and, since the early 1970s, the National Institute on Alcohol Abuse and Alcoholism (NIAAA). In recent years, some public health professionals have urged that the control system be used more self-consciously to reduce drinking and some health problems. Such concerns have by and large been imposed on the system, however, and do not flow from its natural workings.

On the other hand, despite all its flaws, postrepeal alcohol control did succeed in turning consumption away from hard liquor (which is much easier to abuse) and back toward beer and wine. Further, alcohol control (coupled with the Depression and World War II) did keep alcohol consumption below pre-Prohibition levels. In fact, it was not until 1970 that the total alcohol consumption of the drinking-age population reached the levels of 1915 (Levine and Reinarman 1993, 1998; Rorabaugh 1979; Miron and Zwiebel 1991).

In 1936, a second volume of the Rockefeller-sponsored Liquor Study Commission Report was issued. *After Repeal: A Study of Liquor Control Administration* (Harrison and Laine 1936) analyzed the results of liquor control after "a two-year trial" and described the most important changes and innovations in liquor administration instituted since repeal. The overall thrust of the report was that, with some understandable exceptions, alcohol control worked extremely well. Other observers at the time drew similar conclusions (Sheppard 1938; Shipman 1940).

Legalizing alcohol, then regulating it, had accomplished what most temperance and prohibition supporters claimed was impossible: alcohol moved from being a scandal, crisis, and constant front-page news story to something routine and manageable, a little-noticed thread in the fabric of American life. Since 1934, alcohol regulation has quietly and effectively organized and managed the production, distribution, and sale of alcohol, as well as public drinking.

Despite frequent claims to the contrary, alcohol control has, of course, sought to legislate morality. It has not, however, sought to impose the morality of the nineteenth-century Protestant middle class who supported the antialcohol crusade. Rather the alcohol-control system legislates the more modern morality of the new business and professional middle class, of the corporate elite, and to a large extent of the twentieth-century working class. Accordingly, unlike the use of marijuana, heroin, or cocaine, drinking has not been criminalized and pushed beyond the pale of normative and regulatory influence. Moreover, once it ceased to be outlawed, the alcohol industry was no longer dominated by unregulated, illicit entrepreneurs who shot at each other, developed crime syndicates, and paid off police and government officials. The leaders of the major alcohol industries, just like other members of the economic establishment, have a strong investment in maintaining order and obedience to law.

Now, many decades after national alcohol prohibition ended, it is easy to forget that all this was the outcome of self-conscious public policy and not the "natural" result of market forces or national zeitgeist. The alcohol-control system has worked sufficiently well that it usually goes unnoticed, even by students of Prohibition or American history. For purposes of devising new drug policy options, however, it is important to remember that this particular system was the self-conscious creation of a political and economic elite with the power to institute what it regarded as good and necessary. The alcohol-control system they devised is not especially democratic, it does not really address public health or social welfare concerns, and it has produced enormous profits for a handful of large corporations. However, it has achieved what its designers sought to do: to regulate and administer the orderly and lawful distribution of alcoholic beverages in a way that creates little controversy (Bruun et al. 1975; Beauchamp 1981; Levine 1984).

Lessons from Alcohol Control

There are many different lessons that may be drawn from the story of legalization of alcohol production and sales and the establishment of alcohol control in the United States. Two seem particularly relevant for drug policy.

First, the legalization of drug production and sales and the establishment of drug control along the lines of alcohol control *is* a reasonable and practical policy option. Supporters of alcohol prohibition always claimed that alcohol was a special substance that could never be regulated and sold like other commodities because it was so addicting and dangerous. However, as the last seventy-plus years of alcohol control and the experiences of many other societies have shown, the Prohibitionists were wrong. The experiences of drug policy in other nations and of U.S. pharmaceutical and drugstore regulation suggest that most, if not all, psychoactive substances *could* be similarly produced, regulated, sold, and used in a generally lawful and orderly fashion. Therefore, it would mark a significant advance if the current U.S. debate on drug policy could be moved beyond the question of *whether* such a system of legalized drug control is possible. It is. Instead, we think debate should focus on whether a nonmoralistic assessment of the advantages and disadvantages of such a system make it desirable and what different regulatory options might look like.

Second, a workable system of at least partially legalized drug production and sales — of drug control — would have to be a flexible one, geared to local conditions. Edward Brecher recommended this in his landmark study *Licit and Illicit Drugs* (1972), and the Committee of Fifty also stressed the importance of local option over a century ago (Levine 1983). Because towns, cities, counties, states, and countries vary enormously, alcohol and drug policies must be shaped according to local environments.

As with alcohol control, drug control could be implemented so as to reduce substantially, if not eliminate, the illegal drug business and most of the crime, violence, and corruption associated with it. Drug control with a public health orientation would also seek to encourage milder and weaker drugs and to make them available in safer forms accompanied by comprehensive education about risks, proper use, and less dangerous modes of ingestion. In other words, a public health–oriented drug-control regime would seek to reverse the tendencies that appear inherent under criminalization, where production, distribution, and consumption are pushed into deviant subcultures, where purity is uncontrolled and dosage is imprecise.

If a legalized, decentralized drug-control system with local option is implemented, then the experience of alcohol regulation suggests that, in the long run, drug problems would probably not rise significantly above the levels now present under drug prohibition, and overall consumption might not rise either (see also Nadelmann 1989a). Similarly, if such a public health model of drug control were coupled with increased social services and employment for impoverished inner-city populations, then the abuse of drugs like heroin and cocaine might well be expected to decrease (Reinarman and Levine 1997; Brecher 1972; Jonas 1990).

Having said this, it is incumbent upon us to point out that it will be no simple matter to implement such a drug-control system in the United States, or in any other place in the world. As the second part of this chapter shows, drug prohibition is a much larger system than national alcohol prohibition in the United States ever was.

DRUG PROHIBITION IS A WORLDWIDE SYSTEM

Every country in the world now has drug prohibition enforced by its police and military. Every country in the world criminalizes the production and sale of cannabis, cocaine, and opiates (except for limited medical uses). In addition, most countries criminalize the production and sale of other psychoactive substances. Global drug prohibition is a worldwide system structured by a series of international treaties that are supervised by the United Nations. Every nation in the world is either a signatory to one or more of the treaties or has laws in accord with them (Levine 2002, 2003; Bewley-Taylor 1999; Nadelmann 1990; International Narcotics Control Board Web site, www.incb.org, accessed March 14, 2005).

Global drug prohibition is a worldwide system of state power. Drug prohibition is a social fact. For many decades, however, public officials, journalists, and academics rarely identified any form of U.S. drug law as "prohibition." Instead, they referred to national and international "narcotics control." The international organization that still supervises global drug prohibition is called the International Narcotics Control Board (INCB). Outside of some drug policy, harm-reduction, and academic circles, few people have known much about the worldwide drug-prohibition system.

In the last decades of the twentieth century, some people in many countries became aware of *national* drug prohibition. They came to understand that the drug policies of the United States and some other countries are varieties of drug prohibition. Even as this understanding spread, however, the fact that every country in the world has adopted drug prohibition remained a kind of "hidden in plain view" secret. Until recently, the global drug-prohibition system has been taken for granted and nearly invisible. Now that is changing. Global drug prohibition is becoming easier to see and is losing some of its other ideological and political powers.

The Rise of Global Drug Prohibition

In the twentieth century, the cause of drug prohibition was first taken up by committed alcohol prohibitionists. In the United States, national drug prohibition developed out of national alcohol prohibition. National drug prohibition is not "similar to" or "like" alcohol prohibition; it is a historical extension and continuation of it.

National drug prohibition began in the 1920s in the United States as a subset of constitutional alcohol prohibition. The first generation of U.S. narcotics agents worked for the federal alcohol-prohibition agency. In 1930, Congress separated drug prohibition from the increasingly disreputable alcohol prohibition and created a new federal drug-prohibition agency, the Federal Bureau of Narcotics, headed by the committed alcohol prohibitionist Harry J. Anslinger (Epstein 1977; Musto 1987). In 1933, a combination of majority votes in some state legislatures and unprecedented statewide public referendums in other states ended national alcohol prohibition. The question of alcohol policy was turned back to state and local governments to do with as they wished. A few states retained alcohol prohibition for years, and many rural American counties still have forms of alcohol prohibition (Kyvig 1979; Levine 1984, 1985).

Drug prohibition took an entirely different course. Since the early twentieth century, U.S. alcohol prohibitionists found European governments far more willing to consider antinarcotics legislation than antialcohol laws. Alcohol prohibitionists urged adoption of drug prohibition, and over the years, they convinced the United States and other counties to establish various forms of drug prohibition, often called "narcotics control."

In 1919, the founding covenant of the League of Nations explicitly mentioned the control of "dangerous drugs" as one of the organization's concerns. In the 1930s, guided by the Federal Bureau of Narcotics and its chief, Anslinger, the U.S. government helped write and gain acceptance for two international antidrug conventions, or treaties, aimed at "suppressing" narcotics and "dangerous drugs." In 1948, the new United Nations made drug prohibition one of its priorities. The UN Single Convention of 1961 (as amended in 1972, and supplemented by UN antidrug treaties in 1971 and 1988) established the current system of global drug prohibition. In the last eighty years, nearly every political persuasion and type of government has endorsed drug prohibition. (For a discussion of this history, see Bewley-Taylor 1999 and 2003; Bruun, Pan, and Rexed 1972; Walker 1992; King 1972; Epstein 1977; Baum 1996; Gray 1998; Duke and Gross 1993; Musto 1987; Nadelmann 1990; McWilliams 1992; Levine 2002, 2003; Reinarman 2003. Visit www.incb.org for the text of the treaties. For a discussion of why drug prohibition was adopted throughout the world, see Levine 2002 and 2003 and a special issue of the *International Journal of Drug Policy*, 2003, devoted to a critical analysis of the UN treaties and global drug prohibition.)

Drug Use and Policy in the Era of Global Drug Prohibition

The Single Convention of 1961 was put into place just as the world it was designed to govern was being transformed. Over the next two decades, the use of prohibited drugs, especially of cannabis (marijuana), moved from the margins to the mainstream and the middle class. Except for cannabis, none of this use was very large, and most of it was drug use and not abuse.

By about 1979, most forms of illegal drug use in the United States were higher than anytime before or since. By 1993, 22 percent of Americans aged eighteen to twenty-five, and 6 percent over age twenty-five had used marijuana once or more in the last year. And by 1993, 5 percent of Americans aged eighteen to twenty-five and 2 percent over age twenty-five had used cocaine once or more in the last year. With some fluctuations, these rates have remained at roughly the same levels since. Heroin, LSD, psychoactive mushrooms, and other illegal drug use is lower than cocaine use, and the level of MDMA ("ecstasy") use is similar to that of cocaine use (Reinarman and Levine 1997, 28–33).

The rise of illegal drug use in the 1960s and 1970s, and the persistence of use since 1980, have placed enormous pressures on the drug-prohibition systems in many Western countries. Different countries have responded to drug use and abuse in a variety of ways. Global drug prohibition is best understood as a long continuum—with a harsher, more punitive and criminalized end (as in the United States), and a more tolerant, regulated, public health–oriented end (as in the Netherlands and growing numbers of European counties).

U.S. drug prohibition gives long prison sentences for repeated possession, use, and small-scale distribution of forbidden drugs. Many U.S. drug laws explicitly remove sentencing discretion from judges and do not allow for probation or parole. In the United States in the 1980s, the Reagan and Bush administrations substantially increased criminal penalties for drug possession and launched an expensive war on drugs. The United States now has nearly half a million men and women in prison for violating its drug laws. Most are poor people of color imprisoned for possessing an illicit drug or "intending" to sell small amounts of it. The mandatory federal penalty for possessing five grams of crack cocaine, for a first offense, is five years in prison with no parole (Reinarman and Levine 1997; Duke and Gross 1993; Gray 1998; McWilliams 1992).

The cannabis policy of the Netherlands is the best-known example of the other end of the drug-prohibition continuum—of a decriminalized and regulated

form of drug prohibition. Several UN drug treaties require the Netherlands, like
other signatories, to have laws criminalizing the production and distribution of
cannabis and other drugs. However, since the early 1980s, national policy in the
Netherlands allows over eight hundred cafes and snack bars to sell small quantities of cannabis to adults for personal use, on premises and off. These "coffee
shops" are permitted to operate as long as they are orderly and stay within well-
defined limits that are monitored and enforced by the police. Unlike legal businesses, cannabis sales are not taxed, and coffee shops cannot advertise cannabis.

Even as cannabis sales in the Netherlands are open, routine, and *appear* to
be completely legal, importing and commercially producing this cannabis remain illegal. As a result, the coffee shops have always been supplied, as the
Dutch say, "through the back door." This is still formally drug prohibition,
and the Netherlands prosecutes importers, dealers, and commercial growers
who handle large quantities of cannabis—as required by the UN antidrug
treaties. In short, for over two decades, the Netherlands has sustained a
unique system of regulated, open, quasilegal cannabis sales supplied by illegal importers and growers. This is as far as any country has been able to go
within the current structures of global drug prohibition (Leuw 1997; Reinarman and Levine 1997; Engelsmann 1990; Henk 1989).

The prohibition policies of all other Western countries fall in between the
heavily criminalized policies of the United States and the decriminalized and
regulated form of cannabis prohibition of the Netherlands. No Western country and few Third World countries have ever had forms of drug prohibition as
criminalized and punitive as the U.S. regime, and since the early 1990s, drug
policy in Europe, Canada, Australia, and elsewhere has clearly shifted even
farther away from the criminalized end of the prohibition continuum. All
these countries, however, are required by international treaties to have—and
still do have—real, formal, legal, national drug prohibition (Levine 2002,
2003; Andreas 1999; Bewley-Taylor 1999; Reinarman and Levine 1997).

Since the early 1980s, global drug prohibition has had to face a series of
dilemmas or crises. In the final sections of this chapter, we want to discuss
briefly three of these crises: the emergence and development of the harm-
reduction movement within drug prohibition; the growth of a serious, rep-
utable opposition to criminalized and punitive drug policies; and the inability
of drug prohibition to stop the cultivation and use of cannabis throughout the
world.

The Harm-Reduction Movement within Drug Prohibition

The harm-reduction movement was born in the early 1980s as a pragmatic,
remarkably effective response to the spreading hepatitis and AIDS epidemics.

Since then, harm-reduction workers and activists in Europe and, increasingly, throughout the world have sought to provide drug users and addicts with a range of services aimed at reducing the harmful effects of drug use. In the United States, conservative pundits and even liberal journalists have accused harm-reduction advocates of being "drug legalizers" in disguise, but in most other countries, many prominent politicians, public-health professionals, and police officials who are strong defenders of drug prohibition have also supported harm-reduction programs as practical public-health policies (Heather et al. 1993). Even the UN agencies that supervise worldwide drug prohibition have come to recognize the public health benefits of harm-reduction services *within* current drug-prohibition regimes (INCB 2000, 59–60).

It is useful to understand that there are many varieties of drug prohibition, arranged along a continuum from the harsher and more punitive forms to the more tolerant and regulated forms. We want to suggest that harm reduction is a movement that, in effect, though not always in intent, pushes drug policies away from the more criminalized and punitive forms of drug prohibition toward the more decriminalized, tolerant, and regulated forms of drug prohibition. Harm reduction encourages policy makers to shift drug policies away from punishment, coercion, and repression and toward tolerance, regulation, and public health. Harm reduction is not inherently an enemy of drug prohibition. However, in the course of pursuing public health goals, harm reduction necessarily seeks policies that also reduce the punitive effects of drug prohibition (Heather et al. 1993; Reinarman and Levine 1997).

Consider some of the significant programs that the harm-reduction movement has advocated: syringe distribution and exchange, methadone maintenance, hygienic injection rooms, prescription heroin, medical use of cannabis, drug education for users, and pill testing at raves. These programs have sought to increase public health by helping users reduce the harms of drug use. However, in order to carry out their objectives (like reducing the spread of AIDS), the harm-reduction programs have often required changes in laws, policies, or funding that quite clearly also reduce the harshness and intolerance of drug prohibition.

We are suggesting that implicitly and sometimes explicitly the harm-reductionist stance toward drug prohibition is exactly the same as its stance toward drug use. Harm-reduction groups seek to reduce the harmful effects of drug use without requiring users to be drug free. Harm-reduction groups also seek to reduce the harmful effects of drug prohibition without requiring governments to be prohibition free. Harm reduction's message to drug users is: We are not asking you to give up drug use; we just ask you to do some things (like use clean syringes) to reduce the harmfulness of drug use (including the spread of AIDS) to you and the people close to you. In precisely the same way, harm reduction's message to governments is: We are not asking you to give up drug prohibition; we just ask you to do some things (like make clean syringes and methadone available) to reduce the harmfulness of drug prohibition.

Harm reduction offers a radically tolerant and pragmatic approach to both drug use and drug prohibition. It assumes that neither is going away anytime soon and suggests that, therefore, reasonable and responsible people must try to persuade those who use drugs, and those who use drug prohibition, to minimize the harms that their activities produce.

The Growing Opposition to Punitive Drug Policies

In many countries, increasing numbers of people—physicians, lawyers, judges, police, journalists, scientists, public health officials, teachers, religious leaders, social workers, drug users, and drug addicts—now openly criticize the more extreme, punitive, and criminalized forms of drug prohibition. These critics, from across the political spectrum, have pointed out that punitive drug policies are expensive and ineffective at reducing drug abuse, take scarce resources away from other public health and policing activities, and are often racially and ethnically discriminatory. Criminalized drug prohibition violates civil liberties, imprisons many nonviolent offenders, and worsens health problems like the AIDS and hepatitis epidemics. Harm reduction is a major part of the critical opposition to punitive drug policies. Indeed, harm reduction is the first popular, international movement to develop within drug prohibition to challenge openly drug demonization and the more criminalized forms of drug prohibition (Reinarman and Levine 1997; Levine 2002, 2003).

The harm-reduction and drug policy reformers have changed the debate. For example, in 2001 the mainstream Toronto newspaper, the *Globe and Mail* (August 20 and 21), published a two-part editorial strongly urging Canada to "decriminalize all—yes, all—personal drug use, henceforth to be regarded primarily as a health issue rather than as a crime." At the same time, the conservative British business magazine the *Economist* (July 26), devoted an entire issue to drug topics, endorsing decriminalization, harm reduction, and consideration of drug legalization. The *Economist* also reported that U.S. government antidrug publications "are full of patently false claims" and that U.S. drug policy "has proved a dismal rerun of America's attempt, in 1920–1933, to prohibit the sale of alcohol." Since 2001, U.K. drug polices have moved to down-classify cannabis, and the Canadian government has been considering decriminalizing it.

As drug policy reform movements have grown, *supporters* of drug prohibition have been discovering that they cannot make the critics of criminalized prohibition go away. In the reports of the INCB, the UN agency supervising global drug prohibition, and in other publications, the most knowledgeable defenders of drug prohibition warn regularly about the increasing growth of cannabis cultivation and use on every continent and about the increasing legitimacy given to the critics of drug prohibition. These defenders of global drug prohibition recognize that the advocates of decriminalized drug prohibition—and the political, economic, and cultural forces driving that opposition—are gaining strength and legitimacy (see, for example, INCB 2000).

All of this opposition is fairly recent. For much of its history, global drug prohibition has had very few critics. Even today, despite the impressive growth in many countries of the harm-reduction movement and of drug-policy reform activities, worldwide drug prohibition still has very few explicit opponents. One reason for the lack of organized opposition to the drug treaties is that, until recently, the global drug-prohibition system has been invisible.

Furthermore, even now few people understand that by ending or even modifying the Single Convention on Narcotic Drugs of 1961, the question of national drug policy could be returned to individual countries and local governments to handle as they wish. Defenders of global drug prohibition like to evoke an international conspiracy of what they call "drug legalizers," but almost nobody thus far has tried to launch even a half-baked international campaign with slogans like "Repeal the Single Convention" or "End Global Drug Prohibition."

Yet, it may well be that the Single Convention stands in much the same relationship to worldwide drug prohibition that the Eighteenth Amendment to the Constitution and the Volstead Act did in relation to U.S. alcohol prohibition. Once the Eighteenth Amendment was gone, state and local governments were free to create alcohol policy at the local level. If the Single Convention were repealed, or even modified, national governments around the world would be freer to create drug laws and policies geared to their own conditions—including prohibition if they should so desire.

At present, many nations and many more regional and local governments are reforming their drug policies, expanding harm reduction, and adopting less criminalized forms of drug prohibition. But no national government is even discussing withdrawing from the Single Convention and global drug prohibition. In addition to the domestic political obstacles to such a move, a potential "rogue" nation confronts international barriers in the form of economic and political sanctions from the United States and its allies. Therefore, no single country can now formally end its national prohibition regime and completely "defect" from the worldwide prohibitionist system. And it is likely that no single country will be willing or able to defect for a very long time, if ever (Bewley-Taylor 1999, 2002, 2003; Transnational Institute 2002; Andreas 1999; Nadelmann 1990).

The Cannabis Crisis

Global drug prohibition's most glaring weakness and greatest vulnerability is cannabis. As UN experts point out, cannabis is by far the most widely used illegal drug in the world. Cannabis grows wild throughout the world and is commercially cultivated in remote areas, in backyard gardens, and in technologically sophisticated indoor growing operations. Just as it was impossible for prohibitionists to prevent alcohol from being produced and used in the United States in the 1920s, so too is it now impossible to prevent cannabis from being produced and widely used, especially in democratic countries. As a result of this enormous and unstoppable production and use, global cannabis prohibition faces a growing crisis of legitimacy (Zimmer 1997).

Since the 1980s, the Netherlands has successfully administered its system of regulated, decriminalized cannabis sales. A generation of Europeans, Australians, North Americans, and others has learned from the Dutch experience. Politicians, policy makers, police officials, journalists, and ordinary tourists from many countries have seen that decriminalizing cannabis use and regulating cannabis sales have substantial advantages and benefits—especially when compared with the disadvantages and costs of punitive U.S. drug policies. The continued success of the Netherlands's strikingly different and less punitive cannabis policy alternative *within* drug prohibition has undermined the U.S. antidrug crusade and contributed to the spread of de facto and formal cannabis decriminalization in Spain, Switzerland, Portugal, Germany, the United Kingdom, Belgium, Italy, and other countries (Leuw 1997; Webster 1998; Reinarman, Cohen, and Kaal 2004).

Further, since the 1960s, recreational cannabis use has been steadily normalized in many parts of the world, especially among young adults. Prominent middle-aged politicians—including, for example, the current Republican mayor of New York City—admit that they have used cannabis without deleterious effects. As a result, it has become much harder for drug war advocates to portray cannabis persuasively as one of the dangerous, evil drugs. Punitive drug prohibition still requires drug demonization. But defenders of cannabis prohibition find it increasingly difficult to offer plausible justifications for harsh anticannabis laws or even for the Single Convention's cannabis policies. Growing numbers of prominent, influential individuals and organizations are concluding that criminalized cannabis prohibition causes more problems than cannabis use.

In recent years, some veteran drug policy reformers have confronted the problem of the currently invincible drug treaties. Like Professor Peter Cohen (2003) of the University of Amsterdam and Dr. Alex Wodak (2003) of St. Vincent's Hospital in Sydney, they have suggested that the Single Convention and other narcotics treaties are unenforceable "paper tigers," or even "paper corpses." These critics recommend that policy makers disregard the antidrug treaties when considering drug policy reforms within their own countries. With regard to cannabis, public officials in a number of countries seem increasingly open to such arguments. In Europe, political support for harm-reduction approaches and drug policy reform has become so strong that some government officials have discussed systems for licensing cannabis *production.*

Openly licensing, regulating, and taxing cannabis production moves well beyond what the Netherlands has ever done. Licensing production, as well as sales, creates cannabis legalization within one country. Discussion of such measures appears most developed in Switzerland but has been going on as well in the Netherlands and even in Canada. Top U.S. antidrug officials are openly worried about such possibilities.

Switzerland and other countries could choose to license cannabis farms for domestic consumption. In so doing, they would build on the Dutch experience but would completely bypass the Netherlands's complicated problems of illegal, or "backdoor," cannabis supply. When officials have substantial domestic public support, they will be freer to ignore international pressure and to define their own nation's situation as a permissible exception to the antidrug treaties. And countries that may decide, for various reasons, to license sales may also decide to license growers. In short, sooner or later, some Western country, perhaps Switzerland, is likely to be the first to create a system of licensed, regulated, and taxed cannabis sale and production, despite the narcotics treaties.

In political democracies, when laws and policies are unenforceable and unpopular, over time de facto changes usually become de jure (in law). This is what happened with alcohol prohibition in the United States, and this process occurs with international laws as well. For opiates, stimulants, and other drugs, the ongoing trend of increasing decriminalization, harm reduction, and medical use could continue for decades within global drug prohibition. But cannabis is a different story. In some countries, cannabis use and cultivation already threatens to burst the bounds of the international drug treaties. Even drug prohibitionists who study global trends openly worry about their capacity to make worldwide cannabis prohibition a workable system.

Recently, some students of global drug policies have outlined strategies for modifying the drug treaties to bring them more in line with current practice.

(Bewley-Taylor 2002; Transnational Institute 2002). Calls for modifying the treaties are likely to increase in coming years. And whatever happens with efforts to reform the Single Convention and other drug treaties, some Western democracies are likely to continue moving toward creating their own new national policies for cannabis sales, distribution, and production.

One last point: An incisive paper by Martin Jelsma (2002) takes a line from a Monty Python sketch and likens defenders of punitive drug policies and the UN treaties to a pet-shop clerk cheerfully trying to sell a dead parrot. "It's not dead," the salesman tells the incredulous customer, "it's just resting." Jelsma suggests rejecting such arguments and points out that policy makers in a number of countries have urged international discussions about modifying the drug treaties. Since 2001, the U.S. government has become increasingly absorbed in its new War on Terrorism and is itself withdrawing from or openly breaking with several different international treaties. At the same time, support for cannabis policy reform has been growing in the United Kingdom, Canada, and other Western countries. In short, in the next five to ten years, modifying the drug treaties, especially for cannabis, may become a more lively political issue.

THE END OF GLOBAL DRUG PROHIBITION?

Global drug prohibition is in crisis. The fact that it is becoming visible is one symptom of that crisis. In the short run, that crisis seems almost certain to deepen, especially for cannabis prohibition and the more punitive and criminalized drug policies. Over the next century, for a variety of practical and ideological reasons—especially the spread of democracy, information, and trade—democratic governments in Europe and elsewhere are likely to transform and eventually dismantle worldwide drug prohibition.

If and when this happens, it would not mean the end of all local or national drug prohibition. Rather, ending global drug prohibition, like ending constitutional alcohol prohibition in the United States, would clear the path for hundreds of local experiments in drug policy. Many communities and some nations would likely retain forms of drug prohibition and continue to support vigorous antidrug crusades. But most democratic and open societies probably would not choose to retain full-scale criminalized drug prohibition. Over time, democratic societies could gradually develop their own varied local forms of regulated, personal cultivation, production, and use of the once prohibited plants and substances. Many places could also allow some forms of commercial growing, production, and sale—first of all of cannabis.

All of this could take a very long time. Drug prohibitionists in every country can be expected to fight tenaciously to maintain their local regimes. And it is likely that enormous power will be employed to prevent the Single Convention of 1961 and its related treaties from being repealed or even modified.

As a result, in coming years there will be even more public discussion and debate about the varieties of drug prohibition and about the alternatives to it. As part of that conversation, many more people will discover that they have lived for decades within a regime of worldwide drug prohibition. That growing understanding will help push global drug prohibition closer to its end.

We are convinced that someday, as Brecher predicted, most Americans will look back on drug prohibition and judge it to have been (like alcohol prohibition) repressive, unjust, expensive, and ineffective—a failure. In the twentieth century, a dozen major scientific commissions in Britain, Canada, and the United States have recommended alternatives to punitive drug policies. The United States is the only nation where these recommendations have been so consistently ignored (Levine 1994; Trebach and Zeese 1990). For starters, these recommendations should be more widely discussed and better understood in the United States. The experiences of other nations, regions, and cities also provide living examples of decriminalization and harm-reduction programs within global drug prohibition. The full range of alternatives to current U.S. drug policy should be studied and debated—from futuristic visions to pragmatic reforms that could be implemented immediately. For drug policy, as was the case with alcohol policy, discussion of alternatives is an essential part of the transition from prohibition to regulation.

REFERENCES

Alcohol Beverage Control Administration. 1973. *Licensing and enforcement.* Edited by B. W. Corrado, rev. ed. Washington: Joint Committee of the States to Study Alcoholic Beverages Laws.

Allen, F. L. 1931. *Only yesterday: An informal history of the 1920s.* New York: Harper.

Allsop, K. 1961. *The bootleggers and their era.* London: Hutchinson.

Andreas, P. 1999. When policies collide: Market reform, market prohibition, and the narcotization of the Mexican economy. In *The global economy and state power.* Edited by F. Richard and A. Peter. New York: Roman & Littlefield.

Baron, S. 1962. *Brewed in America: A history of beer and ale in the United States.* Boston: Little, Brown.

Baum, D. 1996. *Smoke and mirrors. The War on Drugs and the politics of failure.* Boston: Little, Brown.

———. 2003. Jake Leg: How the blues diagnosed a medical mystery. *The New Yorker.* September 15, 50–57.

Beauchamp, D. 1981. *Beyond alcoholism: Alcohol and public health policy.* Philadelphia: Temple University Press.

Bewley-Taylor, D. 1999. *The United States and international drug control, 1907–1997.* London and New York: Wellington House.

———. 2002. Habits of a hegemon: The United States and the future of the global drug prohibition regime. In *Breaking the impasse—polarisation & paralysis in UN drug control.* Amsterdam Drugs and Conflict Debate Paper no. 5. Amsterdam: Transnational Institute, available at www.tni.org/reports/drugs/debate.htm (accessed March 8, 2005).

———. 2003. Challenging the UN drug control conventions: Problems and possibilities. *International Journal of Drug Policy* 14:171–79.

Billings, J. S. 1905. *The liquor problem: A summary of investigations conducted by the Committee of Fifty and the origins of alcohol control.* Boston: Houghton Mifflin.

Blocker, J. 1989. *American temperance movements: Cycles of reform.* New York: Twane.

Brecher, E. 1972. *Licit and illicit drugs: The Consumers Union report on narcotics, stimulants, depressants, inhalants, hallucinogens, and marijuana—including caffeine, nicotine, and alcohol.* Boston: Little, Brown.

Bruun, K., G. Edwards, M. Lumio, K. Makela, L. Pan, R. E. Popham, R. Room, W. Schmidt, O. J. Skog, P. Sulkunen, and E. Osterberg. 1975. *Alcohol control in public health perspective.* Helsinki: Finnish Foundation for Alcohol Studies.

Bruun, K., L. Pan, and I. Rexed. 1972. *The gentlemen's club: International control of drugs and alcohol.* Chicago: University of Chicago Press.

Burnham, J. C. 1968. New perspectives on the prohibition "experiment" of the 1920s. *Journal of Social History* 2(51):1–67.

Cashman, S. D. 1981. *Prohibition, the lie of the land.* New York: Free Press.

Cohen, P. 2003. The drug prohibition church and the adventure of reformation. *International Journal of Drug Policy* 14(2) (April): 213–15.

Duke, S., and A. C. Gross. 1993. *America's longest war: Rethinking our tragic crusade against drugs.* New York: G. P. Putnam's Sons.

Englesmann, E. 1990. The pragmatic strategies of the Dutch "drug czar." In *Drug prohibition and the conscience of nations.* Edited by A. S. Trebach and K. Zeese, 49–55. Washington, D.C.: Drug Policy Foundation.

Epstein, E. J. 1977. *Agency of fear: Opiates and political power in America.* New York: G. P. Putnam's Sons.

Everest, A. S. 1978. *Rum across the border.* Syracuse, N.Y.: Syracuse University Press.

Fosdick, R. B., and A. L. Scott. 1933. *Toward liquor control.* New York: Harper.

Gordon, E. 1943. *The wrecking of the 18th Amendment.* Francestown, N.H.: Alcohol Information Press.

Gray, M. 1998. *Drug crazy: How we got into this mess and how we can get out.* New York: Random House.

Gulick, L. 1977. Letter to Richard S. Childs, copy to Laurence S. Rockefeller, in Rockefeller Archives, Rockefeller Center, New York, May 2.

Gusfield, J. R. 1968. Prohibition: The impact of political utopianism. In *Change and continuity in twentieth-century America.* Edited by John Braeman, Robert H. Bremner, and Everett Walters. Columbus: Ohio State University Press.

———. 1986. *Symbolic crusade: Status politics and the American temperance movement,* 2nd ed. Urbana: University of Illinois Press.

Harrison, L. V., and E. Laine. 1936. *After repeal: A study of liquor control administration.* New York: Harper.

Heather, N., A. Wodak, E. Nadelmann, and P. O'Hare. 1993. *Psychoactive drugs and harm reduction: From faith to science.* London: Whurr.

Henk, J. V. 1989. The uneasy decriminalization: A perspective on Dutch drug policy. *Hofstra Law Review* 18:717–50.

Hofstra Law Review. 1990. *A symposium on drug decriminalization* 18(3).

INCB. 2000. *Report of the International Narcotics Control Board for 2000.* Vienna: UN publication, available at www.incb.org/e/ind_ar.htm (accessed March 8, 2005).

Jelsma, M. 2002. *Diverging trends in international drug policy making: The polarisation between dogmatic drugs and democracy program.* Amsterdam: Transnational Institute, available at www.tni.org (accessed March 8, 2005).

Jonas, S. 1990. Solving the drug problem: A public health approach to the reduction of the use and abuse of both legal and illegal recreational drugs. *Hofstra Law Review* 18:751–93.

Kerr, J. A. 1985. *Organized for Prohibition: A new history of the Anti-Saloon League.* New Haven, Conn.: Yale University Press.

King, R. 1972. *The drug hang-up: America's fifty-year folly.* Springfield, Ill.: Charles C. Thomas.

Kobler, J. 1973. *Ardent spirits: The rise and fall of Prohibition.* New York: G. P. Putnam.

Kyvig, D. E. 1979. *Repealing national prohibition.* Chicago: University of Chicago Press.

Leuchtenburg, W. E. 1958. *The perils of prosperity: 1914–1932.* Chicago: University of Chicago Press.

Leuw, E. 1997. Recent reconsiderations in Dutch drug policy. In *Cannabis science: From prohibition to human right.* Edited by L. Böllinger. Frankfurt am Main: Peter Lang, available at www.bisdro.uni-bremen.de/boellinger/cannabis/inhalt.htm (accessed March 8, 2005).

Levine, H. G. 1978. The discovery of addiction: Changing conceptions of habitual drunkenness in America. *Journal of Studies on Alcohol* 39:143–74.

———. 1983. The Committee of Fifty and the origins of alcohol control. *Journal of Drug Issues* 13:95–116.

———. 1984. The alcohol problem in America: From temperance to prohibition. *British Journal of Addiction* 79:109–19.

———. 1985. The birth of American alcohol control: Prohibition, the power elite, and the problem of lawlessness. *Contemporary Drug Problems* 12:63–115.

———. 1994. Drug commissions, the next generation: "To boldly go. . . ." *International Journal of Drug Policy* 5(4):209–15.

———. 2002. The secret of world-wide drug prohibition. *The Independent Review.* 7(2) (fall):165–80.

——. 2003. Global drug prohibition: Its uses and crises. *International Journal of Drug Policy* 14(2) (April):145–53.

Levine, H. G., and C. Reinarman. 1993. From prohibition to regulation. In *Confronting drug policy: Illegal drugs in a free society*. Edited by R. Bayer and G. M. Oppenheimer. New York: Cambridge University Press.

——. 1998. The transition from prohibition to regulation. In *How to legalize drugs*. Edited by J. Fish. Northvale, N.J.: Jason Aronson, Inc.

Lyle, J. H. 1960. *The dry and lawless years*. Englewood Cliffs, N.J.: Prentice Hall.

MacAllister, W. B. 2000. *Drug diplomacy in the twentieth century: An international history*. London: Routledge.

Mäkelaä, K., R. Room, E. Single, P. Sulkunen, B. Walsh, R. Bunce, M. Cahannes, T. Cameron, N. Giesbrecht, J. de Lint, H. Makinen, P. Morgan, J. Moser, J. Moskalewicz, R. Miller, E. Osterberg, I. Wald, and D. Walsh. 1981. *A Comparative Study of Alcohol Control*. Vol. 1 of *Alcohol, Society, and the State*. Toronto: Addiction Research Foundation.

Manchester, W. 1974. *The glory and the dream: A narrative history of America, 1932–1972*. Boston: Little, Brown.

McWilliams, J. C. 1992. Through the past darkly: The politics and policies of America's drug war. In *Drug control policy: Essays in historical and comparative perspective*. Edited by W. O. Walker III. University Park: Pennsylvania State University Press, 5–41.

Mertz, C. 1970. *The dry decade*. Seattle: University of Washington Press.

Miron, J. A., and J. Zweibel. 1991. Alcohol consumption during prohibition. *American Economic Association Papers and Proceedings* 81:242–47.

Moore, M., and D. R. Gerstein, eds. 1981. *Alcohol and public policy: Beyond the shadow of Prohibition*. Washington, D.C.: National Academy Press.

Morgan, J. 1991. Was alcohol prohibition good for the nation's health? Working paper, School of Medicine, City University of New York.

Murphy, S., D. Waldorf, and C. Reinarman. 1991. Drifting into dealing: Becoming a cocaine seller. *Qualitative Sociology* 13(4):321–43.

Muscatine, D., M. Amerine, and B. Thompson. 1984. *The University of California book of California wine*. Berkeley: University of California Press.

Musto, D. 1987. *The American disease: Origins of narcotic control*, exp. ed. New York: Oxford University Press.

Nadelmann, E. 1989a. Drug prohibition in the United States: Costs, consequences, and alternatives. *Science* 245:939–47.

——. 1989b. Response to letters. *Science* 246:1102–3.

——. 1990. Global prohibition regimes: The evolution of norms in international society. *International Organization* 44(4):479–526.

Odegard, P. 1928. *Pressure politics: The story of the Anti-Saloon League*. New York: Columbia University Press.

Piven, F. F., and R. Cloward. 1971. *Regulating the poor: The functions of public welfare*. New York: Pantheon.

——. 1977. *Poor people's movements*. New York: Pantheon.

Reinarman, C. 2003. Geo-political and cultural constraints on international drug control treaties. *International Journal of Drug Policy* (2) (April 14):205–8.

Reinarman, C., and H. G. Levine. 1989. Crack in Context: Politics and Media in the Making of a Drug Scare. *Contemporary Drug Problems* 16:535–77.

———, eds. 1997. *Crack in America: Demon drugs and social justice.* Berkeley: University of California Press.

———. 2004. Crack in the rearview mirror: Deconstructing drug war mythology. *Social Justice* 31(2): 182–99.

Reinarman, C., P. D. A. Cohen, and H. L. Kaal. 2004. The limited relevance of drug policy: Cannabis in Amsterdam and in San Francisco. *American Journal of Public Health* 94:836–42.

Room, R. G. W. 1988. The dialectic of drinking in Australian Life: From the Rum Corps to the wine column. *Australian Drug and Alcohol Review* 7:413–37.

Rorabaugh, W. J. 1979. *The alcoholic republic: An American tradition.* New York: Oxford University Press.

Rumbarger, J. J. 1989. *Profits, power, and Prohibition: Alcohol reform and the industrializing of America, 1800–1930.* Albany: State University of New York Press.

Schmoke, K. L. 1990. An argument in favor of decriminalization. *Hofstra Law Review* 18:501–25.

Schuler, J. T., and A. McBride. 1990. Notes from the front: A dissident law-enforcement perspective on drug prohibition. *Hofstra Law Review* 18(3):893–942.

Sheppard, J. S. 1938. After five years, what has repeal achieved? *New York Times Magazine*, December 4.

Shipman, G. 1940. State administrative machinery for liquor control. *Law and Contemporary Problems* 7:600–20.

Sinclair, A. 1964. *Era of excess: A social history of the prohibition movement.* New York: Harper.

Single, E., P. Morgan, and J. Delint, eds. 1981. *The Social History of Control Policy in Seven Countries.* Vol. 2 of *Alcohol, society, and the state.* Toronto: Addiction Research Foundation.

Thornton, M. 1991. *The economics of prohibition.* Salt Lake City: University of Utah Press.

Timberlake, J. H. 1963. *Prohibition and the Progressive movement, 1900–1920.* Cambridge, Mass.: Harvard University Press.

Transnational Institute. 2002. *Breaking the impasse: Polarisation and paralysis in UN drug control.* Drugs and Conflict Debate Paper no. 5. Amsterdam: Transnational Institute.

Trebach, A. S. 1989. Ignoring the Great Commission reports. *The Drug Policy Letter* (September–October):5.

Trebach, A. S., and K. B. Zeese, eds. 1990. *Drug prohibition and the conscience of nations.* Washington, D.C.: Drug Policy Foundation.

Tyrell, I. 1979. *Sobering up: From temperance to prohibition in antebellum America, 1800–1860.* Westport, Conn.: Greenwood Press.

United Nations. 1998. Secretary-general calls on all nations to say 'yes' to challenge of working towards drug-free world. Press release GA/9411, June 8.

Waldorf, D., C. Reinarman, and S. Murphy. 1991. *Cocaine changes: The experience of using and quitting.* Philadelphia: Temple University Press.

Walker, W. O., III, ed. 1992. *Drug control policy: Essays in historical and comparative perspective*. University Park: Pennsylvania State University Press.

Warburton, C. 1932. *The economic results of Prohibition*. New York: Columbia University Press.

Webster, P. 1998. Rethinking drug prohibition: Don't look for U.S. government leadership. *International Journal of Drug Policy* 9(5):297–303.

Wickersham Commission [National Commission on Law Observance and Enforcement]. 1931. *Report on Enforcement of the Prohibition Laws of the United States*. 71st cong., 1st sess., HR 722.

Williams, C. D., F. S. Stinson, S. L. Steward, and M. C. Dufor. 1995. Apparent per capita alcohol consumption: National, state, and regional trends, 1977–93. NIAAA Surveillance Report #35, U.S. Department of Health and Human Service, Public Health Service, Institute of Health, Washington, D.C., December.

Williams, T. 1989. *Cocaine kids: The inside story of a teenage drug ring*. Reading, Mass.: Addison-Wesley.

Wodak, A. 2003. The international drug treaties: "Paper tigers" or dangerous behemoths? *International Journal of Drug Policy* 14(2) (April): 221–23.

Zimmer, L. 1997. The ascendancy and decline of worldwide cannabis prohibition. In *Cannabis science: From prohibition to human right*. Edited by L. Böllinger. Frankfurt am Main: Peter Lang, available at www.bisdro.uni-bremen.de/boellinger/cannabis/inhalt.htm (accessed March 8, 2005).

Zinberg, N. E. 1984. *Drug, set, and setting: The basis for controlled intoxicant use*. New Haven, Conn.: Yale University Press.

II

CONCEPTUAL BACKGROUND

4

Five Drug Policy Fallacies

Jefferson M. Fish

Many false beliefs about drugs and erroneous inferences about the dangers of legalization result from five well-known methodological fallacies. Erroneous conclusions that do not take into account the effects of selection bias (Cook and Campbell 1979) or base rates (Meehl and Rosen 1955), that are based on reified concepts, or that refuse to consider probabilistic predictions or cost-benefit analyses are often used to justify bad policy. This chapter will briefly explain these fallacies and their relevance to drug policy.

SELECTION BIAS

Have you ever sneezed when you were with a lot of people and "discovered," to your amazement, that you were in the midst of a flu epidemic? One person says that she is just getting over a cold, another has an uncle who has been in bed for a week with the flu, and someone else's friend has just called with a cough and sniffles to postpone a get-together. These instances are not sufficient to conclude that a flu epidemic is raging, and the making of such an inaccurate inference can be seen as an instance of selection bias.

Selection bias is the term experimenters use for the way in which the nonrandom selection of subjects for different treatment groups can produce inaccurate or biased results. The concept can easily be extended outside the laboratory to understand many social phenomena where people inaccurately assume they are observing the behavior of a random sample of others. (In a related methodological problem, the observer may even evoke unusual behavior in others. For example, overseas tourists may mistakenly assume that those around them are displaying culturally typical behavior, when it is the tourists' unusual presence that is leading the "natives" to act in unusual ways [Fish 1996].)

In the case of the "flu epidemic," those who said they were sick or knew others who were did not constitute a random sample of the people around you. Their comments were made in response to your sneeze—in the terms of this chapter, they were "selected" by your sneeze. In order to gather evidence as to whether or not you are in the midst of an epidemic, you might begin by asking everyone present—not just those who speak up—whether they know anyone with a cold or flu to see how large the proportion really is. You might try to find out how representative the group itself is (in terms of age, education, gender, ethnicity, socioeconomic status, and so forth) of people in your region. You might even try to reassemble them on the same date the following year and compare numbers.

The point is that each of us lives in a particular social world that is not representative of the larger society, and our behavior itself evokes responses from a nonrandom sample of others. For this reason, we have to exercise caution and engage in critical thinking when we draw inferences about apparent social patterns we see around us.

People who act in uncommon, unpopular, deviant, or stigmatized ways draw attention to themselves (like someone sneezing) and create an opportunity for inaccurate generalizations. Where social stereotypes or prejudices already exist, selection bias provides an easy way to confirm them.

Consider the example of homosexuality—never a popular form of behavior and, until recently, considered a mental illness. When psychiatry finally removed it from the list of mental disorders, many therapists rebelled. "How can you say that homosexuality is normal? I have treated many homosexuals, and they all had psychological problems."

The therapists were telling the truth, but they were not engaging in critical thinking. The people they see in therapy are self-selected for having psychological problems. The same reasoning would lead to the conclusion that heterosexuality is abnormal since all their heterosexual clients also have psychological problems. However, since the therapists presumably did not come from a wide enough social circle to have had contact with well-adjusted homosexuals, their provincial life experience gave them no reason to question conventional stereotypes.

Once one begins to think in terms of selection bias, it is easy to locate many examples. Matchmakers have a more positive view of marriage than divorce lawyers because the two occupations select different client groups. Matchmakers are surrounded by people who want to get married; divorce lawyers are in constant contact with those who want to get divorced.

Thus, it is not surprising that many law enforcement officials, judges, and others who work with addicts and drug-related criminals should have a negative view of drugs and oppose legalization. It is not surprising, but it is not any more defensible intellectually than the position of therapists who viewed homosexuality as a mental illness because of their lack of experience with well-adjusted homosexuals. Those involved in drug enforcement might equally well conclude (and, sadly, some of them do) that poor people or members of minority groups are criminals because the only poor people or members of minority groups they know are in trouble with the law. They do not, however, conclude that all men are criminals because they are at least cosmopolitan enough to be acquainted with many men who are not.

People involved in drug enforcement often see the worst of the worst and develop a biased view of reality because of the unrepresentative social world in which they work. They are not in contact with the huge majority of those who are experimenting with drug use or who are casual, occasional, recreational users. The distortion of their view of drugs and drug use, which has become the official version of reality, can be seen by comparing it to the view of alcohol held by those working in a skid row mission. They view people who have a glass of wine with dinner several times a week as beginning the slippery slope toward alcoholism, degradation, and death—although moderate drinkers would be appalled at being seen in this way. Yet, it is not unusual to hear, "I started as a social drinker," in the skid row mission.

This is selection bias, pure and simple. Those in a skid row mission are not a random sample of all drinkers, and addicts in the criminal justice system are not a random sample of illicit drug users. Most people who drink do so occasionally or in moderation and for a variety of reasons. These include the intrinsic pleasure of intoxication as well as its purported enhancing effect on other activities (sex, TV sports); participation in social events (cocktail parties, wine-and-cheese receptions) or religious activities (mass, Passover seder); self-medication (after getting fired or at the end of a relationship); and health promotion (moderate drinking reduces the risk of heart attack). In the same way, most people who use illicit drugs do so occasionally or in moderation and for the most diverse reasons.

Failure to think critically in terms of selection bias has led to the invention of statistically indefensible concepts like "gateway drugs." Thus, some who would acknowledge that marijuana is not dangerous still argue that it should remain illegal because it leads to the use of substances that are. They base their view on stories of addicts who, like the skid row alcoholics, describe their experimentation with marijuana as the first step on the road to cocaine or heroin addiction. The fallacy is the same. If, instead of addicts, they had interviewed college honors students, they might have reached the equally erroneous conclusion that weekend marijuana use relaxes people and leads to greater overall achievement.

The relevant question is not, What proportion of heroin users used marijuana first? since they also drank water or breathed air first, but rather, What proportion of marijuana users goes on to use heroin? (Fish 2000). An estimated 94,946,000 Americans have used marijuana at least once, and 3,668,000 have used heroin at least once (U.S. Department of Health and Human Services 2002). From these numbers, it is easy to see that—even if every single person who tries heroin uses marijuana first—there is a 96 percent probability against someone who uses marijuana even trying heroin one time.

In addition to exaggerating the dangerousness of drugs, selection bias has also been used to exaggerate the effectiveness of drug treatment. Alcoholics Anonymous and other drug-treatment programs sometimes claim high rates of success for "all people who complete the program." Here, instead of interviewing addicts about their history of drug use and falsely claiming that it is typical, one interviews ex-addicts about their history of recovery and falsely claims that it is typical. High dropout rates are common in such programs, so a large percentage of a small proportion winds up as not very much. The relevant response to such assertions of effectiveness is, What is the rate of success for all people who enter the program? In addition, one would want to know how representative the people in the program are of alcoholics in general or addicts in general.

Thinking in terms of selection bias does not equate to thinking that all drugs are the same or that no treatment works. It does remind us, though, that when a claim is made in this emotionally charged field, it should be evaluated in part on the representativeness of the sample on which it is based.

REIFICATION OF CONCEPTS

We live in a world not just of things but of socially constructed meanings. Different cultures, at different times and in different places, invent different concepts to organize their world and to make communication possible about matters of common interest. Even when it comes to objects in nature, cultures differ in the concepts they invent. For example, English speakers consider almonds, cashew nuts, and peanuts all to be examples of "nuts," a category that does not exist in Portuguese and that does not correspond to the way botanists would classify these edible parts of different plants. Cultures invent new concepts when circumstances demand—"cyberspace" is a recent example.

Culturally invented concepts differ in the degree to which they correspond to observable phenomena—"ghosts" and "unicorns" are also familiar concepts in our culture, although evidence that they refer to observable phenomena is hard to come by. Many Americans' actions are governed by these concepts (avoiding graveyards at night or painting pictures of unicorns), just as they are by the concept of "nuts"—in contrast to the behavior of people from cultures with none of the three concepts. And the actual behavior of people in the real world has real consequences for them and others, regardless of whether or not they are acting in terms of observable phenomena. Real people have been put to death for witchcraft, despite the lack of scientific evidence for the concept.

Reification of a concept is the fallacious process of treating a concept as a thing; when people act with reference to reified concepts, undesirable consequences often result. Unfortunately, the field of drug prohibition is rife with reified concepts that have led to untold mischief. Some of these are "drugs" (as opposed, for example, to "food"), "gateway drugs," and "codependency." One could easily write a chapter, or even a book, about such concepts, and those who are interested in exploring the matter further would do well to consult the relevant works of Thomas Szasz (1974, 1992).

For the purposes of this chapter, I will briefly explore the reified concept of "addiction" since it is the cornerstone on which other reifications, misguided thinking, and counterproductive policy are built. The following is the supposed phenomenon in nature that is described by the concept of addiction:

> Certain potent substances exist, called drugs. Drugs that are not medicine are evil because they have the power to destroy the lives of upstanding individuals. These substances, for reasons rooted in human biology, give people such overwhelming pleasure, or so effectively blot out their misery, that they crave and use more and more. Because the substances are irresistible, society must make them illegal; but individuals hooked on drugs will pay any price and risk any danger to get them. Thus, they descend into poverty, prostitution, and crime on the antisocial and self-destructive road to an early death.

In reading this dramatic narrative, certain features are evident. There is the emphasis on the substance itself rather than on the person who uses it, the circumstances under which it is used, or other individual, social, or cultural factors. The substance is viewed as evil and thus becomes an enemy that society can declare war on. Furthermore, addiction is understood as a unitary and repetitive phenomenon so that a variety of substances can be lumped together as "drugs," all of which cause addiction. Finally, by shifting the emphasis from an objective description of people and their behavior to a moral crusade against drugs and addiction, one is relieved of responsibility for discovering what happens to whom in the domain of substance use under differing social policies.

It is important to recognize that people can be found who behave like the addicts just described, but this is not adequate evidence that the concept of addiction describes a natural phenomenon. We have seen from the discussion of selection bias how easy it is to make such mistakes. For example, we could invent the "Sherlock Holmes syndrome" to describe people who take cocaine, play a musical instrument, and are interested in criminology. We could then look around us and find people who suffer from the syndrome, as well as borderline cases who sing or are interested in the sociology of deviance. But we would be deluding ourselves if we thought that the Sherlock Holmes syndrome really existed and doing damage if we based social policy on this reified concept.

In other words, reification goes beyond the description of behavior (cocaine + musical instrument + criminology) to the creation of an entity, like a disease (The poor man is suffering from Sherlock Holmes syndrome). Once a concept has been reified, it can be used for fallacious explanations (e.g., He takes cocaine because he has Sherlock Holmes syndrome) and as a basis for social policy (e.g., banning the sale of musical instruments as Sherlock Holmes syndrome–related paraphernalia).

Like the Sherlock Holmes syndrome, the concept of addiction—as it is understood by the general public and by too many legal and health professionals— does not describe the ways in which people use drugs. We have long known, as Edward Brecher (1972) indicates, that the effects of a licit or illicit drug depend on "who is taking the drug, in what dosage, by what route of administration, and under what circumstances" (xi). The effects of "set and setting," the drug taker's learned expectations of the effects of the drug, and the social circumstances under which he or she takes it, are of central importance (Zinberg 1984). At low dosages, drug effects are often indistinguishable from placebo effects, and given the irregular supplies of black markets, low dosages are not uncommon. Furthermore, there is wide variation among individuals in their patterns of drug use, as well as great variation over time in the drug-taking behavior of any given individual.

It is true that different drugs have different physiological effects (although these vary from person to person) and may have characteristic withdrawal syndromes (which also vary among people), but these physiological aspects do not bear a strong relationship to social behavior, which is the object of drug policy. All of the supposed equations associated with the concept of addiction—(a) pleasurable or pain-reducing subjective effects of a drug = (b) behavioral evidence of intoxication = (c) need for increased dosage, or tolerance = (d) intensity and duration of withdrawal symptoms = (e) difficulty in quitting use of the drug—are known to be inaccurate. These five indices vary separately from one another and form different patterns for different drugs (as do other indices);

they also vary among different users. In discussing heroin, for example, Stanton Peale (1990) points out that "a substantial number of patients who report potent addictive symptoms have taken little or no heroin, while regularly maintained narcotics users often express feeble or inconsistent withdrawal" (206).

As if this were not devastating enough to the notion of addiction as an empirical, substance-caused phenomenon, the term is also applied to behavior where no substance is involved (gambling) and that is necessary to sustain and reproduce life (eating and sex). It is a methodological commonplace that a concept that can be used to explain everything explains nothing.

Since patterns of drug use do not conform to our concept of addiction, one might ask how the concept arose. Not surprisingly, Peale (1990) and Harry G. Levine (1978) find the answer in history. They discuss the evolution of the concept of addiction and show how it was shaped by social forces—such as the religiously inspired temperance movement and Alcoholics Anonymous, and government institutions like Harry Anslinger's Federal Bureau of Narcotics—rather than by scientific data. Hence, attempts to understand the complexities of drug usage show the concept of addiction to be a misleading reification, and attempts to understand the concept of addiction lead us to historical forces unrelated to scientific accuracy.

(Since there are people with significant problems in living associated with drug usage, it is sometimes necessary, in order to communicate, to refer to them as a group despite their diversity. One can use the term "addict" as shorthand to refer to those who repeatedly take high levels of psychoactive substances despite what observers view as significant negative consequences to themselves or others. But when such terms are used for convenience [e.g., in the next section], it is important to make sure that they are not reified.)

When drug policy is based on reified concepts like addiction, it is bound to have unfortunate consequences. If we want to make the world a better place, we have to base our actions on reality as we find it rather than on concepts that we treat as real. If we want to improve our current drug policy, we should base our thinking on observable evidence and logic rather than on reified concepts that reflect current social prejudices.

BASE RATES

Consider the following "proof" that marijuana is a slow-acting poison:

1. Everyone who smoked marijuana before 1875 is dead.
2. Over 99 percent of those who smoked marijuana between 1875 and 1900 are dead.

3. Over 90 percent of those who smoked marijuana between 1900 and 1925 are dead.
4. As the date of first smoking marijuana gets closer to the present, the number of resulting deaths decreases because, for increasing numbers of people, too little time has elapsed for the slow-acting poison to take its toll.

Statisticians would say that this "proof" is fallacious because it does not take base rates into account. The base rate is defined as the percentage of the target condition in the parent population. In this case, the target condition is death and the first parent population is all people alive before 1875. Thus, the base rate is 100 percent. Since the number of deaths among those who smoked marijuana does not exceed the base rate, one cannot infer that marijuana contributed to their deaths. In a similar way, the death rate among those who smoked marijuana does not exceed the base rate for the general population during the periods 1875 to 1900, 1900 to 1925, or subsequently.

Base rates can be used to evaluate the effectiveness of doing something to people—such as treating or jailing them—to prevent them from becoming addicts. They can also be used to evaluate the effectiveness of the judicial system by examining the ratio of those unjustly convicted to those justly convicted. The following extended example illustrates what such comparisons show us.

Suppose we thought it would be a good idea to make drug addiction a crime so that we could send addicts to jail so that they would cease using drugs and remain drug free after release for fear of reincarceration. (This is a dubious premise, especially considering the ubiquity of smuggled drugs in our prisons, and it ignores the ethical issue of punishing individuals for something they do to themselves rather than to others. I should mention in passing that some people make the claim that addicts harm others, such as family members, not only by assaulting or robbing them—which are quite separate crimes—but also by making them feel bad. This kind of logic would criminalize someone who broke up with an unwilling girlfriend or boyfriend or a teacher who made a student feel bad by giving a failing grade. In any event, the rationale of criminalizing addiction does lie behind much current drug policy, such as making it illegal to possess certain psychoactive substances, so it is worth considering.)

Let us further suppose that we did not want to send nonaddicts to jail, even if they did occasionally use illicit drugs. This is because jailing them is costly to taxpayers, harmful to the nonaddicts, and takes up jail space better occupied by violent criminals. The problem then arises—how can the courts differentiate between addicts, who should be sent to jail, and nonaddicts, who should not?

Table 4.1. Courts Unable to Differentiate between Addicts and Nonaddicts

Conviction Certain Knowledge	Addict	Nonaddict	Number of Cases
Addict	50	50	100
Nonaddict	50	50	100
Number of Cases	100	100	200

Table 4.1 illustrates the hypothetical situation of courts unable to differentiate between addicts (however defined) and nonaddicts. It tallies two hundred cases, half of whom are known to be addicts, and half of whom are known not to be. Since the courts cannot tell the difference, fifty of the hundred addicts are correctly identified, and fifty are misidentified as nonaddicts. Similarly, fifty of the hundred nonaddicts are correctly identified, but fifty are misidentified as addicts. The courts correctly convict fifty addicts, at the expense of sending fifty nonaddicts to jail.

Let us assume that the courts can do better than this. Table 4.2 illustrates the hypothetical situation of courts that are able to differentiate reasonably well between addicts and nonaddicts. Despite crowded calendars and limited resources, they are able to make correct decisions 70 percent of the time. Table 4.2 once again presents two hundred cases, half of whom are known to be addicts, and half of whom are not. Since the courts are 70 percent effective, seventy of the hundred addicts are correctly identified and thirty are misidentified as nonaddicts. Similarly, seventy of the hundred nonaddicts are correctly identified, but thirty are misidentified as addicts. The courts correctly convict seventy addicts, at the expense of sending thirty nonaddicts to jail.

In a system where, to guarantee individual liberties, it is supposed to be preferable to free ten guilty people rather than send one innocent person to prison, this is not an outstanding record. Nevertheless, the balance is positive; and people who view drugs as a terrible menace might say that the lessening of the "justice ratio" from ten to one to seven to three is defensible.

Table 4.2. Courts 70 Percent Accurate in Differentiating between Addicts and Nonaddicts

Conviction Certain Knowledge	Addict	Nonaddict	Number of Cases
Addict	70	30	100
Nonaddict	30	70	100
Number of Cases	100	100	200

In the real world, however, addicts and nonaddicts do not come in groups of equal sizes. Addicts are a small proportion of those who use illicit drugs— say 5 percent, though the actual figure is lower. (They do, of course, use a disproportionate amount of the illegal drugs. One rule of thumb is that 80 percent of the drugs are used by 20 percent of the users. This is a ratio of sixteen to one in the consumption rates between the top fifth and bottom fifth of users—and the behavior of most of the top fifth would not meet any conceivable definition of addiction.)

Table 4.3 illustrates what happens when courts that are 70 percent effective attempt to convict addicts from a population with a base rate of 95 percent nonaddicts. The courts correctly convict seven of the ten addicts, while misidentifying three as nonaddicts. They are similarly accurate in identifying 133 of the 190 nonaddicts, while inaccurately convicting the remaining 57.

Let us examine more closely the results of applying this 70 percent–accurate legal procedure to the population under discussion. Of 64 people who go to jail, only 7 are addicts. This is an "injustice ratio" of more than eight to one! That is, by applying a 70 percent–valid legal procedure to detect a condition that occurs only 5 percent of the time, one winds up making more than eight wrong decisions for every correct one.

In contrast, by rejecting the valid legal procedure and making decisions based on base rates alone, one can be accurate 95 percent of the time. This can be verified by looking at the last column of table 4.3. By consulting no evidence and applying no procedure whatsoever, one could declare all two hundred people to be nonaddicts. This classification is correct in 190 of the cases and incorrect in only 10. (It might be mentioned in passing that this 95 percent accuracy implies a policy of not jailing addicts.) To restate the contrast, by using a 70 percent–valid procedure, one makes wrong decisions eight times to one over right ones, and by using base rates, one makes correct decisions nineteen times to one over wrong ones. The discrepancy between the two is in excess of 150 to 1.

This discrepancy is indefensibly unjust. When the effectiveness of the procedure one is using does not exceed the base rate, bad outcomes are bound to

Table 4.3. Courts 70 Percent Accurate in Differentiating between Addicts and Nonaddicts with a Base Rate of 95 Percent Nonaddicts

Conviction *Certain Knowledge*	*Addict*	*Nonaddict*	*Number of Cases*
Addict	7	3	10
Nonaddict	57	133	190
Number of Cases	64	136	200

Table 4.4.   Courts 70 Percent Accurate in Differentiating between Addicts and Nonaddicts with a Base Rate of 95 Percent Nonaddicts among All Americans

Conviction Certain Knowledge	Addict	Nonaddict	Number of Cases
Addict	3,500,000	1,500,000	5,000,000
Nonaddict	28,500,000	66,500,000	95,000,000
Number of Cases	32,000,000	68,000,000	100,000,000

occur. While our incarceration rate is the highest in the world, table 4.4 indicates that there is ample room for things to get much worse. If one hundred million Americans have used an illegal substance at least once (the actual figure is higher), and if 5 percent of them are addicts, a zero-tolerance policy avidly enforced could lead to the imprisonment of tens of millions of additional people, the overwhelming majority of whom would have been convicted unjustly.

In addition, when a policy creates so much room to be applied unjustly, there is an opportunity for it to be used in a discriminatory manner. Unfortunately, it is clear that such discrimination is taking place. Using U.S. government statistics, Mare Mauer (1996) reported that African Americans represent 12 percent of the U.S. population, 13 percent of drug users, 35 percent of arrests for drug possession, 55 percent of convictions for drug possession, and 74 percent of prison sentences for drug possession. Such unjust applications are ethically indefensible and socially divisive, and they undermine respect for and the integrity of our criminal justice system.

In summary, a consideration of base rates leads to the following conclusions. First, addicts constitute a small proportion of drug users. Second, any policy aimed at addicts will be imperfect at identifying them. Therefore, not only will the policy miss some addicts, but it will also affect many more nonaddicts than addicts because the number of nonaddicts is huge in comparison to that of addicts. This discrepancy produces unjust outcomes on a massive scale. Whatever one thinks of illicit drugs, a consideration of base rates makes one wonder whether the undesirable results of drug prohibition—like the undesirable results of alcohol prohibition before it—make a change of policy worth considering.

PREDICTIONS ARE PROBABILISTIC

Some people say, "Unless you can assure me that drug legalization won't make us a nation of addicts, I can't support it." While the reified term "addiction" was discussed above, and other difficulties with the statement are discussed in the next section, I would like to focus on its demand for certainty.

A moment's reflection tells us that nothing in life is certain. Even though the sun has risen every day, we cannot be certain that it will rise tomorrow. The fallacy in the demand for certainty is that of a false dichotomy—the implication that one must choose between total certainty and total uncertainty.

In other words, when people say, "We cannot know with certainty what will happen following drug legalization," and "Evidence from nineteenth-century America or from other countries today can't give us that certainty," they are really saying, "I refuse to think about this matter." The trouble with refusing to consider alternatives without certainty is that such a position constitutes an ideological support for the status quo, no matter how bad it may be, simply because it is conceivable that an alternative might be worse.

Instead of demanding certainty, one can and should seek probabilities. That is, we can ask, Based on evidence and reason, what are the most likely consequences of various approaches to legalization? This is in contrast to asking, based on fear and prejudice, What are the most awful consequences imaginable? Improbable worst-case scenarios will lead us (indeed, have led us) to policies that are counterproductive because they are divorced from reality.

What are some of the kinds of predictions that would emerge from such analyses? In very general terms, they are ones like the following. I list these four predictions, along with suggestions of the evidence supporting them, to illustrate the difference between reasonable predictions and the demand for certainty that cannot, in principle, be met.

No Matter Which Drugs Are Legalized in What Ways, Tobacco and Alcohol Will Remain, by Far, Our Severest Problems

In the case of tobacco, this prediction is made because people find it so difficult to stop using nicotine—it is approximately as difficult to give up as heroin—and because smoking is so deadly (over 400,000 deaths per year in the United States). In addition, cigarettes are popular because the mind-altering effects of nicotine are subtle, allowing people to work, drive, operate machinery, and carry on social relationships without noticeable impairment.

While a much smaller percentage of those who use alcohol have difficulty stopping, the population of users is so huge that even a small percentage of abusers is a very large number of people. Furthermore, alcohol does affect coordination and judgment. Unfortunately, people using alcohol often are both unaware of these effects and manage to conceal them from others (e.g., He knows how to hold his booze.). For these reasons among others, alcohol remains extremely popular, even though it is associated with well over 100,000 deaths per year. In the nineteenth century, when opiates, cocaine, and marijuana were all legal and available, the Prohibition movement was directed at alcohol rather than other substances. It was obvious at the time that the numbers of people affected and the scale of the associated psychological, social, and physical misery were much greater than those of other substances. Under any system of legalization, this will likely continue to be the case.

In contrast, opiates and cocaine are each associated with only a few thousand deaths per year. Both substances interfere with people's ongoing work and social lives, thereby imposing real costs on their users and making the substances less attractive. While excessive use of alcohol creates similar problems, people find it easier to moderate their consumption of alcohol than of opiates and cocaine. Thus, if these substances became legal, the demand for them among occasional users of psychoactive substances would probably not be great. Furthermore, those who did want to try opiates or cocaine would probably experiment with low dosages so as to minimize the associated risks.

Marijuana is probably the only illegal substance whose use would increase significantly following legalization because it enables occasional users to become intoxicated with so few disadvantages. Marijuana has never caused a death from overdose, and this positive feature would likely continue after legalization.

The interaction of the legal use of marijuana with the legal use of alcohol is likely to produce a variety of positive and negative public health effects. Many who might otherwise use alcohol would be likely to use marijuana instead. This decrement should ultimately result in a saving of life among those who would otherwise go on to use alcohol heavily. This health benefit might be partially undercut by a slight increase in accidents among those using alcohol and marijuana simultaneously over those using alcohol alone, as well as by accidents among marijuana users. Furthermore, although low use of alcohol may confer some health benefits, marijuana smoke is more carcinogenic than tobacco smoke. On the other hand, marijuana is used in very small amounts in comparison to tobacco, and people find it much easier to stop using. Therefore, the increase in cancer mortality from marijuana legalization is likely to be slight and limited to tobacco users. Nevertheless, since the carcinogens in both marijuana and tobacco are different from the nicotine and THC that people seek from these plants, legalization will provide yet another argument for developing safer ways to smoke. Since cannabinoids are volatile at a temperature below that at which marijuana burns, vaporizers that heat but do not burn the leaves offer a public health benefit.

Finally, since marijuana stays in the body longer than alcohol, there is an incentive for users to hold down consumption (e.g., so that an intoxicated evening will not interfere with work performance the next day).

There Will Not Be Much Change in the Numbers of Severe Drug Abusers under Any System of Legalization

This prediction is based on the relatively stable numbers of such people over extended periods of time and under differing legal sanctions. Unfortunately, there will always be a small percentage of individuals who are chronic alcoholics or abusers of other drugs, just as there will always be some psychotics, criminals, and other social misfits. This state of affairs appears to be unavoidable. We can experiment with social policies to minimize severe substance abuse and to minimize the harm severe abusers do to themselves and others (e.g., by making clean needles available to prevent the spread of AIDS), but attempts to stamp severe abuse out by force are doomed to failure—as we have reconfirmed decade after decade, ad absurdum and ad nauseam.

On the other hand, the way of life of this relatively small population is so clearly stigmatized that ending drug prohibition would be unlikely to contribute substantially to its numbers. Although long-term expectations are for no major change in severe abuse, there might be an initial increase following legalization. Still, our experience—in the last century when everything was legal as well as following the end of Prohibition—gives no reason to worry that these numbers would exceed the current range of fluctuations as fads in substance abuse wax and wane over time.

Experimentation by Occasional Users Will Increase

In contrast to severe abuse, occasional experimentation should increase. This is because the main effect of prohibition is not to curtail use by severe abusers—who make sure they get their substances one way or another—but by occasional users. Adults who hold down jobs and are raising families might have a drink or two in the evening but would not risk drinking heavily or trying an illegal substance because the potential negative consequences for them are too great. Once prohibited substances become legal, they might experiment with them in the same prudent way.

Dosage Levels for Occasional Users Will Decrease

The economics of the black market lead producers to concentrate as much of an illegal substance as possible in as small a space as possible. This is another way of saying that the black market encourages high dosage levels—dosages that interfere more with people's lives and that are associated with more negative consequences. As chapter 3 indicates, Prohibition changed us from a nation of beer drinkers to one of whiskey drinkers, but after the end of Prohibition, we gradually drifted back to beer with its lower dosage level of alcohol. More specifically, because alcohol is legal, a range of dosage levels is available for all preferences—from beer to wine to cocktails to straight whiskey. Only a small proportion of people prefer the highest levels of alcohol, while the largest proportion of drinkers prefer the lowest levels. Similarly, only a small proportion of those who drink do so to excess, while the great majority do so in limited quantities.

Drug prohibition has similarly led to the progression from opium to morphine to heroin, from coca to powdered cocaine to crack cocaine, and to the creation and use of marijuana with higher THC levels. Making any prohibited substance legal—even if a wide range of dosage levels is permitted—should lead to the kind of preference for lower dosages that we see with alcohol. Because occasional users are committed to their work, families, and social relationships, they seek occasional mild intoxication for brief periods of time. They do not want intense or long-lasting intoxication, with all its attendant problems, from currently illegal substances any more than they want to get drunk or go on a bender from alcohol, even though they have plenty available in their liquor cabinets.

These four probabilistic predictions can be seen as an alternative to the unfulfillable demand for certainty that is sometimes used to justify the status quo.

COST-BENEFIT ANALYSES

As indicated above, people sometimes argue against drug legalization by saying that it would lead to an increase in the use of drugs. This argument is an example of a more general one: maintain (or change) policy *x* because to do otherwise will have undesirable consequences. (There are other ways to discuss the argument, but they are not relevant to the purposes of this chapter, and they appear elsewhere in the book.)

While it is amazing that such arguments continue to be made, it is still worth pointing out their shortcoming. *All policies have undesirable consequences.* They also have desirable consequences. The problem in comparing a proposed new policy with the current one is to consider the relative costs and benefits of each—in both economic and social terms—in order to arrive at an overall decision as to which is best.

There are two kinds of errors that one might make: an erroneous rejection of current policy in favor of a proposed alternative, and an erroneous continuation of current policy in lieu of the alternative. Table 4.5 illustrates the way

Table 4.5. Desirable and Undesirable Consequences of Current and Alternative Policies

	Current Policy	*Alternative Policy*
Desirable consequences	a	m, n, o, p, q, r, s, t, u, v
Undesirable consequences	b, c, d, e, f, g, h, i, j, k, l	w, x, y, z

in which the desirable and undesirable consequences have to be weighed for both current policy and a proposed alternative policy.

For example, we might want to compare current marijuana policy to an alternative policy of making the drug legal for adults and regulating it much as we do alcohol and tobacco. In this case, table 4.5 might be interpreted as follows:

- *Desirable consequences of current policy*
  a. Demonstration of society's disapproval for using marijuana
- *Undesirable consequences of current policy*
  b. Growth of a huge black market
  c. Death, injury, and property loss from marijuana-related crimes
  d. Injuring (occasionally killing), confiscating the property of, and jailing of many users who are no danger to anyone
  e. Huge marijuana-related economic costs of prisons and the legal process
  f. Increasing dependency of local law enforcement on federal funding and forfeiture income
  g. Infringement of civil rights by antimarijuana drug war legislation
  h. Corruption of police and politicians with marijuana-related money
  i. Early release of violent prisoners to make space for prisoners serving mandatory minimum sentences for marijuana-related convictions
  j. Loss of respect for government and the legal system
  k. False information about the effects of marijuana, leading to a loss of respect for drug education (and probably to increased use as well)
  l. Increased physical suffering and disability from many conditions because physicians cannot prescribe and patients cannot use marijuana
- *Desirable consequences of alternative policy*
  m. Availability of marijuana to treat many medical conditions
  n. Destruction of the black market for marijuana, which would decrease crime, including innocent bystander injuries and deaths from turf war battles
  o. Long-term increased economic potential for poor areas resulting from diminished crime
  p. Decrease in alcohol-related disease and accidents for those who use marijuana instead

q. End to property loss, injury, and death from mistaken marijuana-related law enforcement action
r. Disappearance of marijuana-related crime, enabling police to devote more resources to violent crime
s. Decreased corruption among police and politicians
t. Decreased cost of law enforcement
u. An end to jail crowding, making adequate space available to contain violent criminals
v. Increased respect for government and the legal system
• *Undesirable consequences of alternative policy*
w. Increased unemployment for jailers due to decreased number of prisoners
x. Short-term financial losses in poor areas resulting from the loss of black market income
y. Governmental loss of forfeited marijuana-related assets
z. Possible increase in accidents and lung cancer (if marijuana smoking increases)

This enumeration of the desirable and undesirable consequences of current marijuana policy and an alternative policy is not necessarily complete or indisputable. For example, it omits a discussion of taxation and the use of such revenues (e.g., to pay for drug education and drug treatment). But it does illustrate the use of cost-benefit analyses in considering policy alternatives.

In summary, then, an understanding of selection bias, reification of concepts, base rates, probabilistic predictions, and cost-benefit analyses is helpful in making informed judgments about drug policy.

REFERENCES

Brecher, E. 1972. *Licit and illicit drugs*. Boston: Little, Brown.
Cook, T. D., and D. T. Campbell. 1979. *Quasi-experimentation: Design and analysis issues for field settings*. Boston: Houghton Mifflin.
Fish, J. M. 1996. *Culture and therapy: An integrative approach*. Northvale, N.J.: Jason Aronson, Inc.
———. 2000. Rethinking our drug policy. In *Is our drug policy effective? Are there alternatives?* Edited by J. M. Fish, 9–19. New York: *Fordham Urban Law Journal* 23(1). Proceedings of the March 17 and 18, 2000, joint conference of the New York Academy of Sciences, New York Academy of Medicine, and Association of the Bar of the City of New York.

Levine, H. G. 1978. The discovery of addiction: Changing conceptions of habitual drunkenness in America. *Journal of Studies on Alcohol* 39:143–74.

Mauer, M. 1996. The drug war's unequal justice. *Drug Policy Letter* 28:11–13.

Meehl, P. E., and A. Rosen. 1955. Antecedent probability and the efficiency of psychometric signs, patterns, or cutting scores. *Psychological Bulletin* 52:194–216.

Peale, S. 1990. Addiction as a cultural concept. In *Psychology: Perspectives and practice*. Edited by S. M. Pfafflin, J. A. Sechzer, J. M. Fish, and R. L. Thompson, 205–20. Annals of the New York Academy of Sciences 602. New York: New York Academy of Sciences.

Szasz, T. S. 1974. *Ceremonial chemistry: The ritual persecution of drugs, addicts, and pushers*. New York: Anchor/Doubleday.

———. 1992. *Our right to drugs: The case for a free market*. New York: Praeger.

U.S. Department of Health and Human Services, Substance Abuse and Mental Health Services Administration. 2002. *National survey on drug use and health: Population estimates 2002*, Washington, D.C.: U.S. Department of Health and Human Services.

Zinberg, N. E. 1984. *Drug, set, and setting: The basis for controlled intoxicant use*. New Haven, Conn.: Yale University Press.

5

Competing Rationales for Drug Policy Reform

Douglas Husak

Commentators who propose a fundamental rethinking of our nation's drug policy are impatient for the debate to proceed to the next level. Their impatience is understandable. Many thoughtful critics have found the arguments against the status quo to be compelling—and frustratingly repetitive. Every month, an academic from one discipline or another discovers anew that the War on Drugs has been a disaster. Each successive book recites familiar arguments about the failures of what might be called our *criminal justice drug policy*, according to which, the best way to deal with drugs used largely for recreational purposes—in particular, marijuana, cocaine, ecstasy, and heroin—is to severely punish the persons who use them.[1]

Even those commentators who have not been wholly persuaded by these arguments are anxious to see the controversy move in a different direction. To some theorists, the case in favor of fundamental change cannot be decisive in the absence of a blueprint for reform. These more cautious critics withhold judgment about our criminal justice policy until a detailed description of a new strategy for dealing with drugs becomes available for evaluation. Although deeply skeptical of the status quo, these commentators know it is naive to suppose that "things can't get much worse."

Why do most theorists decline the invitation to provide the specifics of a better drug policy? Many explanations are possible, apart from the obvious fact that attacking a proposal is always easier than defending a solution. In this chapter, I attempt to account for this state of affairs by contrasting two distinct bases for dissatisfaction with contemporary drug policy. Many thinkers who are unified in their opposition to the status quo divide in their reasons to oppose it. The shape of an ideal drug policy cannot be specified without a relatively clear idea of why our criminal justice approach is so deficient.

The two bases for opposition to our criminal justice drug policy might be called the *harm-reduction* and *rights-based* perspectives. Although these two perspectives are logically compatible, and in many ways are complementary, this chapter highlights the respects in which they are in tension with one another. After describing some of the strengths and weaknesses of each perspective, I contrast their implications for drug policy reform and argue that no one should profess to be able to describe more than the outlines of an ideal drug policy without choosing between a harm-reduction and a rights-based perspective. The details of a new drug policy depend not only on which of the two perspectives is adopted but also on further subdivisions and refinements within each perspective. Careful reflection about the deficiencies of our criminal justice drug policy is required before the debate can be taken to the next level and the details of a better strategy can be described.

THE HARM-REDUCTION PERSPECTIVE

In this section, I describe the harm-reduction perspective on drug policy reform. Because I tend to favor the competing rights-based perspective, I focus here largely on what I take to be the difficulties with the harm-reduction approach. Of course, harm-reduction theorists do not speak with a single voice. In particular, they disagree with one another about matters of fact—about how harm is best reduced. In what follows, however, I explore theoretical rather than empirical problems within the harm-reduction movement.

Many commentators have concluded that our criminal justice drug policy does not work. Our policy is alleged not to work because it is largely ineffective in reducing both the supply and the demand for drugs—and no realistic measures to improve our efforts are on the horizon. In addition, our policy is alleged not to work because it is counterproductive. I will not recount the several respects in which our criminal justice drug policy is counterproductive.[2] These reasons are familiar to anyone who is not a novice to drug-policy debates.

What would it mean for a policy to work? One answer is that the best drug policy would minimize harm. This reply makes no presuppositions about which kind of policy will emerge as optimal. Contrary to the accusations of some of its opponents, harm-reduction is not a disguise for a drug-decriminalization agenda.[3] Many theorists are persuaded that harm would be minimized by abandoning criminal penalties to deter drug use.[4] But deterrence might be a component of the most effective approach; some supporters of the status quo are prepared to defend our criminal justice policy on harm-reduction grounds.[5] In any event, the question of what policy works is contingent on careful research and a dispassionate assessment of alternatives.

Perhaps the greatest virtue of the harm-reduction perspective is that its ultimate objective seems beyond serious reproach. As Ethan Nadelmann asks, "who, in their right mind, could oppose the notion of reducing harm?"[6] This alleged consensus about the proper goal of drug policy accounts for the wide ideological diversity of persons who have joined in the call for fundamental reform on harm-reduction grounds. Both liberals and conservatives should welcome a drug policy that works.

Theorists who advocate a harm-reduction perspective should be well aware, however, that their objective is not really so platitudinous. A harm-reduction perspective is incompatible with what might be called *legal moralism*.[7] According to the legal moralist, the criminal law should punish immoral behavior, apart from any harm that such conduct might cause. Legal moralism provides the theoretical foundation for many defenses of our criminal-justice drug policy. Former "drug czar" William Bennett states, "The simple fact is that drug use is wrong. And the moral argument, in the end, is the most compelling argument."[8] Another former czar, Barry McCaffrey, echoes this sentiment in the context of defending the disparate treatment of licit and illicit drugs. He writes, "The reason drugs are wrong and dangerous is not that they're illegal but that they're destructive of a person's physical, emotional and moral strength—and also of their families. That central assertion also applies to alcohol. Nicotine may be more of a health problem, but these other drugs are dangerous because they pull you apart physically and emotionally."[9] President George W. Bush remarks that "legalizing drugs would completely undermine the message that drug use is wrong."[10]

Many commentators join political appointees in invoking legal moralism to support a punitive approach to drug policy. James Q. Wilson writes,

> If we believe—as I do—that dependency on certain mind-altering drugs *is* a moral issue, and that their illegality rests in part on their immorality, then legalizing them undercuts, if it does not eliminate altogether, the moral message. That message is at the root of the distinction we now make between nicotine and cocaine. Both are highly addictive; both have harmful physical effects. But we treat the two drugs differently, not simply because nicotine is so widely used as to be beyond the reach of effective prohibition, but because its use does not destroy the user's essential humanity. Tobacco shortens one's life, cocaine debases it. Nicotine alters one's habits, cocaine alters one's soul.[11]

Moral judgments against drug use are expressed again and again. Even those commentators who are ambivalent about our existing drug policy and cautiously defend various reforms admit to moral reservations about illegal drug use. John Kaplan confesses, "I cannot escape the feeling that drug use, aside from any harm it does, is somehow wrong."[12]

How do theorists who adopt a harm-reduction perspective respond to these legal moralists? They cannot easily incorporate the supposed wrongfulness of drug use into their harm-reduction calculus. The alleged immorality of drug use is not simply another kind of harm—"moral harm"—to be included along with physical, psychological, or economic harm. The concept of "moral harm" is rejected by most harm-reduction theorists as incoherent.[13] Some harm-reduction theorists are explicit in regarding allegations about the immorality of drug use as irrelevant to their framework.[14] The fact that the harm-reduction perspective aspires to moral neutrality is yet another reason its defenders find this approach so appealing. In an era in which many persons profess skepticism about moral discourse and believe normative controversies to be intractable, a perspective that claims not to depend on moral judgments, but only on reducing harm, seems enlightened and progressive.

In what follows, I raise a number of difficulties that arise in the reply that harm-reduction theorists offer to the legal moralists. I do not insist that any of the problems I discuss are fatal to the harm-reduction perspective, so that all talk of harm-reduction should be abandoned. I have no interest in dividing drug reformers against one another; thus far, they have presented a fairly unified front against a common enemy: our criminal justice policy. Perhaps the difficulties I examine should be construed as invitations for further conceptual work on the part of those theorists who embrace a harm-reduction perspective. Commentators who have refined this perspective have done an enormous service in identifying several respects in which our criminal justice drug policy is ineffective and counterproductive. In addition, they are pledged to improving drug policy and have pointed out several practical steps that would help to do so.[15] I am prepared to concede that a harm-reduction perspective may ultimately prove the more successful in stimulating drug policy reform in the court of public opinion. Nonetheless, I believe that the questions I raise indicate some of the relative merits of a rights-based perspective, even though this approach faces considerable problems of its own.

I have already mentioned the central difficulty. Legal moralists who defend our criminal justice drug policy by alleging that much drug use is wrongful— apart from its harmful consequences—cannot be expected to subscribe to a perspective that purports to avoid the moral dimension of drug use as too controversial or otherwise irrelevant in shaping policy. From their point of view, any methodology that fails to acknowledge the wrongfulness of drug use misses the crucial point and ignores the primary rationale that drug policy should be designed to serve. Many retributivists believe that the punishment of wrongdoers is intrinsically good, even if the institutions that apprehend and convict these wrongdoers are inefficient.[16] Harm-reduction critics of our criminal justice drug policy may disagree with this judgment. They should not, however, beg the question by applying a criterion to choose between competing drug policies that assumes that moral judgments play no proper role in the decision.

Allegations about the immorality of drug use should not be dismissed as anachronistic, unscientific, or irrelevant. These allegations must be addressed directly; persons who insist that illicit drug use is wrongful are owed a reply. A philosopher would like to respond to their arguments. Unfortunately, arguments for the alleged immorality of drug use are almost never produced; this judgment is typically put forward as a kind of brute moral fact or uncontrovertible moral intuition.[17] In the absence of an argument for this judgment, it is hard to know how a reply should be structured. When commentators do not defend their views, conflicts between moral intuitions are nearly impossible to resolve. Still, I believe it is necessary to offer some response to the legal moralists, even if I cannot critique an argument they are unable or unwilling to provide.

One matter is clear: allegations about the wrongfulness of drug use should not be ignored simply because they are moral judgments. I suspect that many harm-reduction theorists are disingenuous if they claim to regard moral judgments as irrelevant to the formation of public policy. Commentators would be unwilling to put aside their moral views if asked to choose between competing policies about which they hold strong opinions of their own. Take any example about which there exists a social consensus about the immorality of conduct. Suppose we agree that domestic violence is wrong. Imagine that some clever theorist argued in favor of a policy to minimize the harm of domestic violence that dispensed with the use of criminal punishment. After all, it is always a contingent matter whether the best policy for reducing the harm caused by persons who batter their spouses will include criminal sanctions. How should these arguments be received? Few of us would be prepared to entertain these arguments seriously. We would be reluctant to allow spouse batterers to escape their just desserts simply because we became convinced that less harm would be caused by a nonpunitive approach.

Consider also the converse phenomenon. Take any example about which there exists a social consensus that conduct is morally permissible. Suppose we agree that watching television is not wrongful. Imagine that some clever theorist argued in favor of a policy to minimize the harm of watching television that included the use of criminal punishment. After all, it is always a contingent matter whether the best policy for dealing with the harms caused by television will include criminal sanctions. Again, few of us would be prepared to entertain these arguments seriously. We would be unwilling to punish persons who watch television simply because we became convinced that less harm would be caused by a criminal justice approach. I conclude that if we really believe that a given kind of conduct is wrongful or firmly hold it to be morally permissible, we will not happily embrace a methodology that regards the moral status of that conduct as irrelevant to the formation of public policy. Legal moralists have a point when they respond that the supposed moral neutrality of the harm-reduction perspective need not be welcomed by any reasonable person.

But can the harm-reduction perspective really maintain moral neutrality? I think not. My skepticism arises from attempting to understand the nature of the "harm" that these reformers propose to minimize.[18] What is harm? Theorists are likely to respond by reciting a list of uncontroversial examples of the negative consequences of our criminal justice drug policy: overcrowded prisons, violence by drug dealers defending turf, emergency medical treatment for persons who ingest contaminated drugs, and the like. But I am not simply asking for examples or for a list of harms. In inquiring what harm is, I am asking what makes something a harm. By virtue of what property or properties does something qualify for inclusion on the list?

One cannot simply identify a given consequence as a harm in the same way that one can identify a person's height or shoe size. Smokers who die premature deaths help to keep the Social Security fund solvent. Are their early deaths a harm? The problem is not simply the existence of contested, borderline examples. The problem is that no empirical test can answer this kind of question. Without making judgments about which consequences we do want or do not want, the contrast between the harmless and the harmful cannot be drawn. And which consequences should we not want? We should not want those consequences that are bad. A harm, I think, is any consequence that is bad. Philosophers and economists call it "disutility." "Bad," of course, is not a morally neutral concept. If I am correct, harm is not a morally neutral concept either.[19] Perhaps the moral content of harm is not widely recognized because we tend to think of moral questions as controversial, and there is nothing controversial about judgments such as "drug-related killings of children to protect turf are bad." But a moral judgment is not transformed into something other than a moral judgment simply because its truth is so evident. Not all moral questions are intractable; some moral judgments are obviously true.

The realization that harm is a moral concept casts the harm-reduction perspective in a new and different light. The harm-reduction approach to drug policy, no less than that of the legal moralist, depends on moral judgments. If so, the harm-reduction perspective does not offer a morally neutral alternative to the enforcement of morality. At best, it simply proposes a different version of the morality to be enforced.[20]

Further evidence that the harm-reduction perspective incorporates a moral point of view is easily provided. Harm-reduction theorists divide over a number of issues that cannot be resolved empirically. I will mention two such issues. First, is harm to users to be given the same status as harm to nonusers? On the one hand, it is difficult to treat harms to users differently from harms to nonusers. The death of a smoker from lung cancer and the death of a nonsmoker as a result of secondary, side-stream smoke each count as a fatality caused by tobacco. If our objective is to reduce harm, should we not strive equally hard to prevent each death? On the other hand, it is difficult to treat harms to users comparably to harms to nonusers, and few harm-reduction theorists are prepared to do so. After indicating that "drug use is viewed as neither right or wrong in itself," one prominent defender of a harm-reduction perspective continues, "Rather, drug use is evaluated in terms of harm to others, and, to some extent, harm suffered by users. The latter is regrettable but acceptable if it arises from 'informed choice.'"[21]

According to this train of thought, not all harms are alike. Some kinds of harm—those arising from "informed choice"—are "acceptable." No theorist who adopts this stance can pretend that his approach is morally neutral. Any basis for concluding that some harms "don't count" in the harm-reduction calculus is almost certain to be derived from a theory that presupposes some conception of the autonomy of agents. Unlike harms to others, self-inflicted harms caused through informed choice are exempted because they are the product of autonomous choice. Needless to say, any defense of this conclusion—an account of the nature and importance of autonomy—involves moral reasoning.

Consider a second moral issue that divides theorists in the harm-reduction camp. Notice that the goal of harm-reduction seems curiously incomplete. Consider two policies, A and B. Suppose that policy A produces less harm than policy B. Is policy A therefore preferable? Not always. In order to choose between A and B, we need to know not only which policy minimizes harm but also which maximizes benefits. A moral argument is needed to show why harms should count but benefits should not. Most harm-reduction theorists would probably agree that the best drug policy would not simply minimize harm but would do so while maximizing benefits. If "harm" is equated with "cost," the best drug policy achieves the most favorable ratio of benefits to costs.[22]

Two problems arise if the focus is shifted away from the simple goal of harm-reduction toward the more complex goal of achieving the most favorable ratio of benefits to costs (or harms). The first problem is to identify the benefits to be balanced against the harms or costs; the second is to balance them. Neither problem can be solved without making moral judgments.

Begin with the benefits to be balanced against the harms or costs of drug use. What is the nature of these benefits? If I am correct that harm is a moral concept—equivalent to anything bad—it should come as no surprise that benefit is a moral concept as well—equivalent to anything good. And what is good about drug use? Much has been said and written about the harms of drug use—and, from harm-reduction theorists, about the harms of prohibiting drug use—but a discussion of the benefits of drug use is conspicuously absent in the cost-benefit literature. Some commentators, to be sure, have emphasized the artistic creativity, spiritual enlightenment, and consciousness expansion that drug use may produce.[23] These effects should not be dismissed as unimportant. Such benefits do not, however, capture the motivation behind most recreational drug use. The explanation of why many persons consume drugs is no more mysterious than the explanation of why many persons consume so much fat or sugar: they enjoy the experience. The main benefit persons obtain is pleasure or euphoria—the "high" of drug use.

Does pleasure count as a benefit in the cost-benefit calculus? An affirmative answer seems obvious; to demand a defense of the significance of pleasure is odd.[24] Yet, there is a puzzling reluctance among commentators to mention pleasure as the main benefit of drug use. Despite occasional allegations that Americans are puritanical, we do not really regard pleasure per se as objectionable or suspicious; we engage in all kinds of activities that are important to us solely (or at least primarily) because of the pleasure we derive from them. Although there is some nutritional value in potato chips, almost no one devours them for that reason. Eye-hand coordination is developed by video games, but few play them to gain that skill. These activities are popular because they are almost purely *recreational*—they are pursued for fun. No one could afford to ignore the superior taste of ice cream relative to wheat germ if asked to prepare a cost-benefit analysis of these foods. Licit recreational drugs such as alcohol would fail a cost-benefit test if the pleasure of intoxication were omitted from consideration. Like the pleasure derived from eating, playing video games, or any other activity, the pleasure of illicit drug use must be included in the cost-benefit calculus—unless there is some basis for disqualifying it.[25] But any basis for claiming that not all pleasures count equally has the same status as the foregoing claim that not all harms count equally. The rationale for differentiating between kinds of pleasures in a cost-benefit analysis—for alleging that some pleasures are good and other pleasures are bad—must be moral in nature.

The second problem in attempts to achieve the most favorable ratio of costs and benefits is to justify a decision about how the various factors should be

weighed and balanced. Even if all the costs and benefits of various drug policies could be predicted with reasonable accuracy, there is simply no common
denominator by which it is possible to decide whether the costs outweigh the
benefits or vice versa. The balancing metaphor suggests the existence of a
common denominator, or a common currency, in which all costs and benefits
can be expressed. Unfortunately, no such common denominator is available.
One theorist will judge that the costs of a given activity outweigh its benefits,
while another will reach the opposite conclusion. He will judge that the pleasure of a drug high (or of a jelly doughnut) outweighs the health risks that
such activities create. The point is not simply that there is no way to decide
who is correct—many empirical disagreements seem quite intractable. Instead, the point is that the disagreement is moral rather than factual. Here
again, the tendency of theorists who subscribe to a cost-benefit analysis to depict themselves as empirical and scientific is inaccurate. Like those who employ a perspective they typically resist, they too are engaged in moral debate.

With this conclusion in mind, return again to Nadelmann's rhetorical question, "Who, in their right mind, could oppose the notion of reducing harm?"
Of course, he asks this question in the context of identifying the best drug policy, and perhaps a harm-reduction perspective is supposed to apply *only* to
drug policy. Yet, confining a harm-reduction approach to drug policy seems
suspiciously ad hoc. Of course, theorists who aspire to the improvement of
society must begin somewhere, and I sympathize with those who believe that
the greatest payoffs will occur by overhauling our drug policy. Still, in principle, Nadelmann's rhetorical question could be raised in any context. Is it
equally sensible—no more or no less—to implement a harm-reduction perspective to any issue whatever? After all, harm-reduction seems just as viable
when applied to educational policy, defense policy, or anything else about
which we may want a policy. For example, Americans do not eat as well as
we might. Who in his right mind could oppose harm-reduction when formulating food policy? Americans do not read as much as we might. Why not
pursue a harm-reduction approach to reading policy?

Something has gone wrong here. On some matters it is inappropriate to implement a policy. No one talks about the need for harm-reduction in design-
ing a speech policy, not because no harms are caused by speech or because
nothing could possibly be done to reduce them. A harm-reduction perspective
should not be applied to a controversy about whether a given speaker should
be tolerated or persecuted because it seems clear that rights are at stake in
matters of speech. When rights are implicated, the very suggestion that controversies should be decided by reference to a policy seems misguided. Harm-
reduction or cost-benefits analyses are largely beside the point when rights
are at stake. I am concerned that the assumption that drug policy should be

formulated on harm-reduction grounds implicitly presupposes that no rights are implicated by drug use.

But are rights at stake in drug use? I now turn to this question.

THE RIGHTS-BASED PERSPECTIVE

In this section, I describe the rights-based perspective to drug policy reform.[26] I believe that this approach has several advantages over the competing harm-reduction perspective, even though it has received far less attention.[27] In particular, it provides a better response to those legal moralists who support our criminal justice drug policy. Still, the rights-based perspective faces considerable problems of its own, which I attempt to address as best I can.

According to the rights-based perspective, drug policy—like any other policy—must respect moral rights. These rights constrain what can be done in the name of policy. Our criminal justice approach is defective because it infringes the moral rights of drug users. Many commentators who endorse a harm-reduction perspective also believe that moral rights are violated by the status quo. Yet, the two perspectives are clearly different and, in some respects, are in tension with each other.[28]

Recall that the harm-reduction perspective deals with the moral dimension of drug use by applying a methodology that dismisses such issues as unimportant. By contrast, the rights-based perspective offers a cogent reply to the legal moralists. One can concede that drug use might be wrongful while still believing it to be protected by a moral right. The supposition that rights can apply to and protect wrongful conduct is familiar to our thinking about rights.[29] Consider just a few examples. No one supposes that privacy rights protect only morally innocent activities. Most people concede the immorality of Nazi politics or racist speech while still believing that these activities are protected by moral rights. To be sure, moral rights do not confer an absolute immunity on persons to engage in such conduct—a point to which I will return. The supposition that recreational drug use is protected by a right does not assume that consequentialist considerations are utterly irrelevant to the resolution of issues about drug use. Still, moral rights can and do offer some degree of protection to wrongful behavior.

I fault harm-reduction theorists above for adopting positions on normative issues while purporting to moral neutrality. Recall that the very distinction between the harmful and the harmless cannot be drawn without a willingness to make moral judgments. Moreover, harm-reduction theorists cannot explain why harm to oneself should count less than harm to others without recourse to moral reasoning. Since a rights-based perspective has no aspirations to moral neutrality, it seems capable of solving problems that embarrassed the harm-reduction perspective. In any respectable theory of rights, for example, consent plays a central role, and persons enjoy a much broader freedom to harm themselves than to harm others.

Nonetheless, some theorists who endorse a cost-benefit (or harm-reduction) perspective on drug policy have expressed skepticism about the cogency of a rights approach. Kaplan concedes that "many people speak of the individual's right to do what he wishes with his own body, his right to harm himself, or his right to eat, drink, or otherwise ingest what he pleases." But, he continues, "the problem with such 'rights' is that they are all assertions. They do not carry any argument with them."[30]

It is not entirely clear what would satisfy Kaplan's demand that defenders of a rights-based perspective produce an argument. I construe his complaint as follows. No one should simply allege that persons have a moral right to eat, drink, or otherwise ingest what they please. Those who defend our criminal justice drug policy will not concede that these rights exist. As I have indicated, legal moralists believe that drug use is wrongful and that drug offenders should be punished for that reason alone. But I have also noted that they have not argued for this position. Both sides seem equally guilty of begging the question against their opponents; each reports moral intuitions the other rejects. The only hope of making progress in this standoff is to produce an argument. Commentators who defend a rights-based perspective must provide a plausible argument in favor of a moral right to use drugs that is infringed by our criminal justice policy.

How might one defend the existence of such a moral right? The best strategy would be to provide a comprehensive theory of moral rights and to show that a right to use drugs is among those particular rights countenanced by the theory. I will not pursue this very ambitious strategy here, although I welcome attempts to do so. Moral philosophers have struggled for centuries to provide an adequate theory of rights, and I have no confidence that success is on the horizon. A general theory of moral rights would be just as controversial as the existence of any particular right—such as a right to use drugs—that might be derived from it.

In the absence of a comprehensive theory of rights, how might one proceed in reforming drug policy from a rights-based perspective? One alternative is to rely on analogies. If one believes any recreational activities to be protected by a moral right, one must explain why recreational drug use is not similarly protected. But even if two recreational activities are similar in all relevant respects, this strategy is still vulnerable to a difficulty that plagues all analogical reasoning. Someone may simply deny that moral rights protect any recreational activity.

In what follows, I pursue a third strategy. I inquire whether a right to use drugs might be derived from some other, more general right, the existence of which all parties to the debate are likely to accept. Many arguments that proceed in the name of rights have followed this strategy. They have not posited new rights, which are always rejected as "odd, frightening, or laughable,"[31] but have expanded the scope of existing rights. Consider, for example, the controversy about flag burning. No one who believes that criminal laws to prevent flag burning are justified is likely to change his mind because a commentator retorts that persons have a right to burn the flag. The existence of such a right must be the conclusion of an argument, not its premise. A cogent defense of a right to burn the flag would derive this particular right from a more general right, the existence of which is likely to be accepted on both sides of the controversy. In the case of flag burning, of course, that right is freedom of speech. Once a general right to freedom of speech is invoked, debates about flag burning move to a new level, where the hope of progress becomes more realistic. Opponents of flag burning are far more likely to allege that the general right to freedom of speech does not apply to or protect the specific activity of flag burning than to reject that general right altogether.

What more general moral right(s) might be infringed by proscriptions of drug use? This question raises the greatest single challenge to the rights-based perspective on drug policy reform. Of course, the zealous enforcement of our criminal justice drug policy has jeopardized familiar and easily identifiable rights.[32] But legal moralists who defend our criminal justice policy can apologize for the frequent abuses in law enforcement without surrendering their basic contention that drug use is wrongful. Do drug prohibitions per se infringe rights? If so, what rights do they infringe?

The supposed need to answer this question by reference to a right whose existence all parties to the debate acknowledge may seem too stringent. A right becomes well known not simply because we are confident of its existence but because it has been threatened frequently enough to attract our attention and vigilance. Some rights are less familiar because they have been infringed so rarely that they are taken for granted. Everyone is aware that states have often sought to interfere with freedom of speech, and civil libertarians are quick to sound the alarm when any such interferences are proposed. But apart from interference with food additives, modern Western states have not, to my knowledge, sought to interfere with our decisions about what foods we eat.[33] Thus, a right to eat whatever foods we like sounds unfamiliar and controversial. If the state really did endeavor to interfere with our decisions about the foods we eat, I would anticipate howls of protest at least as loud as those that greet attempts to interfere with rights that are much better known, such as our right to freedom of speech.

Still, my argument does not depend on controversial and unfamiliar rights, such as an alleged right to eat whatever foods we like. Which general rights presumed to exist by a broad social consensus can serve as candidates from which a right to use drugs might be derived? The Constitution provides the best source of such rights. I assume that most of the rights included in the Bill of Rights have both a legal as well as a moral status. Although some moral rights may not be included in the Constitution, the advantages of deriving a right to use drugs from some Constitutional source are clear. Despite contemporary skepticism and disagreement about moral issues, few people seem prepared to reject the existence of rights that are protected by our Constitution.

The two most obvious candidates from which to derive a moral right to use drugs are the general rights of equal protection and privacy.[34] How should we decide whether either of these rights apply to and protect drug use? I answer this question by invoking the general theory of interpretation defended by Ronald Dworkin. As Dworkin notes, rights are described with varying degrees of generality or specificity. The rights to equal protection and privacy are very abstract, and no abstract right can be applied to concrete cases "except by assigning some overall *point* or *purpose* [to it]."[35] One must decide whether the point or purpose of the rights to equal protection or privacy is promoted or frustrated by applying these rights to drug use.

Of course, these questions have been litigated; courts have had ample opportunity to decide whether drug proscriptions infringe the rights of equal protection or privacy. A number of constitutional challenges to our criminal-justice drug policy have been brought, and it is instructive to examine how courts have responded. Almost all of these constitutional challenges have failed, although a few have succeeded. I propose to assess the reasons that courts have given when forced to decide whether the rights to equal protection or privacy are infringed by drug proscriptions. Thus, I briefly examine some recent (but not too recent) constitutional history in perhaps the two leading cases in which the rights of drug users were litigated. I conclude that the rights of equal protection and privacy provide a plausible basis from which a right to use drugs might be derived.

In *Ravin v. State*,[36] the constitutionality of Alaska's marijuana prohibition was challenged. The defendant alleged that this statute violated both his right to equal protection and his right of privacy under the federal and Alaska State constitutions. Five years later, in *NORML v. Bell*,[37] a similar challenge was brought to that part of the federal Controlled Substances Act that prohibited the private possession and use of marijuana. Although neither court held that drug proscriptions violated a right to equal protection, *Ravin*, unlike *NORML*, prevailed on the privacy issue.

I begin by assessing the equal protection arguments. Both the litigants in *Ravin* and *NORML* alleged that marijuana proscriptions were underinclusive as well as overinclusive. Marijuana proscriptions were alleged to be underinclusive because the statutes failed to attach comparable punishments to the use of relevantly similar substances, most notably tobacco and alcohol. The intuitive force behind this argument is easy to appreciate. How is it fair for the state to prohibit the drugs preferred by some persons but not the drugs preferred by others? Unless there is good reason to believe that the drugs permitted are less dangerous than those proscribed, this discrimination would seem to deny persons the equal protection of the laws. The statute was also alleged to be overinclusive on the ground that the use of marijuana was punished as severely as the use of relevantly dissimilar substances, most notably cocaine and heroin.[38]

Neither court was persuaded by these allegations. To succeed in a challenge based on underinclusiveness, a plaintiff must show that a statutory classification is "clearly wrong, a display of arbitrary power, not an exercise in judgment."[39] Almost no challenge can sustain such a heavy burden of proof. Legislatures are granted wide latitude in attacking social ills one step at a time. A statutory prohibition should not be overturned simply because the legislation did not cover every evil that might conceivably have been addressed. The fact that alcohol and tobacco may have adverse affects that resemble those of marijuana does not necessitate that these substances must be regulated by the same statutory scheme that applies to marijuana.

The *NORML* court had more difficulty disposing of the allegation that marijuana proscriptions were overinclusive. The plaintiffs contended that marijuana does not satisfy the criteria for placement on Schedule I—the part of the Controlled Substances Act that regulates the most dangerous drugs. The court responded that Congress was warranted in punishing the use and possession of marijuana as severely as the use and possession of more harmful substances. Congress had a rational basis for rejecting attempts to impose less severe punishments for marijuana possession, "fearing that such action would create the impression that marijuana use was acceptable."[40] The court expressed reservations about whether marijuana satisfied the criteria for placement on Schedule I. Still, when correctly interpreted, these criteria were said to be satisfied. In what may be the most confusing aspect of the court's reasoning,[41] these statutory criteria were construed not as "dispositive"—that is, as necessary conditions—but as mere "guides in determining the schedule to which a drug belongs."[42] Thus, the constitutional challenge based on the overinclusiveness of the statute fared no better than the challenge based on its underinclusiveness.

I admit that courts are ill equipped to upset whole statutory schemes on the ground that allegedly similar substances are treated dissimilarly. In light of medical uncertainty and disagreement, judges should tend to defer to good-faith legislative judgments about whether different drugs merit comparable treatment. Just because judges should be reluctant to second-guess legislators, however, does not mean that legislators acted correctly in the first place. The prior decision to prohibit some drugs while allowing others does not appear to reflect an impartial judgment about their relative dangers.[43] As I have indicated, drug czars have tended to resort to legal moralism to defend the distinctions between licit and illicit substances. The use of some drugs but not others is alleged to be wrongful. This basis for distinguishing among various drugs poses a genuine threat to equal protection. May the state prohibit the drugs preferred by some persons while allowing the drugs preferred by other persons because the preferences of the former class are alleged to be immoral? I do not insist that moral reasons can never be invoked on behalf of a legislative discrimination, but unless these moral reasons are produced and evaluated, one comes to suspect that the state is simply using its raw power to discriminate against some persons because it disapproves of their preferences.[44] If so, drug users are denied the equal protection of the laws.

Next, consider the privacy issue. Here *Ravin*'s constitutional challenge—unlike *NORML*'s—ultimately prevailed. Why did the courts reach different results on very similar allegations? Several answers might be given.[45] Most importantly, the *Ravin* court was prepared to struggle to formulate a general conception of the right of privacy to determine whether the use of marijuana might be protected by it. The court characterized privacy as "a right of personal autonomy in relation to choices affecting an individual's personal life"[46] and, even more generally, as a "right to be let alone."[47] On the basis of these conceptions, the court concluded that "this right of privacy would encompass the possession and ingestion of substances such as marijuana in a purely personal, non-commercial context."[48]

How do the foregoing conceptions of privacy differ from that articulated in *NORML*? Remarkably, no answer can be given since the *NORML* court failed to articulate any conception of privacy at all. It simply claimed that the right of privacy was limited to those matters to which the Supreme Court had previously applied it. Subsequent cases have followed this trend. Courts have been reluctant to apply the right of privacy to issues of personal autonomy other than those involving marriage, reproduction, and the family.[49] One can only guess as to why such matters are unique in meriting protection by the right of privacy.

The most difficult challenge confronting attempts to show that the right of privacy protects drug use is to defend a general conception of privacy that applies to this activity.[50] If either of the conceptions formulated in *Ravin* are accepted—if privacy is construed either as a "right to be let alone" or as a "right of personal autonomy in relation to choices affecting an individual's personal life"—its application to drug use seems relatively clear. This challenge also confronts those theorists who believe that the right of privacy does not protect drug use. Their task is to formulate a general conception of privacy that protects such activities as the use of contraceptives but does not apply to drug use. The court in *NORML* evaded this challenge.

Why did the *Ravin* court bother to articulate a general conception of privacy at all? The need to characterize this right—and to do so broadly—was necessary to enable the court to make sense of some of its own precedents. In *Breese v. Smith*, "one of the most significant decisions [in which] this court has dealt with the concept of privacy," Alaska had found a school hair length regulation to be unconstitutional.[51] The *NORML* court's failure to provide a general conception of privacy makes it impossible to decide whether such matters as hair length would receive any degree of constitutional protection.

The *Ravin* court found that the right of privacy applied to decisions about both marijuana use as well as hair length, but the court did not deem the right to use marijuana a fundamental constitutional right, even though the court had found the liberty interest in *Breese* to be fundamental. "Hair-style," the court said, "is a highly personal matter involving the individual and his body."[52] Why did the court not reach the same conclusion about marijuana use? Isn't it, too, a "highly personal matter involving the individual and his body"? The court answered, "Few would believe they have been deprived of something of critical importance if deprived of marijuana, though they would if stripped of control over their personal appearance."[53] This answer was quoted with approval in *NORML*.[54]

This basis for contrasting the degree of protection offered to hair length in *Breese* from that offered to marijuana use in *Ravin* is deficient. First, no empirical data is cited to support the court's conjecture about what "few would believe." Persons who smoke marijuana might feel just as strongly about their preference as persons who violate a school ordinance governing hair length. Second, it is unclear that the degree of protection offered by the right of privacy should depend on the numbers of persons who have or lack the relevant beliefs. Third and most significantly, the question is rigged to enable the court to justify its answer. I concede that more persons would be outraged if "stripped of control over their personal appearance" than if "deprived of marijuana," but the terms of the comparison are flawed and misleading. The first part of the comparison is very general, and the second is very specific. Imagine how the question would have been answered if the first part of the comparison were very specific and the second were very general. How would persons feel if "stripped of control over what they are allowed to put into their bodies" relative to a "deprivation of shoulder-length hair"? Clearly, the outcome of such a determination would be very different. To be meaningful and unbiased, the issues to be compared must be expressed at the same level of generality. On that basis, it is hard to decide whether persons care more about control over what they are permitted to put into their bodies than about control over their personal appearance. I see no reason to regard either matter as more important, basic, or fundamental than the other.

I conclude that plausible interpretations of either the right of equal protection or the right of privacy can be applied to offer some degree of protection to drug use. Perhaps other moral rights are implicated as well.[55] If I am correct, the greatest obstacle in defending a rights-based perspective to drug-policy reform has been overcome.

DIFFERING POLICY IMPLICATIONS OF THE TWO PERSPECTIVES

The shape of an ideal drug policy that improves on our criminal justice approach cannot be described in any detail without deciding which of the two foregoing rationales for reform should be accepted. A policy that implements a harm-reduction perspective and seeks to maximize the ratio of benefits to costs will differ substantially from a policy that is geared to respect moral rights. The specifics of a new drug policy depend not only on which of the two perspectives is embraced but on further subdivisions and refinements within each perspective. I briefly support these claims in this final section. I am especially concerned to identify a few specific issues on which a harm-reduction and a rights-based perspective are likely to disagree. Of course, my efforts take only the smallest step in determining the direction of drug policy reform. All I can hope to accomplish is to provide some of the reasons why a blueprint for change has been so hard to produce.

Which variables affect the shape of a drug policy designed to implement a harm-reduction perspective? Changing circumstances are the most important such factors. A policy that minimizes harm today might not continue to do so tomorrow. The ratio of costs to benefits is in a state of flux as newer and more effective means to reduce the harms of drugs become available. For example, harm-reduction theorists are frequently skeptical about our prospects for reducing supplies from drug-producing countries, but a breakthrough might radically change this assessment. Suppose, for example, that coca-eating moths could be unleashed in the Andes, devouring much of the world's supply of coca. I do not know whether this particular "technological fix" is realistic. My point is that any such innovation would radically alter the balance of costs and benefits of drug policy.

Apart from changing circumstances and technological innovations, the details of drug policy will be influenced by the answers that harm-reduction theorists provide to two of the questions I raised above. I asked, first, whether the harm-reduction calculus treats the harm that drug users do to themselves on a par with the harm they do to others. If each kind of harm is comparable, theorists who implement a harm-reduction perspective will have a great deal of harm to try to reduce. After all, drug users themselves suffer most of the harm caused by drugs, so policy makers would have a greater incentive to decrease this harm by curtailing use. Suppose, on the other hand, that self-inflicted harms are exempted from the harm-reduction calculus when they are the product of autonomous choice. By this simple stroke of the accountant's pen, the amount of harm caused by drugs is drastically reduced. Harm-reduction theorists should concentrate only on reducing those harms that drug users cause to others. Since self-inflicted harms are important only when they are not the product of autonomous choice, harm-reduction theorists should endeavor to create the conditions under which drug use is autonomous. Needless to say, this objective makes little sense if harms to self have the same status as harms to others.

I can think of at least three reasons why some instances of drug use might be regarded as nonautonomous. First, since adolescents are typically believed to lack the capacity for autonomous choice, harm-reduction theorists should adopt strategies to decrease drug use among adolescents. Second, since false beliefs are generally thought to undermine autonomous choice, harm-reduction theorists should devote substantial resources to drug education. Finally, since addiction might render drug use nonautonomous, harm-reduction theorists should favor whatever programs have been shown to help addicts.[56] Of course, these reasons provide no basis to conclude that all drug use is nonautonomous. Once an informed adult uses drugs autonomously, any detrimental consequences his acts create for himself may be far less important from a harm-reduction perspective. If so, measures to reduce drug use per se would become much less appealing.

I also asked whether pleasure counts as a benefit on the cost-benefit calculus. If pleasure is not placed on the balance, little can be said in favor of drug use that could possibly outweigh all that might be said against it. Again, abstinence becomes an attractive ideal. Suppose, on the other hand, that pleasure counts in the cost-benefit calculus and, therefore, must be weighed against harm. If so, an entirely new set of issues become relevant. Abstinence would be a much less desirable objective since it would sacrifice all of the benefits that could be gained by drug use.

Once pleasure is included in the balance, two very different strategies might be followed to improve the cost-benefit ratio of drug use. This ratio could be improved not only by making drugs less harmful but also by making them more pleasurable. This option is largely unexplored in the harm-reduction literature, but cost-benefit theorists who include pleasure in their calculus should be enthusiastic about proposals to create new and more exhilarating drugs. Here the possibilities quickly strain the imagination.[57] Even without producing entirely new substances, measures to increase the pleasure of existing drugs are not so hard to imagine. Perhaps the simplest strategies would involve improving the delivery systems by which drugs are consumed. Although harm-reduction theorists have said a lot about how to increase the safety of delivery systems, they have said little about how to make these systems more pleasurable. Consider just two suggestions. First, the discomfort caused by needles may be the greatest barrier to more widespread heroin use. If so, harm-reduction theorists who take their pleasure seriously should applaud the recent trend of first-time users to smoke rather than to inject heroin.[58] Second, the greater use of filters, vaporizers, and water pipes should decrease the irritation to the lungs and throat caused by smoking marijuana. Obviously, defenders of our criminal justice policy will be appalled at the prospects of making drug use more pleasurable.

Although it is difficult to specify the characteristics of a drug policy that implements a cost-benefit, harm-reduction perspective, the details of a drug policy that is designed to respect moral rights are no more apparent. Which variables affect the shape of a drug policy designed to implement a rights-based perspective? I will mention only two such factors. The first is the nature of the general right from which a specific right to use drugs is derived. Suppose that drug proscriptions are thought to infringe a right of privacy. If so, the details of drug policy will depend on how the distinction between the public and the private is drawn. A policy would be expected to attach great significance to the place at which drugs are used. For example, a right of privacy might protect conduct in the home that is unprotected elsewhere.[59] Recall that the right to consume marijuana upheld in *Ravin* was restricted to the home.[60]

Suppose, however, that drug proscriptions are thought to infringe a right to equal protection. If so, a comprehensive rethinking of all drugs—licit and illicit—is needed. After all, unjust discrimination among the preferences of drug users can be remedied in either of two ways. First, drugs currently classified as illicit—marijuana, cocaine, and heroin—might be subjected to lesser restrictions. Alternatively, drugs not currently classified as illicit—tobacco and alcohol—might be subjected to greater restrictions. Commentators who propose a fundamental change in our criminal justice drug policy tend to favor the former alternative. Until recently, the latter option seemed unthinkable. Today, however, various strategies have reduced tobacco use substantially—without resorting to criminal punishments. Some commentators predict more extensive regulation of the liquor industry. The important point is that either means to produce a uniform system of drug regulation respects the right to equal protection that is allegedly infringed by our criminal-justice policy.

I will devote somewhat more attention to the second variable that affects the shape of a rights-based drug policy. The details of this policy will be influenced by the nature of the considerations that are regarded as sufficient to override whatever right is infringed by proscriptions of drug use. It is one thing to say that a right is infringed by drug prohibitions and quite another to say that the infringed right is absolute.[61] An absolute right, as I understand it, is not subject to being overridden by more stringent moral considerations. I doubt that any moral right is absolute. But even if I am mistaken and some rights are absolute, it is hardly plausible to include the right to use drugs among those few absolute rights that exist. Surely there can be good reasons to override whatever moral rights are infringed by recreational drug use. Perhaps the consequences of drug use might provide such a reason.

Theorists unequivocally committed to drug decriminalization are unlikely to be thankful for this result. What is the practical difference, they will ask, between saying that no right is infringed by our criminal justice drug policy and saying that the right infringed by our criminal justice drug policy is overridden by more stringent moral considerations? In fact, the difference between these two statements can be important. A higher standard must be satisfied to justify overriding a right than to prohibit an activity that is not protected by a right in the first place. Simple utilitarian considerations—the outcome of a cost-benefit analysis—can justify prohibiting an activity that is unprotected by a right. When a right is implicated, however, mere utilitarian considerations are insufficient to justify the infringement.[62] If utilitarian reasons are inadequate, what considerations are sufficiently weighty to override a right to use drugs? Providing a theory of the conditions under which rights may be overridden is yet another major challenge confronting defenders of a rights-based perspective. Not only must the theorist show that a right applies to and protects drug use, but he must also decide whether this right may be infringed by whatever objectives drug prohibitions are designed to achieve. Once we have identified whatever reasons might tempt us to prohibit the use of a particular drug, the next question is whether these reasons are sufficient to allow that right to be infringed.

This question is difficult. No standard theory of the conditions under which rights may be overridden is widely accepted. Fortunately, we are not totally dependent on philosophical speculation for help in answering this question. Justifiable infringements of the rights that drug prohibitions might infringe—equal protection or privacy—have been developed over time by constitutional lawyers. The "clear and present danger" test, for example, was devised to identify a circumstance under which the right of free speech could be infringed. But few of the familiar reasons for punishing drug users fall within any of the established justifications for infringing rights.

Consider, for example, Bennett's rationale for punishing casual users in the War on Drugs. Bennett insists that the "non-addicted casual" drug user "remains a grave issue of national concern," even though such a person "is likely to have a still-intact family, social and work life" and "to 'enjoy' his drug for the pleasure it offers." Nonetheless, Bennett argues, the casual drug user should be punished severely because he is "much more willing and able to proselytize his drug use—by action or example—among his remaining non-user peers, friends, and acquaintances. A non-addict's drug use, in other words, is *highly* contagious."[63] Whatever one might think about this rationale if rights were not involved, it is clearly inadequate to justify the infringement of a right. In no other context is a right overridden on the ground that its exercise might induce other persons to exercise their rights as well. Many other rationales for drug prohibitions fare no better. For example, in no other context is a right overridden on the ground that its exercise might set a bad example for adolescents.[64]

Let me tentatively advance a strong hypothesis about the nature of the moral considerations that suffice to override a moral right: only the violation of a competing, more stringent right can justify the infringement of a right. I will not attempt to defend this hypothesis here, but if it is accepted, many familiar rationales for drug prohibitions will fail to justify infringing the rights of drug users. Consider, for example, Wilson's allegations that drug users tend not to be "healthy people, productive workers, good parents, reliable neighbors, [or] attentive students."[65] These allegations are seldom supported by empirical evidence,[66] but if they are true, the social disutility of drug use is clearly established. Mere utilitarian considerations, however, are insufficient to justify the infringement of a right. According to my tentative hypothesis, these allegations provide a good reason to infringe the rights of drug users only if the behaviors Wilson describes violate some competing, more stringent right. A comprehensive theory of rights would be needed in order to demonstrate that these behaviors do not violate any rights. Even in the absence of a comprehensive theory, however, the inadequacy of these allegations is apparent. Apart from the context of drug use, no one pretends that anyone possesses a right that others be healthy, that workers be productive, that parents be good, that neighbors be reliable, or that students be attentive. If such rights did indeed exist, many of our social practices and institutions would have to be changed dramatically. Any activities that tended to make persons less reliable, for example, would become eligible for punishment on the ground that they violate the rights of their neighbors. Thus, I conclude that a rights-based perspective, when supplemented by my hypothesis about how rights may be overridden, will reject these allegations as good reasons to infringe moral rights. These reasons fail to justify our criminal justice drug policy.

Is my hypothesis too strong? Is the violation of a competing, more stringent right always needed to justify the infringement of a right? I am unsure. In any event, not all rationales for drug prohibitions will fail my stringent test. Surely one can imagine a drug that is sufficiently threatening to the rights of others that no reasonable person would want to allow it to be used. Fiction provides the least controversial examples of drugs that should be prohibited on this ground. Dr. Jekyll took a substance that transformed him into the evil Mr. Hyde. Would anyone doubt that the state has authority to proscribe a substance that actually turned persons into homicidal monsters?[67] Any right to use a given drug would surely be overridden by the competing right that innocent persons not be endangered by crazed villains. Such extreme cases are clear and demonstrate that a rights-based perspective can be sensitive to consequentialist considerations, and need not allow persons to use any conceivable drug that might ever be created. But less extreme cases raise hard questions. How great a risk of harm to the rights of others must a drug create before the state has good reason to prohibit it?[68]

A policy designed to respect moral rights has additional implications for reform. Theorists who defend a harm-reduction perspective often endorse a medical model that emphasizes mandatory treatment for drug users.[69] This "medicalization" alternative is defended as a progressive measure that produces less harm than our criminal justice approach.[70] But if persons have a right to use drugs, subjecting persons who exercise this right to mandatory treatment is only a marginal improvement over the status quo. Although a medical model might be recommended from a harm-reduction perspective, it is hard to see how it would respect a right to use drugs.

I conclude by briefly commenting on the single matter that is perhaps more likely than any other to divide harm-reduction theorists from those who defend drug policy reform from a rights-based perspective. Harm-reduction theorists are especially sensitive to an accusation that commentators who support our criminal justice drug policy inevitably bring up. Any relaxation of criminal prohibitions, it is said, is bound to trigger a massive explosion in the number of drug users.[71] Harm-reduction theorists can hardly ignore this accusation or pretend that it is irrelevant. Their responses are varied.[72] Most reply that the impact of their recommendations on the incidence of drug use is far less clear than their critics suppose. Others promise that the benefits of harm-reduction will more than compensate for any costs incurred by the increased numbers of drug users. Still, the specter of a massive increase in drug use is worrisome to theorists who adopt a harm-reduction perspective on policy reform.

Those who endorse a rights-based perspective have far less reason to be concerned about how their approach to reform would affect the number of drug users or the quantity of drugs they consume. No one believes that the question of whether the act of burning the flag is protected by a right depends on how the answer will affect the incidence of flag burning. Nor does anyone believe that the question of whether a right to burn the flag may be overridden depends on how the answer will affect the number of flag burners. If persons have a right to burn the flag—or, by parity of reasoning, to use drugs— dire predictions about how the lack of deterrence will increase the number of persons who engage in these behaviors seem immaterial. The supposition that decriminalization will lead to a dramatic growth in drug use, even if true, will not justify infringements of the right to use drugs. If our criminal justice approach infringes moral rights, as I have suggested, the punishment of drug users is objectionable, even if the absence of criminal sanctions increases the incidence of drug use.

I hope to avoid misunderstanding. Predictions about how various reforms will affect the number of drug users are not totally irrelevant to the formation of all aspects of drug policy. According to the rights-based perspective I favor, these predictions are irrelevant only to the issue of whether drug users should be punished. But criminal punishment is not the only means by which society may protect itself from the disutility that would result from an explosion of drug use. Defenders of a rights-based perspective are pro-choice and pro-rights, not pro-drug. Thus, they may support any number of devices to discourage drug use short of criminal punishment. These devices might include taxes, tort liability for injuries caused by drug users, zoning and licensing restrictions, drug education programs, prohibitions against advertising, and the like. A society may not, however, resort to punishment. The fear that too many persons might join those who exercise their rights is simply not a good reason to infringe and override a right to use drugs.

CONCLUSION

I have described two rationales for critiquing our criminal justice drug policy—a harm-reduction and a rights-based perspective. I have been especially concerned to contrast these rationales without dwelling on the several respects in which they are complementary. If these rationales are as different as I have suggested, it is relatively easy to understand why the details of an ideal drug policy are so hard to provide. A policy designed to respect moral rights is likely to differ fundamentally from a policy designed to achieve the optimal ratio of costs and benefits. In particular, theorists who embrace these perspectives are able to offer different responses to those who fear that a radical rethinking of our criminal justice policy will greatly increase the incidence of drug use. I believe that the response to this concern provided by rights-based theorists is preferable to that offered by harm-reduction theorists. For this reason, among others, I tend to favor the former framework for drug policy reform. But I want to close on a more conciliatory note. The disputes between rights-based and harm-reduction theorists are far less important than their agreement that our criminal justice drug policy is indefensible.

NOTES

1. Two qualifications are needed. First, of course, the criminal justice system plays a much more modest role in governing the recreational use of many other drugs, primarily tobacco and alcohol. For convenience, however, I will refer to our present drug policy as reflecting a criminal justice orientation. Second, I should not be misunderstood as saying that our approach relies exclusively on punishment. Considerable amounts of money are expended on drug education and treatment. Still, by any measure, our approach to drugs is mostly punitive.

2. The best summary is Ethan Nadelmann, "Drug Prohibition in the United States: Costs, Consequences, and Alternatives," *Science* 245 (1989): 939. More recent and detailed accounts of the respects in which our criminal justice drug policy is ineffective and counterproductive appear frequently. See, for example, Richard Davenport-Hines, *The Pursuit of Oblivion* (London: Weidenfeld & Nicolson, 2001).

3. "The relationship between the 'harm reduction' approach and the notion of drug legalization remains ambiguous." Ethan Nadelmann, "Progressive Legalizers, Progressive Prohibitionists and the Reduction of Drug-Related Harm," in *Psychoactive Drugs & Harm Reduction: From Faith to Science*, ed. Nick Heather, Alex Wodak, Ethan Nadelmann, and Pat O'Hare (London: Whurr Publishers, 1993), 34, 36.

4. Some theorists who adopt a harm-reduction perspective actually define their methodology to underscore their reservations about the desirability of deterring use. According to one commentator, "the most logical definition of [harm reduction] is those policies and programs which are designed to reduce the adverse consequences of mood altering substances without necessarily reducing their consumption." See Alex Wodak, "Harm Reduction: Australia as a Case Study," *Bulletin of the New York Academy of Medicine* (1995): 339, 340.

5. One theorist concludes that "a rational, hard-nosed prohibitionist could profitably employ the harm-reduction platform, as I suspect many are beginning to realise." Stephen Mugford, "Harm Reduction: Does It Lead Where Its Proponents Imagine?" in Heather, Wodak, Nadelmann, and O'Hare, *Psychoactive Drugs & Harm Reduction*, 21, 24.

6. Nadelmann, "Progressive Legalizers, Progressive Prohibitionists and the Reduction of Drug-Related Harm," 37.

7. For the classic description of legal moralism, see Joel Feinberg, *Harm to Others* (New York: Oxford University Press, 1984), 12.

8. William Bennett, "The Plea to Legalize Drugs Is a Siren Call to Surrender," in *Drugs in Society*, ed. Michael Lyman and Gary Potter (Cincinnati: Anderson Publishing Co., 1991), 339.

9. William Raspberry, "Prevention and the Powers of Persuasion," *Washington Post National Weekly Edition*, July 15–21, 1996, 29.

10. Remarks by President Bush in announcing the new head of the Office of the National Drug Control Policy, May 10, 2001.

11. James Q. Wilson, "Against the Legalization of Drugs," in *The American Drug Scene*, ed. James Inciardi and Karen McElrath, 4th ed. (Los Angeles: Roxbury Publishing Co., 2004), 496, 503.

12. John Kaplan, *Marijuana: The New Prohibition* (New York: World Publishing Co., 1970), xi.

13. See Feinberg, *Harm to Others*, 65–70.

14. "Drug use is viewed as neither right nor wrong in itself. Rather, drug use is evaluated in terms of harm." Mugford, "Harm Reduction." Comparable claims are made by other harm-reduction theorists. One writes, "The true champion of harm reduction is not necessarily anti-drugs; nor necessarily pro-drugs. . . . A pre-determined position on drug use as intrinsically 'bad' or 'good' has no meaning in this context." John Strang, "Drug Use and Harm Reduction: Responding to the Challenge," in Heather, Wodak, Nadelmann, and O'Hare, *Psychoactive Drugs & Harm Reduction*, 3.

15. The specific measure that is perhaps the most easily defended on harm-reduction grounds is a needle exchange program to retard the spread of AIDS. See Institute of Medicine, Panel on Needle Exchange and Bleach Distribution Programs, Commission on Behavioral and Social Sciences and Education, and National Research Council, *Preventing HIV Transmission: The Role of Sterile Needles and Bleach*, ed. Jacques Normand, David Vlahov, and Lincoln E. Moses (Washington, D.C.: National Academy Press, 1995).

16. For a powerful defense of this retributivist position, see Michael Moore, *Placing Blame* (Oxford: Clarendon Press, 1997). Moore himself, however, contends that drug use per se is morally unobjectionable.

17. The most respectable arguments for the immorality of illicit drug use invoke a conception of virtue or human excellence. Apart from other difficulties, these arguments provide an inadequate basis for criminal policy. For further discussion, see Douglas Husak, *Drugs and Rights* (New York: Cambridge University Press, 1992), 64–68.

18. Courts have not agreed on the precise nature of the harm(s) that drug prohibitions are designed to prevent. See Stanton Peele and Douglas Husak, "'One of the

Major Problems of Our Society': Imagery and Evidence of Drug Harms in U.S. Supreme Court Decisions," *Contemporary Drug Problems* 25 (1998): 191–233.

19. To be sure, some harm-reduction theorists do not drape themselves in the cloak of moral neutrality. See, for example, Robert MacCoun and Peter Reuter, *Drug War Heresies* (Cambridge: Cambridge University Press, 2001).

20. For further discussion, see Douglas Husak, *Philosophy of Criminal Law* (Totowa, N.J.: Rowman & Littlefield, 1987), 224–48.

21. Mugford, "Harm Reduction," 5, 21.

22. Kaplan maintains that the case for or against drug decriminalization "boils down to a careful weighing of the costs of criminalizing each drug against the public-health costs we would expect if that drug were to become legally available." Presumably, he would evaluate policy alternatives other than decriminalization by the very same standard. See John Kaplan, "Taking Drugs Seriously," *The Public Interest* 92 (1988): 32, 37.

23. Perhaps the most intriguing such defense is provided in Andrew Weil, *The Natural Mind*, 2d. ed. (Boston: Houghton Mifflin Co., 1986).

24. For an interesting discussion, see Henry Clark, *Altering Behavior: The Ethics of Controlled Experience* (London: Sage Publications, 1987), 64–77, 178–181.

25. See the discussion in Sheridan Hough, "The Moral Mirror of Pleasure: Considerations about the Recreational Use of Drugs," in *Drugs, Morality, and the Law*, ed. Steven Luper-Foy and Curtis Brown (New York: Garland Publishing Co., 1994), 153.

26. For further discussion, see Husak, *Drugs and Rights*.

27. To date, most of the work on a rights-based perspective on drug policy reform has been undertaken by libertarians. See, for example, Thomas Szasz, *Our Right to Drugs: The Case for a Free Market* (New York: Praeger Publishing Co., 1992). Where are the liberals? They tend to say little more than that the massive incarceration of drug offenders is ineffective and counterproductive. Moral and political philosophers—indeed, philosophers generally—have been strangely silent in the drug policy debate. Perhaps their absence accounts for the relative popularity of a harm-reduction perspective, which tends to be favored by social scientists.

28. Some theorists explicitly subordinate rights to policy. See Strang, "Drug Use and Harm Reduction," 15–16: "From the pure harm-reduction perspective, the support of the personal freedom of one or other group of drug users should be determined solely by the extent to which one or other course of action can be shown to result in an overall reduction of harm accrued."

29. See Jeremy Waldron, "A Right to Do Wrong," *Ethics* 92 (1981): 21.

30. John Kaplan, *The Hardest Drug: Heroin and Public Policy* (Chicago: University of Chicago Press, 1983), 103.

31. See Chris Stone, "Should Trees Have Standing?" *Southern California Law Review* 45 (1972): 450, 455.

32. For one discussion, see Stephen Wisotsky, "Crackdown: The Emerging 'Drug Exception' to the Bill of Rights," *Hastings Law Journal* 38 (1987): 889.

33. Noninterference with food should not be taken for granted. See Alan Hunt, *Governance of the Consuming Passions: A History of Sumptuary Law* (New York: St. Martin's Press, 1996).

34. I do not discuss the libertarian attempt to derive a right to use drugs from a general right to property. According to some libertarians, "producing, trading in, and using drugs are property rights." See Szasz, *Our Right to Drugs*, 2.

35. Ronald Dworkin, *Freedom's Law* (Cambridge, Mass.: Harvard University Press, 1996), 199.

36. 537 P.2d 494 (Alaska 1975).

37. 488 F.Supp. 123 (1980).

38. Drug proscriptions are overinclusive on other grounds as well. The typical drug user will not cause or even substantially risk causing most of the harms alleged to justify drug proscriptions. See Jacob Sullum, *Saying Yes: In Defense of Drug Use* (New York: J. P. Tarcher, 2003).

39. 488 F.Supp. 123 (1980), 137.

40. 488 F.Supp. 123 (1980), 139.

41. For a more detailed discussion, see Husak, *Drugs and Rights*, 27–37.

42. 488 F.Supp. 123 (1980), 140.

43. See David Musto, *The American Disease: Origins of Narcotics Control*, exp. ed. (New York: Oxford University Press, 1987), 260.

44. See David T. Courtwright, *Forces of Habit: Drugs and the Making of the Modern World* (Cambridge, Mass.: Harvard University Press, 2001).

45. Two considerations other than the factor I discuss help to explain the different judgments. First, *Ravin* was decided under the Alaska State constitution, which contains an enumerated right of privacy, as well as under the federal constitution, which does not. States may construe their own constitutions to provide broader protection to individual rights than that afforded by the federal government. Second, the state of Alaska applied a different standard to test the constitutionality of governmental action that abridges a defendant's liberty. The *NORML* court assessed this statutory interference with liberty under the "rational basis" test and had no difficulty finding the government's interest in prohibiting marijuana to be rational. The *Ravin* court, however, invoked a more demanding test: it asked whether the means chosen bear a "substantial relationship" to whatever governmental interest is properly served by restricting the use of marijuana. This standard is much harder to satisfy than the rational basis test.

46. 537 P.2d 494 (Alaska 1975), 500.

47. 537 P.2d 494 (Alaska 1975), 500.

48. 537 P.2d 494 (Alaska 1975), 504.

49. The domain of unenumerated personal liberty now includes the right to marry, to choose a marital partner, to define family relationships, to procreate, to rear and educate one's children, to determine one's sexual relationships, to prevent conception, to terminate a pregnancy, and to seek medical treatment and care. See Edward Keynes, *Liberty, Property, and Privacy: Toward a Jurisprudence of Substantive Due Process* (University Park: Pennsylvania State University Press, 1996), 158.

50. See Norbert Gilmore, "Drug Use and Human Rights: Privacy, Vulnerability, Disability, and Human Rights Infringements," *Journal of Contemporary Health Law and Policy* 356 (1996): 355.

51. 501 P.2d 159 (Alaska 1972).

52. 537 P.2d 494 (Alaska 1975), 502.

53. 537 P.2d 494 (Alaska 1975), 502.

54. 488 F.Supp. 123 (1980), 133. Perhaps I should say that this answer was *mis-quoted* in *NORML* since a crucial part of the quotation is missing. The court quotes *Ravin* as saying that "few would believe they have been deprived of something of critical importance if deprived of marijuana." The court deletes the remainder of the sentence: "though they would if stripped of control over their personal appearance." It is easy to see why the second half of this sentence was deleted. According to the conception of privacy applied in *NORML*, privacy has no more application to personal appearance in general or to hair length in particular than to drug use.

55 Arguably, persons have a right not to be punished—a right not to be subjected to hard treatment and condemnation—in the absence of an excellent reason. If no good reasons in favor of punishing drug users can be provided, the case in favor of prohibition collapses. I explore this line of argument in Douglas Husak, *Legalize This!* (London: Verso, 2002).

56. See James Inciardi, Duane McBride, and James Rivers, *Drug Control and the Courts* (London: Sage Publications, 1996).

57. See the discussion in Clark, *Altering Behavior*.

58. See J. Strang, M. Gossop, P. Griffiths, and B. Powis, "First Use of Heroin: Changes in Route of Administration over Time," *British Medical Journal* 304 (1992): 1222.

59. The most important case in favor of this proposition is *Stanley v. Georgia*, 394 U.S. 557 (1969).

60. This restriction was not due solely to the fact that the decision was reached on privacy grounds but also because drug use outside the home posed more of a threat to important state interests, such as highway safety.

61. Thus, I have spoken of drug proscriptions as infringing rather than violating rights. I adopt that terminology according to which rights violations, as opposed to rights infringements, are always wrongful. See Judith Thomson, "Some Ruminations about Rights," *Arizona Law Review* 19 (1977): 45.

62. The metaphor of rights as trumps is developed in Ronald Dworkin, *Taking Rights Seriously* (Cambridge, Mass.: Harvard University Press, 1977). Even if rights should not be regarded as trumps, I believe it is clear that rights withstand utilitarian arguments against allowing them to be exercised.

63. Office of the National Drug Control Policy, *National Drug Control Strategy* (Washington, D.C.: Office of the National Drug Control Policy, 1989), 11.

64. See the thoughtful discussion of drug policy for adolescents in Franklin Zimring and Gordon Hawkins, *The Search for Rational Drug Control* (Cambridge: Cambridge University Press, 1992), 115–36.

65. James Q. Wilson, "Drugs and Crime," in *Drugs and Crime*, ed. Michael Tonry and James Q. Wilson (Chicago: University of Chicago Press, 1990), 521, 524.

66. Causal links between drug use and various social problems is not unidirectional. See David Boyum and Peter Reuter: "Reflections on Drug Policy and Social Policy," in *Drug Addiction and Drug Policy: The Struggle to Control Dependence*, ed. Philip B. Heymann and William N. Brownsberger (Cambridge: Harvard University Press, 2001), 239.

67. Some libertarians actually have doubts. See Walter Block: "Drug Prohibition: A Legal and Economic Analysis," in Luper-Foy and Brown, *Drugs, Morality, and the Law*, 199.

68. I discuss some of these matters further in Douglas Husak, "The Nature and Justifiability of Nonconsummate Offenses," *Arizona Law Review* 37 (1995): 151–83.

69. See, for example, the discussion in James L. Nolan Jr., *Reinventing Justice: The American Drug Court Movement* (Princeton, N.J.: Princeton University Press, 2001).

70. See, for example, Eva Bertram, Morris Blachman, Kenneth Sharpe, and Peter Andreas, *Drug War Politics: The Price of Denial* (Berkeley: University of California Press, 1996).

71. See, for example, Mark Moore, "Drugs: Getting a Fix on the Problem and the Solution," *Yale Law & Policy Review* 8 (1990): 701.

72. See MacCoun and Reuter, *Drug War Heresies*, 72–100.

POLICY CONSIDERATIONS

6

Legalization: An Introduction

Richard M. Evans and Stanley Neustadter

Thorough outlines of drug policy options inevitably include "legalization," but rarely is that concept examined in any detail. Does legalization mean that marijuana will be sold in vending machines or advertised on TV? That coca will return to cola? That all pharmaceuticals will be available over the counter? The purpose of this chapter is to look at how some legislators and writers have glimpsed the particulars of legalization and to suggest a menu of questions that will have to be confronted if and when legalization comes under serious scrutiny as an alternative to prohibition.

Imaginers of drug legalization, like nineteenth-century science fiction writers imagining interplanetary rocketry, have little to go on besides their wisdom and creativity. There is scant literature or data on the subject. They share some basic premises and not much more. One of those premises is that drug prohibition and the war of enforcement that has been waged for an entire generation have failed to protect the public from the problems associated with illegal drugs and have done a lot more harm than good in the effort. A second premise is that public support could plausibly emerge for coming to terms with drugs in ways other than with police, prisons, and propaganda. If legalizers were to have their way, the acquisition, possession, and use of the now-illegal drugs by responsible adults would cease to be the business of the state; thus, a person's liberty or property would not be put in jeopardy as a result of such use. Within that broad standard lies a menagerie of schemes. Although the criminal- and civil-justice apparatuses would retain a prominent role in protecting the public health and public safety, under legalization the government would not intrude upon personal autonomy with regard to drug acquisition or consumption by adults that is not visibly harmful.

As the sine qua non of legalization is legal access to drugs for responsible adults, this chapter excludes consideration of "medical marijuana" or "hemp" reforms. These measures and initiatives—worthy though they may be for medical or industrial purposes, and welcome though they may be to antiprohibitionists—bear little connection to legalization. Exempting small categories of people from the prohibition laws (chemotherapy patients, licensed hemp farmers) has little to do with repealing prohibition entirely and granting access to most adults. The availability of "medicinal" alcohol during Prohibition (1920–1933) did little to abate the ills of the "noble experiment."

A variety of policy renderings have been put forward in the name of legalization. Most seem to fit into one of three general categories: *decriminalization* plans, *limitation* plans, and *regulation-and-taxation* plans. Falling outside this grouping are calls for outright legalization, where drugs would be produced, bought, and sold like any ordinary commodity. The most eminent advocate of treating drugs like ordinary goods is Thomas Szasz, M.D., whose prolific and eloquent writings make a strong case for a free market in drugs, independent of government involvement.[1] Some reformers speak affectionately of the tomato model, where commerce in and use of drugs would carry a level of government regulation comparable to tomatoes, viz., with merely the usual agricultural regulations and pure-food rules and, perhaps, an ordinary sales tax.

If drugs are to be treated under the law like tomatoes, magazines, over-the-counter medicines, or toothpaste, it is hardly necessary to conjure a new set of rules about where and to whom they can be sold, to what extent they may become ingredients in other products, how they are to be taxed, if their potency is to be regulated, and in what forms they may be sold. All that is needed is to latch upon the existing commodity that best illustrates the favored approach. Free market proponents can bring clarity and spirit to the debate over how to legalize drugs by simply filling in the blank: drugs should be as legal as umbrellas or _____.

DECRIMINALIZATION

In the context of drugs, the word "decriminalization" entered the popular lexicon during the 1970s and described changes to the marijuana laws in eleven states.[2] The changes were modest. Under them, marijuana remained illegal under both state and federal law, and one could still be prosecuted and punished for simple possession of marijuana. The difference was that such possession of a small quantity was no longer an offense under state law for which one could lose one's liberty (i.e., be arrested) upon being caught. And, typically, such charges did not carry the risk of creating a permanent criminal record. As a result, prosecutions for marijuana were said to resemble prosecutions for speeding or other traffic offenses — offenders were given a ticket and fine and possibly had to appear in court, but they were not arrested on the spot and taken in.

In terms of a policy alternative to prohibition, such decriminalization represented a mere tinkering with the statutory law, not any major policy change. It was merely a kinder, gentler version of prohibition. Leaving the laws the way they are and simply enforcing them less stringently can achieve a similar result. In his book *Marijuana: Costs of Abuse, Costs of Control*, Mark A. R. Kleiman calls this approach "enforcement reduction" and recommends it as the "best alternative for dealing with the nation's marijuana problem."[3] Veterans of the 1960s and 1970s recall a time when marijuana was used widely with minimal concealment, even in states that did not decriminalize it. A modicum of discretion was sufficient to retain one's liberty. Police and the public were tolerant, if not approving, of personal marijuana use.[4]

The clearest picture of de facto decriminalization of drugs by enforcement reduction can be seen in Amsterdam. There, "soft" drugs (marijuana and hashish) remain illegal but are widely tolerated by law enforcement authorities. Cannabis is openly available for purchase in coffee shops. The drug-prohibition laws remain on the books but are not enforced against soft drugs.

Among avenues of drug law reform, de facto decriminalization has the distinct advantage of not requiring the complicity of the legislature. Police officers, one recalls from elementary civics, work for the executive branch of government, whose job it is to execute and carry out the laws. All it takes to institute such a policy of reduced enforcement is the will of a single executive — a mayor, governor, or president — and the political moxie to carry it off.

Decriminalization can be achieved judicially as well. The best example of court-made decriminalization is the 1975 case of *Ravin v. State of Alaska*, in which the Supreme Court of Alaska, having considered the right-to-privacy amendment to the Alaska constitution, found "no adequate justifications for the state's intrusion into the citizen's right to privacy by its prohibition of possession of marijuana by an adult for personal consumption in the home," a decision that had the result of removing criminal penalties for the violation of the statutory prohibition laws to the extent declared unconstitutional.

Notwithstanding challenges from political fronts, *Ravin* remains good law in Alaska, ratified and reinforced in 2004 in a case called *State of Alaska v. Leo Richardson Crocker*,[5] wherein the Alaska Court of Appeals threw out a search warrant that did not establish probable cause that a person possessed a quantity of marijuana beyond the scope constitutionally protected by *Ravin*.

Although decriminalization is frequently mentioned as a preferable alternative to prohibition, a principal problem haunts it as a permanent policy option. That problem is that under decriminalization, as the term is used here, the drug market remains illegal, and underground networks of illegal suppliers and distributors continue to supply the public demand for drugs. With no legal commerce, there are no taxes paid or collected, no FDA-like controls over purity and dosage, and no legal and peaceful remedies for settling the industry disputes that inevitably occur. Criminal organizations remain in control of drug production and distribution (except, one speculates, in the case of cannabis, where backyard gardens may well supply most consumers). If the goals of legalization are to protect the public safety and public health, prevent abuse, and halt the crime associated with prohibition, decriminalization, whether de jure or de facto, is not an attractive candidate for significant and long-term reform, as the war continues against production and supply networks. A secondary problem is that decriminalization fails to address problems arising out of excessive or otherwise inappropriate consumption of drugs. Hence, a number of legalization advocates have urged schemes to protect people from drugs by drawing lines in new and different ways.

LIMITATION

The basic idea is that if people's access to drugs is limited, their problems with drugs will be limited. Limits can be imposed on the categories of people who are permitted access, on the quantity of drugs they can obtain, and the circumstances under which they are available.

A familiar example of the limitation approach is today's prescription drug model, where only those holding permits (prescriptions) from physicians are given access, and then only in limited quantities. Some have suggested that access to recreational drugs should be subject to a physician's prescription, but it's dubious whether the medical profession would gladly become arbiters of Saturday nights.

Should drug users be licensed, like drivers? The suggestion has been made that in order to use drugs legally, people should take a class and pass an examination, proving to the satisfaction of authorities that they can handle drugs.

By granting to qualified individuals a right of legal access to drugs, limitation schemes do not replace the prohibition laws but instead carve out exceptions to them. For those who do not qualify under the exceptions, the prohibition laws remain in place, with a law enforcement apparatus equipped to come down on drug use and commerce that remains off limits. Thus, limitation plans could not be expected to change the prohibition landscape significantly in terms of illegal drug markets. Unlimited supplies of drugs will remain available illegally for those who do not qualify for legal access, raising serious questions about the point of imposing limits in the first place.

REGULATION AND TAXATION

It is the absence of such limits that characterizes regulation and taxation, the principal function of which is to drive out the illegal market by recognizing a legal market with which the illegal market cannot compete. Its essence is that just about any adult can obtain drugs legally—and, if using them responsibly, avoid scrutiny of the police. In other words, if the taxes are paid and the other rules observed, production and distribution of drugs carry no criminal penalties.

Current alcohol and tobacco schemes are fairly characterized as regulation and taxation, although neither stands as a compelling model for other drugs. Given the nearly half-million deaths caused annually by alcohol and tobacco and the close association between violence and alcohol, one cannot argue persuasively that American alcohol and tobacco policies are a total success (although prohibition is rarely proffered as a alternative). Since a regulation-and-taxation scheme for drugs would likely build on that experience but take a different form, it is not correct to say that where drugs are regulated and taxed, they are treated "just like wine" or "just like cigarettes."

A variety of bills introduced in state legislatures and several initiatives proposed have as their aim some sort of regulation-and-taxation plan for drugs. Typically, they received a polite, if not serious, reception. None has been vigorously scrutinized or debated. Like castles in the sky, they are visions sculpted in exquisite detail, but visions nonetheless.

The first drug-legalization and taxation schemes applied only to marijuana. In 1971, a bill was introduced in the New York senate by Sen. Franz Leichter,[6] which would set up a Marijuana Control Authority to license and control commerce in cannabis, as commerce in alcohol is presently licensed and regulated, except that advertising would be forbidden. The Leichter bill was introduced regularly during the 1970s and by 1979 had attracted a number of cosponsors, including Sen. Joseph L. Galiber, who in 1989 expanded the scope of the Leichter bill to include all illegal drugs and who proffered a bill that he unambiguously called "A Bill to Make All Illegal Drugs as Legal as Alcohol."[7] Under the Galiber bill, all "controlled substances" could be sold by licensed doctors or pharmacists under a license issued by the State Controlled Substances Authority, which would be granted authority to make all necessary rules for drug production, distribution, and sales.

A comprehensive cannabis regulation-and-taxation bill was introduced in Massachusetts in 1981.[8] The Cannabis Revenue and Education Act would regulate commercial production and distribution of cannabis and impose a tax based on THC content. Half of the net tax proceeds collected would go to a Cannabis Education Trust, set up to conduct a public education campaign against marijuana abuse.

The only comprehensive bill for the regulation and taxation of cannabis at the federal level was called the Cannabis Revenue Act (CRA),[9] drafted in 1982 by a group of lawyers and economists called the National Task Force on Cannabis Regulation. This bill was designed as a federal prototype for the regulation and taxation of commercial activity in marijuana. It designates the U.S. Secretary of the Treasury as the chief regulator and requires licenses for commercial cultivation, processing, and retailing of marijuana. The cultivation and possession of personal use amounts are allowed—no more than twenty-five plants or five pounds of crude cannabis—and noncommercial transfers are permitted. The minimum age for purchase or use is eighteen. The processors are obliged to label the product accurately to reveal THC content, species and variety, origin, and the identity of the processor, and the label must also display a detailed warning about the side effects and possible consequences of use.

In the year following publication of the CRA, regulation-and-taxation bills drawing on it were introduced in the state legislatures of Oregon and Pennsylvania. The Oregon bill[10] restricted retail sales to state-operated stores and earmarked all the revenue to local school districts and local law enforcement. The Pennsylvania bill removed all sanctions from personal cultivation and possession (up to 2.2 lbs.) and subjected the commercial cannabis industry to regulation by the Department of Agriculture, restricting retail sales to state-owned liquor outlets.[11]

In the 1990 session of the Missouri legislature, a bill was introduced by Rep. Elbert Walton that would license the production, distribution, and sale of all drugs.[12] The sales tax was set at a flat rate of 25 percent of retail. Unlike the other regulation-and-taxation models, the Missouri bill imposed strict limits on where drugs may be used, prohibiting the use of "controlled substances" "in the presence of a minor under the age of eighteen years or outside the confines of a private residence or in a place of public accommodation or conveyance"—in other words, prohibiting drug use in bars, restaurants, offices, or cars, and even at home if the kids are around.

A novel feature of the Missouri plan was that it expanded the conventional definition of cannabis, giving statutory recognition to the species *cannabis Americana*, a nod to botanists who developed this new domestic species of cannabis as law enforcement focused on border interdiction.

Also in 1990, a creative initiative measure was proposed in Oregon, called the Oregon Marijuana Initiative (OMI). Had OMI reached the voters and obtained their approval, an exception would have been carved out of current cannabis-prohibition laws, allowing personal use and cultivation with a certificate from the county health department, available for $50 each with the revenue going to county drug and health programs.

In a significant article in the summer 1992 issue of *Daedalus*, Ethan Nadelmann suggests what he calls a "right-of-access" or "mail-order" model. Adults would be able to obtain through the mail "a modest amount of any drug at a reasonable price reflecting production costs and taxes,"[13] while other sales of drugs would remain prohibited under local, state, or federal law.

In 1993, a Washington State grassroots organization called the Washington Citizens for Drug Policy Reform (WCDPR) sponsored an initiative for a new marijuana policy to be known as "regulated tolerance." Under the WCDPR's plan, private adults would be able legally to grow and possess up to a "personal use quantity" without sanction by the criminal law and without having to obtain any license. Cultivating, transporting, and selling more than a "personal use quantity" would require a license from a cannabis-control authority (CCA). Determining a "personal use quantity" would be left to the courts. The proposed law prescribed a tax of $15 per ounce of cannabis "at standard cured moisture content" to be collected and paid by sellers.[14]

The measure permitted the retail sale of "cannabis products made from flowering female tops other than seeds," which suggests the prospect of a wide variety of products being marketed containing cannabis, from soft drinks to pastries to chewing gum — all subject to regulation by the CCA. This contrasts with the 1982 CRA, which legalized the sale of cannabis in its natural form only, specifically prohibiting sales in derivative or constituent forms.

In 1997, two "legalization" initiatives were independently promoted in Oregon. The Oregon Drugs Control Amendment would amend the state constitution to require that laws be passed "regulating" controlled substances and to forbid that such laws "prohibit adult possession of any controlled substance."[15] The legislature would be directed to work out the regulatory details for dealing with a list of issues, which is duplicated here as it provides a useful checklist for any new regulatory scheme.

A minimum legal age of not greater than 21 years;
Reasonable limits on adult personal possession;
Adequate public health and consumer safeguards;
Adequate manufacturing, price, import, and export controls;
Penalties for violations, provisions for enforcement;

Exceptions for controlled scientific research;
Exceptions under medical and/or parental supervision;
Exceptions for traditional, spiritual practices;
A defined legal level of impairment;
Promotion of temperance, moderation, and safety;
On-demand substance abuse and harm reduction programs.[16]

Curiously, the amendment provides, "In no case shall the State of Oregon ever make a net profit from the manufacture or sale of controlled substances."[17]

Making such a profit, on the other hand, is a chief objective another Oregon initiative, called the Oregon Cannabis Tax Act, proffered by an organization called the Campaign for the Restoration and Regulation of Hemp. In a lengthy preface, the act traces the history and benefits of industrial, medical, and recreational cannabis and the failings of its prohibition. The existing Oregon Liquor Control Commission is renamed the Oregon Intoxicant Control Commission (OICC) and assigned authority to regulate, by licensing, the cultivation and processing of cannabis. Licensed cultivators sell their crop only to the OICC. After processing, it is sold in OICC stores at such prices as will "generate profits for revenue to be applied to the purposes [of the statute] and to minimize incentives to purchase cannabis elsewhere, to purchase cannabis for resale or for removal to other states."[18] Industrial hemp falls outside the definition of "cannabis," and its regulation is beyond the jurisdiction of the OICC.

The initiative goes on to specify the disposition of "profits" from the issuance of licenses and sale of cannabis. After administrative and enforcement costs, 90 percent goes to the general fund, 8 percent to the Department of Human Resources "to fund various drug abuse treatment programs on demand," 1 percent "to create and fund an agricultural state committee for the promotion of Oregon hemp fiber, protein and oil crops and associated industries," and 1 percent to "to the state's school districts, appropriated by enrollment, to fund a drug education program."

Uniquely among cannabis legalization proposals, the initiative goes on to lay out the essential elements of an acceptable curriculum for young people. Rejecting prohibitionist doctrine, which has traditionally dominated drug education, the proposal instead requires that the curriculum do the following:

1. Emphasize a citizen's rights and duties under our social compact and explain to students how drug abusers might injure the rights of others by failing to fulfill such duties
2. Persuade students to decline to consume intoxicants by providing them with accurate information about the threat intoxicants pose to their mental and physical development

3. Persuade students that if, as adults, they choose to consume intoxicants, they must nevertheless responsibly fulfill all of their duties to others[19]

In the past decade, legislatures have stood mute as to drug policy reform, yielding to the popular initiative process, in those states where it is allowed, to effect changes in the drug laws. Of the forty or so initiatives that have reached, or nearly reached, the ballot, most have been devoted to medical marijuana. One, however, would repeal state laws on marijuana and impose a regulation-and-taxation scheme. The ambitious 2000 Alaska Ballot Measure 5 would have removed penalties for possession, cultivation, distribution, and sale in liquor stores of any amount of marijuana, hemp, and cannabis for consumers over eighteen; grant amnesty to prior marijuana law offenders; and establish an advisory panel to grant restitution to people previously imprisoned for marijuana crimes. It failed by a vote of forty to sixty. A measure on the 2004 ballot in Oakland, California, would direct the city to accommodate the establishment of a taxed and regulated marijuana market and to lobby the state and federal governments to allow it to occur.

BASIC POLICY ISSUES TO BE CONTEMPLATED BY LEGALIZATION DRAFTERS

What Are "Drugs"?

When a policy maker undertakes to craft a scheme called legalization, the threshold issue is determining which drugs, exactly, are to be legalized. At first glance, the question seems simple, even simplistic. One need merely consult the federal Controlled Substances Act (CSA)[20] or its state counterparts. In these prohibition laws, one will find listed, in exquisite detail, the chemical compounds for the "control" of which the war is being waged. Might it follow, then, that the answer as to what we mean by "drugs," when we speak of legalizing them, is right there?

It sounds plausible at first. After all, illegal drugs are what we see on the 11 o'clock news; you do not hear about shootouts between beer distributors. But if the CSA definition is employed, and illegal drugs are made legal, laws are thereby changed as to a huge multitude of chemical compounds. The notion of prescription drugs will cease to exist. Lest advocates of legalization be wrongly accused of going too far, it is incumbent upon them to specify which drugs *exactly* are to be excised from the list of controlled substances and regulated, if at all, in ways not involving criminal or civil sanctions for adults using them responsibly.

Most of the regulation-and-taxation plans described in this chapter relate only to marijuana. If only marijuana is at issue, then the problem of defining "drugs" can be left for another day, as marijuana is easily severable from other illegal drugs economically, culturally, and pharmaceutically. If the intent, however, is to legalize more drugs than marijuana, but not all of those on the prohibited list, then it becomes necessary to draw and explain new lines between the legal and the illegal. Shall we legalize heroin but not cocaine, amphetamines but not barbiturates?

When that problem is solved—when we have determined what drugs, exactly, are to be legalized—another emerges: what happens to those drugs remaining on the prohibited list? Will they fall into the wrong hands, cause harm to abusers, carry risks of contamination and adulteration, and threaten the public safety by perpetuating a violent and criminal production-and-distribution system? To protect the public from those harms, will we continue to wage domestic war but with fewer drugs as targets?

Let us ask the question, what are drugs? a different way: what drugs threaten public health and safety to the extent that the state is justified in imposing restraints and controls? The destructive ones, naturally, but they are already legal! Indeed, opponents of drug legalization often cite the failures of alcohol and tobacco legalization as examples of why drugs should not be legalized. They have a point. When drugs are legalized, the mistakes of alcohol and tobacco policy— aggressive marketing, for example—must be carefully scrutinized.

In terms of morbidity, toxicity, and social disruption, alcohol and tobacco dwarf illegal drugs. If drug policy reform is about measures aimed at protecting us from such destruction, then a posteriori a broader definition of drugs is in order.

The broader definition of drugs is well established, although rarely invoked when talking drug policy. When Congress created the U.S. Food and Drug Administration, it declared that drugs are "articles [other than food] intended to affect the structure or any function of the body."[21] The most prominent drug education program puts it more colloquially to fifth graders: "any substance other than a food that affects the body or the way it works."[22] Alcohol, nicotine, caffeine, laxatives, and headache remedies are, thus, all drugs.

If the point of the drug laws is to protect public health and safety and curb abuse, perhaps a more promising approach lies in urging public cognizance of the broader definition, fixing in the public psyche a new, larger category of substances deserving of serious national concern. Substances in this category will be treated differently: they will not be commercially available to young people; they will be taxed at a level at least to pay for the harm they cause;[23] people who use them irresponsibly will get into trouble; children will learn to avoid problems with them; laws will protect consumers from impurities.

What do we call this larger category? Several years ago, in a small town in Massachusetts, a school committee charged with reviewing the local drug-education curriculum used the acronym "TAOS" for tobacco, alcohol, and other substances. The committee wrote,

> "Drug-free" may be a clever slogan, but it is an unnatural condition. We look around us and see drugs everywhere: not illegal drugs, necessarily, but legal drugs like alcohol, nicotine, caffeine, sleeping pills, wakeup pills, cold pills, prescription medications, inhalants and all the myriad of preparations offered us at drug stores and supermarkets and hawked on the evening news.[24]

The committee called it "the ubiquity of drugs: they seem to be everywhere." Any drug education curriculum that pretended otherwise was defective.

> Children will be exposed to TAOS as they grow older — as they will be exposed to automobiles and dangerous tools and sex and other hazards of adulthood — and what is important is that they act responsibly. It is unrealistic to expect any of our children not to encounter TAOS as they grow up.[25]

Legalizing drugs is about coming to terms with troublesome realities, and one of those realities is the insufficiency of our vocabulary. As the legalization debate develops, one awaits the emergence of a new term to embrace the broader meaning, giving broader swath to the benefits of reform.

Once the threshold question of defining drugs has been overcome, policy makers confront a myriad of others. The following paragraphs identify additional areas of concern to any legislator seriously contemplating introducing a bill to legalize drugs. As will become obvious, any number of these areas, while theoretically distinct, overlap to one degree or another with one or more other issue areas. Though posed here purely as matter of policy, it should be kept in mind that, ultimately, politics, not policy considerations, drives the resolution of these issues.

Allocation of Federal and State Prerogatives

Both levels of government have been legislating in the drug control field for decades, and both levels will certainly want to have a voice in whatever scheme replaces current prohibition. It would seem that there are two polar possibilities. The federal government could enact simple repealers of all federal penal drug statutes and declare the states free to do as they pleased with the issue. The key practical drawback here is that this would inevitably result in at least some, possibly many, "dry" states.

Richard M. Evans and Stanley Neustadter

This can have consequences that some consider undesirable: citizens of bordering states flocking to buy in the "wet" states. Both Amsterdam and Zurich have experienced this phenomenon. Closer to home, so did New York State when its minimum drinking age remained eighteen long after all neighboring states had raised the minimum age to twenty-one; Louisiana has a similar problem today. State-by-state disparities tend to create pressure on wet states to become dry or on low-minimum-age states to become high-minimum-age states. A parallel problem might emerge intrastate: certain counties might want to remain dry or might choose to set disparate minimum age limits.

The other extreme would be to grant the federal government exclusive authority to define and administer the new drug-control regime, completely preempting state prerogatives. While this has the virtue of ensuring clarity and nationwide uniformity, it eliminates the value of having different states devise creative or experimental local methods of deploying and operating a drug-control system. Certainly, states could decide unilaterally to cede responsibility for drug-prohibition enforcement to federal authorities, as New York State did in 1923 when alcohol was the prohibited drug. As one of only a handful of states that repealed or did not enact its own prohibition laws, New York escaped the violent crime that is associated with the era of Prohibition, and that is why the enforcement authorities, in movies of the era, are called the "feds." Cession would be a simple maneuver for states that want to keep drugs illegal but avoid the costs of enforcement. If a state simply repealed its marijuana laws, for example, replacing them with nothing, marijuana would remain illegal, albeit only under federal law, and the enforcement burden would thus be shifted to the feds exclusively. Of course, legalization, as contemplated by this chapter, would not be accomplished.

The more sensible approach to real legalization would seem to reside in a workable middle ground: federal legislation would repeal federal penal drug statutes and would erect a federal regulatory scheme that would allow the states reasonable flexibility in administrative and regulatory detail, but with strong monetary incentives to toe the federal line. In other words, the country's core drug policy would be determined at the national level, and states that adopted policies designed or tending to undermine or frustrate overall federal regulatory policy would suffer fiscal penalties.[26]

Setting the Level of Taxation

Should different substances be taxed differently? What level of taxation can be maintained without driving the final sales price so high that black markets would be encouraged? This latter question has received scant econometric attention[27] but sorely needs it. The various bills mentioned above seem to just pluck numbers from the air, but tax rates must be determined only after serious analysis. An equally thorny problem is reckoning the base cost of cultivating or manufacturing the substances. Because the "crime tariff" (the premium over base cost that the criminal charges for the risk of producing and trafficking in illegal substances) is responsible for most of the retail street price of drugs under the current prohibitionist system, it is difficult to project the true base cost in a free market solely from current price patterns. Moreover, manufacture or cultivation, wholesaling, and retailing would involve significant personnel and regulatory-compliance costs whose dimensions must also be estimated. Without those projections, it is difficult to project a sensible retail sales price, without which no tax rate can be rationally calculated.

Figuring retail prices and tax rates is further complicated by another factor: with cultivation/manufacture open and legal, small-plot farming and garage lab production will disappear and be replaced by economies of technology and scale. In the longer run, this will have the inevitable effect of dramatically reducing the base unit product cost, which will in turn affect taxation policy. For example, an ounce of marijuana whose wholesale cost is $20 in the first year of legalization may well cost only $1 in year five. To the extent the tax rate is based on wholesale product cost, revenues would diminish as production efficiencies increased.

Some, but by no means all, of these problems can be simplified or eliminated if the new drug commerce is operated as a government monopoly. There would be no taxes as such, just "profits" represented by the balance remaining after the state has paid all expenses of cultivation, manufacture, processing, and retailing.

Even after these calculations are made, other questions remain. Who decides what the tax rates should be, the legislature or the regulatory agency? In most jurisdictions, if not all, tax policy may be set only by elected officials, yet regulators are more likely to have a keener grasp of commerce itself and could make wiser, speedier taxation decisions out of public view. If the new drug scheme is a concurrent state/federal one, how should tax revenues be divided? How should the likely competition between state and federal governments for the lion's share of the tax dollar be managed? In any event, should revenues, whether at the federal or local level, be specifically earmarked for, say, drug treatment and education? For reduction in local income or property or sales taxes? For local law enforcement? For government's expenses in administering the new drug scheme? For the general treasury? In any event, should legalization proponents announce an estimate of how much revenue might reasonably be generated by the new regime?[28]

Legislating the Details

How much of the regulatory scheme (e.g., label warning language, sale unit for each drug, time and place of sale, and use restrictions) should be detailed in the legislation? Is it wiser to leave that to the regulatory body that these bills envisage and create? Does that dampen criticism or invite it? To what extent will the politicians, other public figures, defenders of prohibition, and the public insist that the details be spelled out in advance? Politicians might well prefer to pass the buck on those details to the regulatory agency, while others might want to know all the details in advance. To what extent should any new drug legislation expressly answer harsh questions such as, Will an airline pilot be able to go down to the local store and buy crack?

Liability Waivers

Holding manufacturers and sellers harmless from any product liability claims to users is a feature of some of these bills. But what about manufacturer/retailer liability to third parties harmed by users under the influence of legally purchased substances? Is the alcohol/gun model appropriate for liability to the nonusing third party?

Degree of Government Involvement in Legalized Market

Although the analogies are gross and imperfect, the other legalized "sin" markets—alcohol and gambling—provide convenient comparisons. In terms of government involvement, should the new drug scheme resemble, for example, state lotteries or licensed casinos?[29] Lotteries are run virtually entirely by state agencies staffed by state employees; although some peripheral functions are contracted out (e.g., manufacturing the machines that print out the tickets, paying retailers a tiny commission on each ticket sold), the whole system is operated by government functionaries as a monopoly. There is no tax on each sale of a lottery ticket: the government simply keeps the balance of revenue after administrative costs are paid.

Casinos, however, are typically overseen by a state regulatory agency. The actual casino operations themselves, although tightly monitored by the regulators, are entirely managed by licensed private hands, staffed wholly by private enterprise. The state realizes revenues by taxing casino proceeds.

With respect to the drug market, should the government cultivate, process, and sell the product and keep what revenue is left after covering those costs? Should it leave the cultivation and processing to licensed private operators who will then sell it (at what price? free market or fixed?) to the government, which will then operate as the wholesaler/retailer? Many states operate the liquor market in this fashion. Or should the government leave the whole enterprise in private hands, with its involvement limited to licensing and regulatory matters? Should the government/private mix be different for different substances? Should these decisions be made at the national or local level?

Intense government involvement, particularly in the retail phases of the drug market, would be politically attractive to civil service unions, but they might also end up being more costly enterprises, requiring support of ever-increasing total retail prices, creating the risk that underpricing and unregulated black markets would eventually emerge. Even if pervasive government involvement translated into greater government revenues, many might find it unseemly for the government to be in the actual business of importing, cultivating, processing, and retailing substances that once were completely illegal and thought by many to be immoral as well.

Prescription Drugs

Some prescription drugs—for example, valium, barbiturates, opiate-based painkillers—are commonly abused through both overprescription and black market availability; should these drugs be available without prescription under the new scheme? What is the nature of the intersection between the new recreational drug scheme and federal regulation of prescription medication, substances originally designed for the treatment of medical conditions but that have been put to recreational use as well?

Designer Drugs

New substances work their way into use from time to time. How does the new regime deal with this phenomenon?

Home Growers

Of particular importance to pot aficionados, but theoretically a more general, if less widespread, phenomenon with other drugs as well, are the consumers who grow their own. It is worth noting that current alcohol regulations allow individuals to brew limited quantities of their own beer and wine. How about cooking up your own personal use pile of quaaludes or speed? What about growing your own coca leaves to chew yourself or to make into cocaine for your own use? What about buying cocaine through legal retail outlets and rendering it down to crack for your own use? This in turn suggests other questions: does it make sense to legalize/regulate coca leaves but not cocaine, cocaine but not crack, opium poppies but not heroin or morphine?

Licensing Users

Inevitably there will be calls from skeptics and die-hard warriors who say no legalization scheme should even be contemplated unless it requires that users be licensed, the argument being that if we require licenses for the recreational use of cars and guns, why not for drugs? Along the same lines, there may be calls to have retailers keep records of purchasers (perhaps through the issuance of drug ID cards) and amounts sold to each one. Are these wise ideas? If not, how are they to be countered? May the same goals be achieved by measures less onerous to privacy and civil liberties concerns?

Parent-Child Drug Transfers

Current law has an expansive definition of "sale" of drugs and forbids not only typically cash-and-carry transactions but gratuitous transfers—gifts—as well.[30] All legalization bills would lift penal sanctions on adults for licensed sales and for gratuitous transfers between adults, but would retain penal sanctions, often harsh ones, against transfers to those underage.

Yet, parents might well want to introduce their teenage offspring to some drugs both to remove the "forbidden fruit" attraction of drug use (If Mom and Dad do this, how cool could it be?) and to teach responsible use. This, of course, is what many families do today with respect to introducing their children to alcohol, even though, under current alcohol regulations, it is illegal. Should the new legislation deal with this explicitly? Should this particular dog be left to sleep, like parent-child alcohol transfers?

Currently Incarcerated Drug Offenders

How will the new scheme affect them? Not at all, unless the legislation says otherwise. This was a problem when alcohol prohibition was repealed by constitutional amendment (as opposed to ordinary legislative enactment), and where the number of inmates affected was, compared to current drug inmate populations, insignificant.[31]

A number of options suggest themselves: (1) a direct and immediate legislative commutation of all drug sentences; (2) a complete legislative commutation combined with some sort of limited parole supervision, depending upon the severity of the sentence; (3) a staggered legislative commutation depending upon the severity of the sentence either with or without parole supervision; and (4) a case-by-case approach, requiring each defendant to petition the sentencing judge, with legislation providing guidelines to judges, with right of appeal. A parallel issue involves remissions of forfeitures obtained under the former laws.

Drug Testing

Does a legalization scheme call for a different approach to drug testing? Does it warrant testing a broader—or narrower—segment of society on a routine basis or only on a probable-cause basis? Should the criteria change from mere presence of drugs in the system to impairment of function?

Nonpenal Sanctions for Drug Users

This issue is analytically distinct, but closely related to the drug-testing issue noted above. Both issues are likely to be resolved on the basis of whether, and in what manner, the public perceives that drug use will significantly increase after legalization. Many proponents of legalization argue that even if overall usage increases, the drugs available will be safer and, more important, less potent. The theory is that the "iron law of drug prohibition"—that criminal laws virtually guarantee that smugglers will market only the most compact shipments of the most potent substances—will no longer operate in a regulated market and that most drug users, given the choice, would normally opt for milder forms of drugs, preferring a cocktail-like buzz to a blottoed binge.

Even if the future ultimately bears out the truth of these plausible theories, the public's perception of legalization's likely harvest might well be quite different. Citizens might well seek comfort in knowing that the law contains other measures—nonpenal in nature—that would act to deter drug use.

The possibilities are endless. Eligibility for all sorts of public benefits (welfare, housing, veterans, Social Security, Medicare, unemployment insurance, driving and occupational licenses) might be denied on the basis of a failed mandatory drug test or on other proof of drug use. Assuming that the Constitution would impose some limits on the denial of public benefits solely on the basis of using a legal substance, it is not at all clear what would prevent, for example, a legislature from making drug use a ground for divorce or a factor in awarding child custody.

Moreover, the Constitution is unlikely to provide protection from purely private sanctions, like allowing a landlord to evict a tenant for drug use. If measures such as these become part of the legalized drug landscape—plausible so long as opprobrium towards drugs remains at current levels—reformers whose antiprohibitionism is driven largely by libertarian sentiments might find the drug peace scarcely more attractive than the drug war; the brawny arm of the penal law would be replaced by the slithery tentacles of insidiously intrusive "civil" sanctions.

CONCLUSION

Legalization means more than changing laws. In the long run, it means trying to accomplish the same goals as prohibition—protecting public health and safety, curbing abuse, especially among the young, and eliminating the crime and violence associated with illicit drug trafficking. In the short run, legalization means changing the way we think about drugs. When drugs are legal, there will be little confusing of drug use with drug abuse, or confusing the harm done by drugs with the harm done by drug prohibition. Teachers and parents will recognize that educating young people to avoid problems with drugs entails more than infusing them, for now, with fear and scorn. Consumers will understand that the legal status of a drug has little to do with the drug's safety. Drug-related crime will be distinguished from prohibition-related crime.

Legalization confers upon citizens both the benefits and burdens of personal autonomy. Drug users will face less risk to their health and their liberty but will be held accountable for their conduct affecting others. A major challenge to the architects of legalization will be to devise a system that imposes on consumers a profound sense of responsibility for the consequences of their drug use.

When talk is of legalizing drugs, identifying what is meant by "legalizing" and what is meant by "drugs" is a modest but necessary first step before attention is turned to how best to do it. Unlike the "bogus ideal" deprecated by Justice Oliver Wendell Holmes, what it means to legalize drugs must not "dwell in generalities and shirk the details."[32]

NOTES

1. Thomas Szasz, *Our Right to Drugs: The Case for a Free Market* (New York: Praeger Publishing Co., 1992).

2. The eleven states that decriminalized marijuana statutorily are Alaska, California, Colorado, Maine, Minnesota, Mississippi, Nebraska, New York, North Carolina, Ohio, and Oregon.

3. Mark A. R. Kleiman, *Marijuana: Costs of Abuse, Costs of Control* (New York: Greenwood Press, 1989), 182.

4. According to FBI uniform crime statistics, arrests for marijuana have risen from 10 per 100,000 of the population in 1965 to 226 per 100,000 of the population in 2002.

5. *State of Alaska v. Leo Richardson Crocker.*

6. Senate Bill No. 4944, February 16, 1971, 1971–1972 session; Senate No. 3980, Assembly No. 6025, March 15, 1979, 1979–1980 session.

7. S. 1918, 1989–1990 Regular Session of the New York senate.

8. House No. 1737, 1981 session.

9. *The Regulation and Taxation of Cannabis Commerce*, report of the National Task Force on Cannabis Regulation, December 1982. Coauthor Evans was chairman of the task force.

10. Senate No. 497, 1983 Regular Session.

11. Commonwealth of Pennsylvania, the Pennsylvania Marijuana Cultivation Control Act of 1983, introduced by Sen. T. Milton Street.

12. State of Missouri, House Bill No. 1820, 85th General Assembly.

13. Ethan A. Nadelmann, "Thinking Seriously about Alternatives to Drug Prohibition," *Daedalus* 121(3) (summer 1992): 113.

14. Initiative Measure 595 [1993, Section 10(1)].

15. The Oregon Drugs Control Amendment, Section 1 (1997).

16. The Oregon Drugs Control Amendment, Section 3.

17. The Oregon Drugs Control Amendment, Section 6.

18. Oregon Cannabis Tax Act, Section 474.055.

19. Oregon Cannabis Tax Act, Section 474.055(d).

20. U.S. Code 21, § 801 et seq.

21. U.S. Code 21, § 321(g)(1).

22. DARE Officer Training Manual, 1984, 93, revised 1994.

23. Lester Grinspoon, M.D., "The Harmfulness Tax: A Proposal for the Regulation and Taxation of Drugs," *North Carolina Journal of International Law and Commercial Regulation* 15(3) (June 1990).

24. Report of the Committee to Review the Tobacco, Alcohol and Other Substance (TAOS) Curriculum, Ashfield-Plainfield (Massachusetts) Regional School District, Sanderson Academy School Council, June 6, 1994, 6.

25. Report of the Committee to Review the TAOS Curriculum, 7.

26. In fact, the federal government has already used this carrot-and-stick approach in the drug policy arena with considerable effect. The Federal Drug Offenders Driving Privileges Act provides that states declining to enact legislation stripping drivers' licenses from people convicted of drug offenses will have their matching federal highway funds cut off [see U.S. Code 23, § 159(a)(1992)]. Virtually all states got the message and enacted the requisite legislation.

27. See, e.g., Michael R. Caputo and Brian J. Ostrom, "Potential Tax Revenue from a Regulated Marijuana Market: A Meaningful Revenue Source," *Am. J. Econ. & Sociol.* 54: 475 (1994); Garber, "Potential Tax Revenues from a Regulatory Marketing Scheme for Marijuana," *J. Psyched. Drugs* 10: 217. Extrapolating from alcohol and tobacco tax experience and from available statistics on marijuana usage patterns, the authors derive a broad estimate of the range of tax revenues that might be

generated through a legalized marijuana market. However, the authors have no particular legalization model in mind and do not propose any particular tax structure or tax rate. They tacitly assume that the government will be operating (not just licensing others to do so) the entire marijuana industry, from cultivation to processing to retailing, and seem to equate "taxes" with "profits." Yet, the tax issues do not exist in a vacuum and can be confronted or resolved only within the framework of specific legalization models.

28. Cost-benefit and cost-effectiveness analyses have been marshaled by drug-policy debaters but not always sagely because there are so many variables. For trenchant examination of the problem, see Kenneth Warner, "Legalizing Drugs: Lessons from (and about) Economics," *Milbank Quarterly* 69 (1991): 641–62.

29. Another apt contrast would be between racetracks (entirely in licensed, private hands) and off-track betting parlors and lotteries (operated wholly by government employees).

30. For a comprehensive review of the law in all jurisdictions, see *People v. Starling*, 85 N.Y.2d 509, 650 N.E.2d 387 (1985).

31. See, generally, *United States v. Chambers*, 291 U.S. 217, 233 (1934). Note *The Status of Liquor Crimes and Forfeitures Following Repeal*, Geo. Wash. L. Rev. 2 (1934): 395, and annotation at 89 A.L.R. 1514 (1935).

32. Letter to Harry Drinker, quoted in Catherine Drinker Bowen, *Family Portrait* (Boston: Little, Brown & Company, 1970).

7

Acute Toxicity of Drugs versus Regulatory Status

Robert S. Gable

If we are concerned about the external pollutants that threaten our environment, we should be equally concerned about internal pollutants—like marijuana products. For sheer survival, we must defend ourselves against both kinds of pollution.

—Jacques Cousteau (cited in Schuchard 1993)

Consider this: The risks of caffeine are greater than THC in every way. . . . Caffeine is physically addicting (with headache as the most often cited withdrawal symptom) and can cause unnecessary stress, lightheadedness, breathlessness, and an irregular heartbeat or much worse in larger-than-average doses. Marijuana isn't even remotely as dangerous—no deaths by overdose, no physical addiction and minimal health risks.

—D. Larsen (1996)

Opinions about the nonmedical use of psychoactive substances are plentiful and often contradictory. The disputes tend to focus on the dangers of "drugs" in general without thoughtful consideration of the different physical and psychological risks among substances. The public is not to blame. Relevant data are difficult to access and, in some cases, remain highly speculative. Although the number of laboratory reports comparing toxicity and abuse potential within certain classes of drugs (e.g., anesthetics, stimulants, depressants) is substantial, reports comparing substances across classes are relatively rare. Some notable studies making such cross-class comparisons include those by B. Ekwall, E. Wallum, and I. Bondesson (1998), M. Gossop, P. Griffiths, B. Powis, and J. Strang (1992), and M. R. Repetto and M. Repetto (1997).

This chapter briefly reviews empirical criteria for making comparisons of drug toxicity and lists several policy guidelines for developing a broad, evidence-based drug-control strategy.

CRITERIA FOR DRUG COMPARISONS

Acute Physiological Toxicity

The traditional laboratory measure of toxicity has been the *therapeutic index* (Nies 1990). The therapeutic index is computed by first determining the quantity of the drug that is necessary to produce the desired effect in one-half of an animal population (typically rodents). This dosage level is referred to as the *effective dose* for 50 percent of the animals, or "ED_{50}." Similarly, the *lethal dose* is determined by observing the quantity of the drug that causes death in 50 percent of the test animals, the "LD_{50}," within a specified period of time. The ratio of the ED_{50} to the LD_{50} provides a one-point estimate of how selective, or nontoxic, a substance is in producing a desired effect.

Consider our most commonly used recreational substance, alcohol. The effective dose, ED_{50}, of alcohol is assumed to be about 30g, which is roughly equivalent to two 12-oz. beers or malt liquor (assuming 5.5 percent ethanol by volume). The LD_{50} of alcohol is estimated to be about 300g taken orally within five minutes on an empty stomach by a 70-kg human who has not developed a tolerance to the substance. Therefore, the therapeutic index is 10 ($LD_{50}/ED_{50} = 300/30 = 10$).

Obviously, the likelihood of drinking twenty beers, the LD_{50}, within five minutes is a near impossibility because the large fluid volume would trigger regurgitation. Thus, in this situation, the oral route of administration acts as a protective mechanism. With a higher-proof alcohol drink such as whisky, consuming the lethal dose is somewhat more feasible. If alcohol were administered intravenously—as was recommended by at one time as a postsurgical analgesic (Dunham 1951)—it would be much more hazardous.

Common routes of drug administration are injesting orally, smoking, snorting, injecting into muscle, and inhaling. The oral route is the most frequently used and is generally the least susceptible to acute toxic insult because the substance is metabolized in the liver prior to absorption into the bloodstream. However, the slower and variable absorption rate of ingested substances means that adjusting the dosage in order to control drug effects is more difficult. Injection into the vein or muscle produces a more prompt reaction but leaves less margin for error and runs the risk of infection from nonsterile needles. Inhalation also provides rapid absorption and avoids the unpredictability of ingestion; however, nonvolatile materials (such as cigarette smoke and heroin vapor) have been linked to serious chronic illnesses. Intranasal administration (insufflation, snorting) has a slower initial onset of action than inhalation or intravenous injection but is more rapid and controllable than ingestion or intramuscular injection. The route of administration has been positively correlated to the severity of subsequent addiction (Manski, Pepper, and Petrie 2001) as well as to the risk of acute lethality.

The therapeutic index will change as the purpose for use of the drug changes (i.e., the ED_{50} is modified). For example, a sedative-hypnotic such as phenobarbital will be relatively safe if the goal is sedation; it will be less safe if the goal is general anesthesia. A dose still higher than that required for anesthesia may dangerously depress respiratory and vasomotor function and therefore lead to coma and death. Approximately 20 percent of direct chemical deaths among persons fifteen to twenty-four years of age in the United States result from suicide (National Center 2004).

It might seem that a substance with a therapeutic index, or safety margin, of 10 can be used with little risk. This is not necessarily so. In order for a substance to produce a desired response in a large percentage of users (e.g., above 90 percent), a small percentage (e.g., 5 percent) of the users might be reasonably expected to experience severe side effects. Different substances have different "dose-response curves"; that is, the quantity of the substance needed to go from the minimum to the maximum of either a desired or a lethal effect (i.e., the slope of the curve) is unique for each substance. The therapeutic index reflects the relationship of the desired effect and the lethal effect at only *one* point on the curve.

Motivational factors, such as a tendency to repeat dosing, vary among drugs (e.g., cocaine versus MDMA) and affect acute physiological toxicity (cf., Foltin, Fischman, Levin 1995). The influence of environmental factors, such as ambient temperature, on acute toxicity is uncertain (e.g., Malberg and Seiden 1998; Irvine et al. 2003).

Dependence Potential

Dependence potential is a multidimensional construct and can be defined in various ways (cf., Expert Panel 2003). The definition is critical in determining how various substances get evaluated. One measure of addiction hazard is the "capture ratio" of a substance; that is, of the people who try a drug, what proportion of them will encounter some period of time during which their use of the substance is not fully under their voluntary control? By this measure, tobacco could be ranked near the top of addictive substances (cf., Kozlowski et al. 1989); methamphetamine would be more addictive than cocaine (Castro et al. 2000).

A different criterion for dependence potential can be the onset of withdrawal symptoms when the drug is not available after prolonged use. This measure is the traditional negative-reinforcement paradigm of addiction. Alcohol, heroin, and short-acting barbiturates get top billing by this standard (Jaffe and Martin 1990).

Another way to assess dependence potential is to measure the strength of the drug as a positive reinforcer. Users often self-administer a substance in order to induce euphoria, confidence, sensuality, or novel sensory experiences. This form of dependence is motivated primarily by a desire to repeat a rewarding experience rather than to avoid withdrawal symptoms. Cocaine, opiates, and amphetamines are probably the most addicting drugs by this standard (Bozarth 1989).

Finally, another measure of dependency is the drug's toxic severity per unit of time. In other words, how detrimental is the drug to the physical and psychological welfare of the person who is dependent on the substance for, say, a month or a year? By this criterion, smoked cocaine would probably compete with intravenous heroin as the most dangerous. Alcohol would likely rank second among common psychoactive substances (Hall, Room, and Bondy 1999).

COMPARATIVE TOXICITY

A literature review of approximately three thousand articles was conducted over a period of eight years in order to compare the acute lethality of commonly abused psychoactive substances. Readers should consult Gable (2004a, b) to obtain details regarding both the methodology and results of the review. The estimated lethal quantity of a substance was calculated using published data from laboratory-animal studies and from medical-examiner reports. Both the lethal dose and the effective dose listed in table 7.1 assume that the individual is a 70-kg adult human in good health who has not developed a tolerance to the substance as a result of prior use. The quantities refer to the weight or volume of the active material, not to the weight or volume of other substances that may be used as an extender, filler, or vehicle for the primary active ingredient.

An obvious difficulty in estimating lethal doses of illicit substances in nonlaboratory situations is the unknown composition and purity of the administered material. For example, postmortem examination of six fatalities caused by material represented as methylenedioxymethamphetamine (MDMA or "ecstasy") found toxic or fatal blood levels of MDMA in only two decedents;

Table 7.1. Safety Ratio and Dependence Potential of Psychoactive Drugs[1]

Substance	Effective Dose	Lethal Dose	Safety Ratio	Dependence Potential
Narcotics				
Heroin (iv)[2]	8 mg	50 mg	6	Very high
Morphine (or)	20 mg	300 mg	15	High
Depressants (sedative hypnotics)				
Barbiturates				
Pentobarbital (or)	250 mg	5 g	20	Moderate/high
Benzodiazepines				
Rohypnol (or)	1 mg	30 mg	30	Moderate
Alcohol				
Ethanol (or)	30 mg[3]	300 mg	10	Moderate
Stimulants				
Caffeine (or)	100 mg[4]	10 g	100	Moderate/low
Cocaine (in)	80 mg[5]	1.2 g	15	Moderate/high
Ephedra (or)	25 mg	3.5 g[6]	140	Moderate
MDMA (or)	125 mg	2 g	16	Moderate/low
Nicotine (sm)	1 mg[7]	50 mg	50	High
Anesthetics				
Ketamine (in)	70 mg	2.7 g (?)	38 (?)	Low
Nitrous oxide (inh)	3.5 liters	525 liters[8]	150	Moderate/low
Hallucinogens				
LSD (or)	100 mcg	100 mg	1000	Very low
Mescaline (or)	350 mg	8.4 g (?)	24 (?)	Very low
Psilocybin (or)	6 mg	6 g (?)	1000 (?)	Very low
Cannabis				
Marijuana (sm)	15 mg	> 15 g	>1000	Moderate/low

[1] Adapted in part from Gable (2004a,b). The information presented here should not be used as a dosage guide. Significant differences exist with respect to a person's physiological and psychological reactions. The dosage indicated is the estimated median quantity for a 70kg adult human who has not developed tolerance to the substance.

[2] Routes of administration: in = intranasal (insufflation/snorting), inh = inhaled, iv = intravenous, or = oral, sm = smoked.

[3] Approximately two 12-ounce beers or malt liquor at 5.5 percent by volume, or equivalent ethanol in other alcohol drinks.

[4] Approximately 1.5 cups of 148 ml (5 oz.) of fluid coffee per cup.

[5] Assumes three "lines" containing between 20 and 30 mg cocaine each.

[6] Lethal dose not clearly established; estimate based on nonhuman animal studies.

[7] Approximately one cigarette.

[8] Nitrous oxide—when used with sufficient oxygen—has not been demonstrated to be lethal.

toxic or fatal blood levels of the more toxic paramethoxyamphetamine (PMA) were identified in all six cases (Byard, Gilbert, James, and Lokan 1998).

As previously noted, estimates of the effective dose depend, in part, on the intention of the user. The effective doses listed in table 7.1 are those most commonly used in social recreational situations by relatively inexperienced users.

The term "safety ratio" rather than "therapeutic index" is used in table 7.1 because the intended uses of the substances are nonmedical in nature. The numbers are presented solely for the purpose of comparing the relative safety of substances not as a precise quantification.

Even though absolute magnitudes of risk remain uncertain, this quantification can give policy makers a basis for systematically ranking risks and for establishing priorities for intervention programs.

The "Dependence Potential" column in table 7.1 is an attempt to combine the positive- and the negative-reinforcement definitions of dependence potential summarized earlier. Combining physical and psychological dependency appears to result in a significant loss of information only for cocaine powder administered intranasally. The psychological dependence described in research reports for intranasal cocaine ranged from "moderate" to "very high," while the physical dependence ranged from "moderate" to "low."

A graphic representation of dependence and toxicity is presented in figure 7.1. The most dangerous substance (i.e., intravenous heroin) appears in the lower right corner because it has the highest dependence potential and the lowest safety ratio. In contrast, psilocybin ("magic mushrooms"), LSD, and marijuana are clustered in the upper left-hand corner because they have lowest dependence potential and the least acute physiological toxicity. Orally ingested psilocybin, with a safety ratio over 1,000, is one hundred times "safer" than alcohol with a safety margin of 10. Again, these are only estimates, but there seems to be little doubt about the relative position of most (but not all) of the substances with respect to their acute lethality.

A significant limitation of the two-dimensional comparison in figure 7.1 is best illustrated by the location of LSD. Although it is "safe" with respect to potential lethality and addiction, its potency in altering consciousness makes it much less socially benign than, say, caffeine. Driving a car after ingesting LSD is obviously less acceptable than after drinking a cup of coffee. The consciousness-altering potency of a substance and the conditions under which it is used must be factored into any comprehensive assessment of safety.

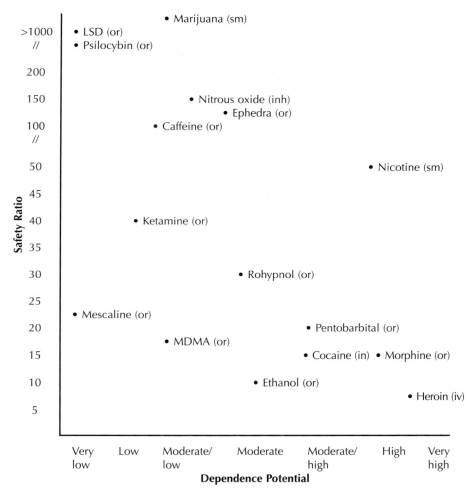

Figure 7.1.   Safety Ratio and Dependence Potential of Psychoactive Drugs

DRUG REGULATION

Drug regulation in some form is generally agreed to be necessary. Unfortunately, many of our present drug laws are more symbolic than evidence based. Consider, for example, the Anti-Drug Abuse Amendments Act of 1988 (U.S. Code 21, § 1504), which stated, "It is the declared policy of the U.S. Government to create a Drug-Free America by 1995." The target date has come and gone, but the increased penalties that Congress imposed in 1988 for a wide range of drug offenses are still on the books. This is not an isolated case of legislative error. There are at least three other well-known, failed attempts to eliminate or prohibit activities involving public health risks: the Delaney Amendment forbidding any carcinogens in food additives (U.S. Code 21, § 348), denial of economic considerations in certain provisions of the Clean Air Act (U.S. Code 42, § 7409), and the zero-tolerance drug policy of the U.S. Customs Service (Thomas 1989). Eventually, all of these laws or regulations were circumvented or rescinded. Realistic and enforceable policies do not come easily in a climate of public fear.

The basic framework for drug regulation in the United States is logically flawed and has not been corrected. The legal definition of a "drug" is, in part, "articles [other than food] intended to affect the structure or any function of the body of man or other animals" (U.S. Code 21, § 321g). This definition is so broad that it could be interpreted to regulate even distilled water if a distributor attached a label claiming (accurately) that the water could improve digestion and prevent renal failure. This amorphous definition was narrowed for regulatory purposes by the Comprehensive Drug Abuse Prevention and Control Act (U.S. Code 21, § 811b), which requires that substances with potential for abuse be classified on the basis of eight factors: (1) actual or relative potential for abuse; (2) scientific evidence of the drug's pharmacological effects; (3) the state of current scientific knowledge regarding the substance; (4) its history and current pattern of abuse; (5) the scope, duration, and significance of abuse; (6) what, if any, risk there is to the public health; (7) the drug's psychic or physiological dependence potential; and (8) whether the substance is an immediate precursor of a substance already controlled.

The Drug Enforcement Administration (DEA) assigns substances with abuse potential to one of five schedules. Schedule I substances have (1) high potential for abuse, (2) no accepted medical use, and (3) a lack of accepted safety under medical supervision. Except for approved research, substances in Schedule I cannot be lawfully distributed. Schedule II substances have (1) high potential for abuse, (2) accepted medical use, and (3) abuse potential that may lead to severe psychological or physical dependence. Substances assigned to the three remaining schedules are to have generally accepted medical use but decreasing abuse potential relative to prior schedules. There is no statutory recognition of, or drug schedule for, psychoactive substances used nonmedically for religious, educational, or recreational purposes. Thus, Schedule I has become a "taxonomic wastebasket" for all substances without medical use, regardless of their toxicity or abuse potential (Gable 1992; cf. generally, Spillane and McAllister 2003). Apparently, the logic of Congress was that if a psychoactive substance has no medical use, it has no benefit and therefore should be totally prohibited.

Based on their acute toxicity and dependence potential, substances such as marijuana, psilocybin, and MDMA that are now in Schedule I appear to be misclassified. Substances such as caffeine (trimethylxanthine) and chocolate (theobromine), with moderate or low abuse potential, are not regulated as drugs because they are considered a "food," unless added to a product as a stimulant ingredient (C.F.R. 21, § 321 et seq.). The caffeine conundrum is a mere tempest in a coffee cup compared to the enigmatic legal history of alcohol and tobacco. Alcohol (ethanol) is not scheduled by the DEA as a result of the 21st Amendment to the Constitution and related administrative actions (e.g., C.F.R. 27, § 201 et seq.) Tobacco (nicotine) escaped scheduling and FDA/DEA regulation because, according to the Supreme Court (529 U.S. 120, 159), "Congress created a distinct regulatory scheme for tobacco products," largely by default, because Congress *could* have done more than simply requiring the labeling of tobacco products.

The DEA is authorized to transfer substances between schedules (U.S. Code 21, § 805), and it has done so by moving, for example, buprenorphine from Schedule V to Schedule III and tetrahydrocannabinal from Schedule I to Schedule II. Nonetheless, transferring substances between schedules does not resolve the fundamental anomaly of having no categories for low- or moderate-abuse substances without medical application.

At least three principles should guide the development of a revised, evidence-based drug-control strategy:

Harm Is Unavoidable

Archaeological studies indicate that psychoactive substances have been used since prehistoric times for more than medicinal purposes (Schultes and Hofmann 1979). Hence, it seems reasonable to proceed on the premise that the use of psychoactive substances, of some type and to some degree, will continue. Laws to control drug use may reduce risks, shift risks, or increase risks, but they cannot eliminate risks (MacCoun 1993). Taxation, regulation, and prohibition are the most common strategies to reduce the consumption of a commodity. All three create their own reaction in terms of substitution, evasion, or black markets. For example, some laboratory (Mello and Mendelson 1978) and sociological (Burglass 1985) studies suggest that, given a free choice, people might prefer marijuana to alcohol. An extensive review of published studies of economic and law enforcement strategies showed, however, quite diverse results with respect to drug substitution (European Monitoring Centre 2002). In short, there are no risk-free options in drug policy. Drug laws and drug pricing should be written so that less harmful substitution is encouraged, even if it means grudging acceptance of a less-than-optimal outcome.

Harm Reduction Is a Desirable but Insufficient Drug-Control Strategy

Harm reduction is best viewed as an initial step in regulatory restructuring. One of its limitations is the exclusive focus on the potential negative consequences of drug use. It ignores the personal, positive values of the drug experience. By analogy, consider a situation in which a person has $100 that she wants to protect from loss. The most direct and cautious action would be to put the money in a safe deposit box. This would be a strict harm-reduction strategy. The money would not, however, earn interest. At a 3 percent annual inflation rate, the $100 would be almost worthless in 30 years, and she would have been burdened with the safe-deposit-box rental fee. In the absence of certain knowledge about the future, the only way to prevent loss of equity is to take a risk and invest the money in some enterprise. Harm-reduction is not a free good.

Because long-term harm reduction can be achieved only by assuming short-term risk in order to gain compensatory benefits, the concept of "risk management," or "harm management," provides a broader alternative to drug prohibition than does harm reduction.

Benefits Should Be Acknowledged

If drugs had no perceived benefits, they would not be used and abused. Just as drug users tend to overlook possible costs (e.g., impurity of illicit substances, chronic toxicity, loss of motivation), nonusers tend to ignore potential benefits. The assertion, for example, that "increased use of marijuana regardless of potency offers a multitude of negative consequences and no benefits" (Vocci 1995, 4) does not explain why marijuana is used in the first place. It also precludes reasonable discussion of how regulatory agencies might go about assessing the benefits and costs of various alternative regulatory strategies.

Numerous first-person reports have been published describing the experiential benefits of psychoactive substances (e.g., Shulgin and Shulgin 1991, 1997). Two early self-studies include those of Victor Robinson (1925), a physician using marijuana, and philosopher William James (1902) using nitrous oxide. Another noteworthy self-study was that of C. C. Bennett (1960), who subjected himself to a series of standardized tests after having eight recreational drugs administered blindly to him.

Regulated access to psychoactive substances—comparable in safety and effectiveness to drugs now prescribed for medical purposes—should be permissible when certain conditions are met (e.g., age, voluntariness, health status). Perhaps at some time in the distant future a constitutional amendment will read, "No citizen shall be deprived of the opportunity to experience the full range of human consciousness." In the meantime, we may insist that elected officials seriously consider the message behind centuries of market demand for nonmedical use of psychoactive substances.

Because we care about our progeny, we want to leave them better off than we were at their age. However, we cannot predict the exact nature of the threats to their well-being; therefore, "better off" must be something in the way of a generalized attitude to toward life — an attitude characterized by resourcefulness, honesty, resilience, and compassion. These virtues are appropriate not only for the next generation but would serve us well, even now, as we work toward a more enlightened relationship with psychoactive substances that have the power to entertain, comfort, inspire, and kill.

REFERENCES

Bennett, C. C. 1960. The drugs and I. In *Drugs and behavior.* Edited by L. Uhr and J. G. Miller, 596–609. New York: Wiley.

Bozarth, M. A. 1989. New perspectives on cocaine addiction: Recent findings from animal research. *Canadian Journal of Physiology & Pharmacology* 67: 1158–67.

Burglass, M. E. 1985. The use of marijuana and alcohol by regular users of cocaine: Patterns of use and style of control. In *The addictions: Multidisciplinary perspectives and treatments.* Edited by H. B. Milkman and H. J. Shaffer, 111–29. Lexington, Mass.: Heath.

Byard, R. W., J. Gilbert, R. James, and R. J. Lokan. 1998. Amphetamine derivative fatalities in South Australia—is "ecstasy" the culprit? *American Journal of Forensic Medicine and Pathology* 19:261–65.

Castro, F. G., E. H. Barrington, M. A. Walton, and R. A. Rawson. 2000. Cocaine and methamphetamine: Differential addiction rates. *Psychology of Addictive Behaviors* 14:390–96.

Dunham, J. S. 1951. Intravenous alcohol in surgery. *What's New* (Abbott Laboratories) 163:26–28.

Ekwall, B., E. Wallum, and I. Bondesson. 1998. MEIC evaluation of acute systemic toxicity, Part V. *ATLA* (Alternatives to Laboratory Animals) 26:571–616.

European Monitoring Centre for Drugs and Drug Addiction. 2002. *European network to develop policy relevant models and socio-economic analyses of drug use, consequences, and interventions.* Final report, Part 7. Lisboa, Portugal.

Expert Panel. 2003. Abuse liability assessment of CNS drugs: Conclusions, recommendations, and research. *Drug and Alcohol Dependence* 70 (supplement): S107–S114.

Foltin, R. W., M. W. Fischman, and F. R. Levin. 1995. Cardiovascular effects of cocaine in humans: Laboratory studies. *Drug and Alcohol Dependence* 37: 193–210.

Gable, R. S. 1992. Regulatory risk management of psychoactive substances. *Law and Policy* 14:257–75.

———. 2004a. Acute toxic effects of "club drugs." *Journal of Psychoactive Drugs* 36:323–45.

———. 2004b. Comparison of acute lethal toxicity of commonly abused psychoactive substances. *Addiction* 99:686–96.

Gossop, M., P. Griffiths, B. Powis, and J. Strang. 1992. Severity of dependence and route of administration of heroin, cocaine and amphetamines. *British Journal of Addiction* 87:1527–36.

Hall, W., R. Room, and S. Bondy. 1999. Comparing the health and psychological risks of alcohol, cannabis, nicotine and opiate use. In *The Health Effects of Cannabis*. Edited by H. Kalant, W. A. Corrigall, W. Hall, and R. C. Smart, 477–506. Toronto: Centre for Addiction and Mental Health.

Irvine, R. J., M. Keane, P. Felgate, and J. M. White. 2003. Physiological effects, blood biochemistry and "club drug" users at a recreational setting. Abstract. 2003 Meeting of the College on Problems of Drug Dependence, available at biopsych.com:81.cpdd03_webFMpro (accessed April 15, 2004).

Jaffe, J. H., and W. R. Martin. 1990. Opioid analgesics and antagonists. In *Goodman and Gilman's the pharmacological basis of therapeutics*. Edited by A. G. Gilman, T. W. Rall, A. S. Nies, and P. Taylor, 8th ed., 485–501. New York: Pergamon.

James, W. 1958 [1902]. *The varieties of religious experience*. New York: Mentor.

Kozlowski, L. T., D. A. Wilkinson, W. Skinner, C. Kent, T. Franklin, and M. Pope. 1989. Comparing tobacco cigarette dependence with other drug dependencies. *Journal of the American Medical Association* 261:898–901.

Larsen, D. 1996. The Vancouver Harm Reduction Club. *Cannabis Canada: Canada's magazine of cannabis and hemp*, December 20, available at www.hempbc.com (accessed March 8, 2005).

MacCoun, R. J. 1993. Drugs and the law: A psychological analysis of drug prohibition. *Psychological Bulletin* 65:613–28.

Malberg, J. S., and L. S. Seiden. 1998. Small changes in ambient temperature cause large changes in 3,4–methylenedioxymethamphetamine (MDMA)–induced serotonin neurotoxicity and core body temperature in the rat. *Journal of Neurosciences* 18:5086–94.

Manski, C. F., J. V. Pepper, and C. V. Petrie, eds. 2001. *Informing America's policy on illegal drugs*. Washington, D.C.: National Academy Press.

Mello, N. K., and J. H. Mendelson. 1978. Marijuana, alcohol, and polydrug use: Human self-administration studies. In *Self-administration of abused substances*. Edited by N. A. Krasnegor. NIDA monograph 20. Washington, D.C.: National Institute on Drug Abuse.

National Center for Health Statistics. 2004. *Deaths from each cause, by 5-year age groups, race, and sex: United States, 2000*. Hyattsville, Md.: 681–84, 2255–58, 2263–66, available at www.cdc.gov/nchs/datawh/statab/unpubd/mortabs/gmwki/ohtml (accessed April 3, 2004).

Nies, A. S. 1990. Principles of therapeutics. In *Goodman and Gilman's the pharmacological basis of therapeutics*. Edited by A. G. Gilman, T. W. Rall, A. S. Nies and P. Taylor, 8th ed., 115–24. New York: Pergamon.

Repetto, M. R., and M. Repetto. 1997. Habitual, toxic and lethal concentrations of 103 drugs of abuse in humans. *Clinical Toxicology* 35:1–9.

Robinson, V. 1925. *An essay on hasheesh*. New York: Dingwall-Rock.

Schuchard, M. K. 1993. Marijuana: An environmental pollutant. *International Drug Report* 34:3–6. Published by PRIDE (Parents' Resource Institute for Drug Education, Inc.), Atlanta, Ga. (Original source of quotation not cited.)

Schultes, R. E., and A. Hofmann. 1979. *Plants of the gods*. New York: McGraw-Hill.

Shulgin, A. T., and A. Shulgin, 1991. *PIHKAL, a chemical love story.* Berkeley, Calif.: Transform Press.

———. 1997. *TIHKAL, the continuation*. Berkeley, Calif.: Transform Press.

Spillane, J., and W. B. McAllister. 2003. Keeping the lid on: A century of drug regulation and control. *Drug and Alcohol Dependence* 70 (supplement): S5–S12.

Thomas, P. 1989. Prosecuting the U.S. drug war: Hard policy versus soft politics. *Los Angeles Times*, August 20, Section 5, 3.

Vocci, F. J. 1995. Letter to Richard Cowan from deputy director, Medication Development Division, National Institute on Drug Abuse. *Ongoing Briefing* (February 7):4.

8

Proposals for De-Escalating the War on Drugs

Jefferson M. Fish

Too often, the debate over legalization is stopped before it begins by a drug warrior asking combatively, "What about cocaine—especially crack cocaine? And what about heroin? Would you sell them in candy stores?"

This kind of worst-case scenario—or most-difficult-substances scenario—has proven a distraction to attempts at drug policy reform. There is a variety of proposals for a variety of ways to deal with cocaine and heroin—several of them discussed elsewhere in this book—but as far as drug policy is concerned, they are almost beside the point. Not that many people use or want to use them, and considerable progress could be made on scaling-down drug prohibition without even addressing them.

We have seen that our current prohibitionist policy is counterproductive because it creates a huge, crime-ridden black market—so that the more we "get tough on drugs," the worse things get. For this reason, it follows that the more we ease up, and the smaller the black market becomes, the better things will get. Thus, any steps we can take toward de-escalating the War on Drugs should improve matters.

This brief chapter consists of a list of suggestions for initial steps toward drug policy reform without addressing heroin or cocaine. The proposals are arranged in an approximate sequence from the easiest to achieve—where we know there are few potential health and social risks—to those more likely to encounter resistance because of fears of the risks involved in comparison to the benefits of change.

In other words, this chapter offers suggestions that are pragmatic rather than programmatic—first steps toward change, rather than final steps completing it. If we can implement these first steps to discover that matters improve dramatically and that the sky does not fall, then maybe we will have the courage to tackle more controversial substances. And if only a few of these are the best we can do for now, at least we will have succeeded in making the problem somewhat smaller and more manageable.

Legalize Drug Paraphernalia (Including Syringes), and Release Those Imprisoned on Drug-Paraphernalia Charges

Here, one can have a tremendously positive effect on public health and a lesser one on unburdening the criminal justice system without even addressing the controlled substances themselves. Implementing needle-exchange programs and legalizing the purchase of syringes (complete with the means for proper disposal—and penalties for improper disposal) will prevent the spread of AIDS and other diseases. In this way, we can save the lives of countless thousands of drug injectors, their current and future sexual partners, those partners' subsequent partners (and so on), and any children resulting from those unions.

Similarly, water pipes for smoking marijuana or tobacco can remove carcinogenic particulates from those substances and, if more widely used, could cut down on the spread of lung cancer—as could vaporizers that heat marijuana enough to release their volatile substances without actually burning the leaves.

As regards other public health–irrelevant "paraphernalia," the reason for making them legal is simply that they never should have been illegal in the first place. The state has no reason to interfere with the marketplace or to punish those who buy, sell, or own such products. We should reserve our prisons for white-collar criminals, thieves, robbers, muggers, rapists, murderers, and other violent or dangerous people.

Create Legal Means for People to Test Illicit Substances

Most drug "overdoses" result from contamination, adulteration, drug mixtures, and other kinds of false labeling of illicit substances, as well as from unpredictable variations in dosage levels. Such dangers to consumers are rampant in a black market but would become all but nonexistent in a free or regulated market. As long as the black market continues, the health of users could be protected by the creation of legal (or at least legally tolerated) laboratories that could inform people of what they have and warn them of unexpected dangers.

End Involuntary Drug Testing, Except Where Public Safety Is Involved

People have a right to their private lives and not to have their physical integrity violated by government or employers examining their breath, blood, urine, or other bodily products or body parts. Any consequences people suffer at work should be related to their job performance and not to private actions in their personal lives.

Replace "Driving While Intoxicated" Laws with "Driving While Impaired" Laws

The principle here is the same as the one regarding nondiscrimination in the workplace. That is, the criteria used for making decisions should be performance based and directly relevant to the behavior involved. The various legal and illegal substances that affect driving by altering perception, coordination, judgment, or other relevant factors do so in different ways and at different dosage levels and affect different individuals differently. Furthermore, these substances cease to have measurable behavioral effects after differing periods of time that do not correspond to the length of time they are detectable by drug testing. For example, traces of marijuana can be detected days after it ceases to have any behavioral effects. In contrast, sleep-deprived drivers are a menace on the roads and are responsible for accidents, injuries, and death on a large scale, despite being free from psychoactive substances.

With modern technology, it is easy for police to film drivers' performance on behavioral tests. It would also be easy to create driving-simulation programs for equipment attached to laptop computers, and these could become standard issue for patrol cars. Police could use such devices to gather evidence that would measure a driver's performance objectively. The use of "driving while impaired" laws would check government's prurient interest in the contents of citizens' bodily fluids and restrict enforcement to the domain of their dangerous behavior.

Along these lines, laws should be aimed at encouraging drivers to pull over to the side of the road as soon as they realize they are impaired. Whether they have become sleepy, or ill, or have belatedly noticed the effects of some substance, if they have not yet done harm and have taken themselves out of action voluntarily, they should not be penalized.

Scale the Classification of and Penalties for Any Prohibited Substances According to Scientific Data

Quite separately from consideration of making prohibited substances legal, the internal coherence of prohibition itself should be addressed. As Robert Gable illustrates in chapter 7, the undesirable properties of illegal substances—which presumably are why they are prohibited—bear little relationship to penalties for their use. While it may be a bad idea to criminalize the use of a psychoactive substance to the extent that we do so, we should still, in the words of Gilbert and Sullivan, "make the punishment fit the crime." Thus, we need to assure that legal classifications of substances are consistent with scientific ones so that more severe penalties are not imposed for less harmful substances or—as the next suggestion posits—for alternative forms of the same substance.

Equalize Any Penalties for a Prohibited Substance for All Its Forms (e.g., the Same Penalty for Equal Amounts of Cocaine in the Form of Powder or Crack)

This suggestion, which flows logically from the previous one, offers an opportunity to remedy a great injustice. By making the penalties for crack cocaine (preferred by inner-city blacks) many times as severe as the penalties for powdered cocaine (preferred by suburban whites), we have packed our jails with young black men and destroyed virtually an entire generation of minority youth. That false, racist stereotypes (black men high on crack brutalizing whites; black women giving birth to crack babies) were used to secure passage of such laws only makes matters worse. Equal justice under law is a basic principle; if cocaine possession remains illegal, then penalties should correspond to the amount of the drug seized, regardless of the form it is in. This principle should apply to all illegal substances.

Legalize the Medical Use of Marijuana and Other Controlled Substances

Marijuana has many medical benefits with virtually no costs, and it is unconscionable that so many people should suffer unnecessarily because it is illegal. However, many other controlled substances also have important medical uses. Perhaps the best example is the undertreatment of pain because physicians are afraid to prescribe adequate dosages of opiates for fear of losing their licenses. As the population ages, increasing numbers of people will suffer painful or debilitating ailments. These citizens vote, and they will not tolerate the government denying them medication. The passage of medical-marijuana initiatives in many states suggests that the voters may already have lost patience with politicians on this issue.

End Mandatory Minimum Sentences and the Confiscation of Property for Possession of Illegal Substances

Even during the depths of Prohibition, possession of alcohol (as opposed to manufacturing or distributing it) was never a crime. We have been filling up the prisons with nonviolent noncriminals on mandatory minimum sentences and releasing violent criminals to make room for them. Meanwhile, allowing law enforcement to seize for its own use the assets of people who have illegal drugs undermines the Bill of Rights, corrupts and delegitimizes the police power of the state, and encourages predatory drug busts for economic gain. Finally, the misallocation of resources required to implement this disastrous policy has led us to build prisons instead of schools and to destroy rather than build the futures of large numbers of our youth.

If penalties cannot immediately be done away with for possession of psychoactive substances, then at least they should be considerably reduced—and judges should be given great latitude to determine what punishment, if any, is appropriate—as a first step toward limiting the damage.

Legalize the Use of Drugs in Established Religious and Cultural Practices

One of the wonders of America is its ability to tolerate, accept, learn from, and assimilate huge numbers of immigrants from all over the planet. While ethnic hatred and genocide continue elsewhere, we have managed to cope with unprecedented diversity (if not always with good humor) by simply recognizing that "different" does not necessarily mean "bad" or "dangerous." Thus, in our drug policy, we should recognize that well-established religious and cultural practices that differ from those of the mainstream must be legitimized in the area of substance use as in other areas. Three common examples are the use of marijuana by Rastafarians from the British West Indies, the chewing of coca leaves and drinking of coca tea by Bolivians, Peruvians, and other immigrants from South America's Alteplano, and the religious use of peyote by members of the Native American Church. Criminalizing these normal, even sacred, practices among culturally different groups is a recipe for ethnic strife.

Legalize Marijuana in a Manner Similar to Alcohol and Tobacco

No one has ever died from a marijuana overdose; yet, the War on Drugs is primarily a war against marijuana. Legalizing marijuana, taxing it, and releasing from prison those who are there solely for its possession would instantly replace huge government expenditures with an important long-term revenue stream, end the shortage of prison space, free up funds for drug treatment, and raise the possibility that consumers seeking intoxication might choose marijuana over the much more dangerous alcohol.

One politically feasible way to go about legalizing marijuana would be to make it subject to the limitations placed on cigarettes and alcohol, whichever are more restrictive. Thus, it would only be sold to those at the older legal age for the other two substances (eighteen or twenty-one), and in the more restrictive location (e.g., liquor stores). Restrictions on advertising, especially advertising to children (as for both alcohol and cigarettes), smoking in public places (as for cigarettes), and on disruptive intoxicated public behavior or driving dangerously while intoxicated (as for alcohol) would also apply. Adults should, however, be allowed to grow the plant for their own consumption.

This tenth suggestion is the first one that actually addresses legalizing a currently illegal substance. If the most change that is workable in our current drug policy goes only as far as to implement these ten suggestions, then the dimensions of the "drug problem" and the "drug war" will have been scaled back from a self-made catastrophe to a serious issue requiring serious changes. Nevertheless, there is room for additional changes that fall short of the more controversial legalization of cocaine and heroin.

Legalize Minimally Processed Coca

Because of the long experience of Andean cultures with chewing coca leaves and drinking coca tea, it is reasonable to assume that Americans can also learn to use minimally processed coca in a responsible manner. (KDrink, produced by Kokka Royal Food and Drink in Peru, is a recent example of a beverage with a slight coca content.) As chapter 3 indicates, Prohibition pushed us from being beer drinkers to whiskey drinkers, and we returned gradually to beer after the end of that era. In a similar way, it is likely that the much lower dosage levels in coca leaves, along with the possible modifying effects of other substances in the leaves, will satisfy much of the public's curiosity and demand. In other words, legal coca leaves would offer consumers a way to experience the plant's stimulant properties without the risks associated with processed cocaine—as was the case when we drank the original Coca Cola. Over time, therefore, a trend away from powdered cocaine and crack—and toward coca leaves—would be expected to develop.

Legalize Psilocybin Mushrooms

As Robert Gable indicates in chapter 7, psilocybin is the lowest risk hallucinogen; as with coca leaves, legalizing the substance in its unprocessed form should also help to hold down dosage levels. Making psilocybin mushrooms legal should reduce demand for other, less predictable, hallucinogens.

Legalize MDMA ("Ecstasy")

As with psilocybin mushrooms, legalizing MDMA would be another way of allowing less dangerous substances into the marketplace so that few people would be willing to take the risk of using those substances that remain illegal. An important point about MDMA is that it is a synthetic substance. With the rapid growth of knowledge in the life sciences and pharmacology, it is inevitable that new psychoactive substances will be invented. Thus, if we wish to keep some substances illegal (and suffer the black market consequences of that policy), we need to be able to distinguish the less dangerous ones from the more dangerous ones and prohibit only the latter. No substance is risk free — every year many people die from bleeding ulcers caused by aspirin, and alcohol kills people by attacking the liver, brain, and other organs.

Decriminalize Possession of Small Amounts of All Substances and Release Those Imprisoned for only This Reason

This last proposal would not go so far as to legalize substances like cocaine and heroin. As such, it would leave their black markets intact, with all their attendant ills. Nevertheless, by reducing the penalties for possession for personal use of any substances that remain illegal to the level of a parking ticket — or a speeding ticket — we would cease packing our prisons with noncriminals.

In implementing this proposal, we can take our guidance from medicine's guiding principle: do no harm. People who use psychoactive substances in the privacy of their own homes should be of no interest to the police.

In addition, I would like to make three other general proposals, also aimed at moving us in the direction of a more rational and humane drug policy.

Increase the Supply of Factual Information and Stop the Use of Scare Tactics

Much is known about the positive and negative effects of legal and illegal psychoactive substances, and that information should be made widely available to the public. The kinds of scientifically accurate warning labels on tobacco and alcohol products should be extended to caffeine products (e.g., concerning withdrawl symptoms and risks for ulcers, anxiety attacks, and insomnia). Any additional substances that are legalized should also have labels warning of the scientifically documented dangers they pose. In addition, because there is a limit to the amount of information that can be put on a label and to the amount that many consumers might be willing to read, it should be made extremely easy for those who are interested to obtain more extensive information. For example, stores could keep information sheets, like inserts currently included with prescription drugs, on hand for free distribution to customers who request them. In addition, the label for each substance — including tobacco, alcohol, and caffeine—could list an Internet address where one could download such information, as well as a toll-free telephone number that one could call to obtain the information for free (e.g., by return mail).

Clear, accurate, and personally relevant information benefits consumers, while scare tactics and false information are counterproductive. They lead to a loss of respect for official sources of drug information and to the inaccurate belief that if official information about drugs is untrue, then illegal substances must be safe after all. We must put an end to propaganda (e.g., a fried egg is your brain on drugs) and misinformation (e.g., all drugs and dosage levels are the same; all use equals abuse), which undermine critical thinking. Instead, by providing factual knowledge and encouraging thoughtful debate, we can help citizens to make informed decisions about an important area of their private lives.

End Coercive "Treatment" (e.g., Therapy or Jail) and Increase the Availability of Therapy and Medical Care for Substance Abusers Who Request Them

To begin with, coercive "treatment" does not work, and its failure has given all drug treatment a bad reputation, despite the fact that voluntary treatment often does succeed. However, even if it did work, coercive treatment should be ended because it undermines the institution of therapy and the honesty, trust, and confidentiality on which it is based. In coercive treatment, clients must pretend to participate in therapy in order to avoid punishment; therapists must pretend to be working for their clients when they are really agents of the state; therapists must lie (or deceive themselves) about their clients' motivation and progress in order to get paid; and therapists must break confidentiality to inform on their clients. Such therapy is a sham. Mental-health professionals who participate in it because they need to earn a living or because they really want to help substance abusers find themselves and their professional ideals corrupted by drug prohibition. The corrosive effects of the War on Drugs pervade the mental health system as well as the criminal-justice system.

In the topsy-turvy world of drug prohibition, some who are caught using proscribed substances—whether or not they are abusing them—may be forced into treatment, even though they do not want it. Usually, these are affluent white people whom the criminal justice system forces to pay a "fine" in the form of lawyers' fees and therapists' fees to avoid going to jail. On the other hand, there is a shortage of treatment available for those substance abusers who truly want to change, especially if they are poor. Such people are often in poor physical health, may have contagious diseases, and can profit from medical care as well as therapy. Treating such people promotes the public health as well as their own and is much cheaper than incarcerating them. Even when therapy fails, society is much better off with such people in their midst than with comparable others who have learned to become criminals in prison.

Legalize in a Way That Is Considerate of the Feelings of Those Opposed to Legalization

In contrast to the behavior of drug warriors, who have prided themselves on their intolerance (as evidenced by slogans like "Zero Tolerance"), it is important to show concern for the sensibilities of others, while protecting the rights of individuals to make their own personal decisions regarding psychoactive substances. For example, alcohol is legal, but drinking in public is not. This is because such behavior offends teetotalers and parents who do not want their children to see it, among others. In the same way, legalizing the use of currently restricted substances can be done in such a way as to minimize the affront to those who find it offensive. Limiting such use to the privacy of people's homes or to places with restricted access, like bars, and prohibiting public intoxicated behavior from whatever substance would protect the sensibilities of those who oppose legalization for whatever reason.

While adopting even a few of these proposals would make matters significantly better, adopting all of them—without legalizing heroin or cocaine—would leave the remaining problems so small that the social issue would largely be solved. (One might also have to legalize newly invented substances from time to time.)

It may well be desirable to find a [ ] galize heroin and cocaine (at least for chronic abusers and under p[ ] lth supervision) so as to minimize or destroy these black markets [ ] be all for it if we could do so, but major change does not require it

9

Economics of Illegal Drug Markets:
What Happens If We Downsize the Drug War?

Mary M. Cleveland

An economic analysis of the illegal drug markets suggests that if the U.S. drug war were downsized (by cutting back interdiction efforts, targeting primarily large or violent dealers, and reducing severity of punishments), the following would happen:

1. *Prices would fall, marijuana prices more than hard-drug prices.* There would be some increase in casual use, especially of marijuana, and a shift to marijuana away from cocaine, heroin, and possibly alcohol.
2. *The black market sales volume would increase, but the number of dealers would decrease.* At present, probably a majority of regular illegal-drug users also deal part-time to help pay for their own use; the lower the price, the fewer who would deal.
3. *The black market would become less dangerous.* Small, teenage dealers would be replaced by larger, less-violent, adult dealers.
4. *The number of problem drug users would probably not increase, but their per capita consumption might increase dramatically.* Problem users who survive by petty theft would probably not steal less if drug prices declined but simply consume more.

Defenders of drug prohibition make a straightforward supply-and-demand argument: Legalization, or any lessening of aggressive enforcement, will lower the high cost of drugs, in terms of price, risk of arrest, severe punishment, and social opprobrium. Consequently, drug abuse will skyrocket. According to Dr. Herbert Kleber, medical director of the Columbia Center on Addiction and Substance Abuse, and former deputy to William Bennett, drug czar under President Reagan,

There are over 50 million nicotine addicts, 18 million alcoholics or problem drinkers, and fewer than 2 million cocaine addicts in the United States. Cocaine is a much more addictive drug than alcohol. If cocaine were legally available, as alcohol and nicotine are now, the number of cocaine abusers would probably rise to a point somewhere between the number of users of the other two agents, perhaps 20 to 25 million . . . [and] the number of compulsive users might be nine times higher . . . than the current number. (1994, 16)

This is a tough challenge to answer. None of us can accurately predict the future; fear of the unknown often makes us rather bear those ills we have than fly to others that we know not of.

Table 9.1. **Prohibitionist Assumptions about Drugs versus Alternative Assumptions**

Prohibitionist Assumptions	Alternative Assumptions
Illicit drugs are all extremely dangerous and addictive. Marijuana is a "gateway" to hard drugs.	Licit and illicit drugs vary greatly in danger and addictiveness. Most marijuana users do not go on to hard drugs.
All use of illicit drugs or underage use of licit drugs like alcohol is "abuse" —assumed to be individually and socially destructive. This assumption is built into official language, such as the U.S. Department of Health and Human Services' "National Household Survey on Drug Abuse."	Most use is not abuse. Drug users, like alcohol drinkers, fall naturally into three categories: a small proportion of problem users, a larger proportion of regular users, and a majority consisting of casual users. Problem users are equivalent to (and often also are) alcoholics. Regular users, like regular drinkers, control the quantity and timing of use so as not to disrupt work or a normal family life.
The addictive properties of illicit drugs cause "abuse." Perfectly normal young people who try drugs are liable to become hooked. By implication, the number of abusers is proportional to the availability and addictiveness of a drug.	Drug and alcohol abuse are symptoms of underlying emotional problems, although substance abuse may make those problems harder to treat. By implication, the number of abusers is proportional to the number of troubled people.
Illicit drugs cause crime, driving users to violent behavior and to theft to support addiction.	While a majority of violent or property-stealing criminals use and/or deal illicit drugs, most illicit drug users do not commit any non-drug-related crimes.
Cost and access are major determinants of illicit drug use.	Personal tastes and social norms are usually more important than cost or access.

However, predictions derived by economic logic depend on the underlying assumptions about reality; change the assumptions, and the predictions change too. Defenders of prohibition make one set of assumptions; critics, myself included, make other assumptions. Table 9.1 briefly paraphrases prohibitionist assumptions, contrasted with alternative assumptions.

Section I of this chapter surveys some evidence supporting the alternative set of assumptions. Section II applies some basic economic principles to these assumptions. Section III examines some policy implications.

THE PRESENT DRUG SITUATION IN THE UNITED STATES

Properties of Licit and Illicit Drugs

If both licit and illicit drugs vary greatly in danger, addictiveness, and other properties, one might expect stricter drug-control policies for more dangerous substances. Appendix 9A reviews the properties of major legal and illegal drugs and the types and harms of drug use. Table 9A.1 provides two rough rankings of three licit and three illicit drugs (see Appendix 9A). Both rankings put alcohol near the top with heroin, and cocaine and marijuana near the bottom with caffeine. If these rankings are valid, they cast doubt on the prohibitionist assumption that illicit drugs are so much more dangerous than licit drugs as to require "zero tolerance."

Patterns of Licit and Illicit Drug Use in the United States

Table 9.2 is compiled from the 2002 National Survey on Drug Use and Health, published annually by the U.S. Public Health Service. It summarizes a survey of use for alcohol, cigarettes, and five categories of illicit drugs. Respondents were polled as to whether they had ever used, used in last year, and used in the last month.

These figures surely understate illicit drug use, both because respondents may be unwilling to admit illegal activity, even in total confidence, and because some of the heaviest illicit drug users are in jail or homeless. Nonetheless, a few points stand out:

- Use of alcohol and cigarettes is many times the use of illicit drugs.
- Use of the "soft" drug marijuana is many times the use of "hard" drugs cocaine and heroin. Some 95 million adults—about 40 percent of the adult population—admit to having tried marijuana; some 34 million admit to having tried cocaine; some 3.7 million admit to having tried

Table 9.2. National Survey on Drug Use and Health: Population Estimates 2002 (in thousands)

Use Substance	Ever	Percent Ever*	Last Year	Percent in Last Year	Last Month	Percent in Last Month
Alcohol	195,452	83.1	155,476	66.1	119,820	51
Tobacco	171,838	73.1	84,731	36.07	71,499	30.4
Total illicit	108,255	46	35,132	14.9	19,522	8.3
Marijuana	94,946	40.4	25,755	11	14,584	6.2
Cocaine	33,910	14.4	5,902	2.5	2,020	0.9
Inhalants	22,870	9.7	2,084	0.9	635	0.3
Stimulants	21,072	9	3,181	1.4	1,218	0.5
Tranquilizers	19,267	8.2	4,849	2.1	1,804	0.8
Sedatives	9,960	4.2	981	0.4	436	0.2
Heroin	3,668	1.6	404	0.2	166	0.1

* Percent of population twelve years and older

Source: Substance Abuse and Mental Health Services Administration, Office of Applied Studies, U.S. Department of Health and Human Services, Public Health Service, Rockville, MD 20857.

heroin. Clearly, only a small proportion of marijuana users go on to try cocaine or heroin, let alone become addicted.

- Licit substances used illicitly constitute a major portion of "abuse." Right after cocaine come inhalants, that is, gasoline, glue, laughing gas, amyl nitrate, and other legal substances. (Inhalants are used primarily by children, who lack access to more serious intoxicants.) Next in magnitude are stimulants, mostly amphetamines. Then come prescription tranquilizers and sedatives used without a prescription.
- Only a small portion of those who have tried illicit drugs still use them; a much larger portion of those who have ever used alcohol and cigarettes still use them.

Three Kinds of Drug Users

Users of drugs—licit or illicit—fall naturally into three rough categories: casual users, regular users, and abusers. Since the term "abuser" is so often applied to all users of illicit drugs, I generally use the less ambiguous term "problem user" for the third category.

- *Casual users or experimenters:* These include light or social drinkers and people who may try drugs when offered by a friend. These also include teenage "beginners." Casual users are largest in number but account for only a small fraction of drug volume.
- *Regular users:* Regular users of alcohol drink daily after work; some may binge on weekends. Regular illegal drug users follow a similar pat-

tern. Regulars lead normal lives, maintaining jobs, families, friends, and health. They consider drug use as a form of relaxation or recreation. Regular users of illegal—or legal—drugs enjoy them and usually share them with friends. Most regular users of illegal drugs also deal them to pay for their own use.

- *Problem users:* Unlike regular users, problem users characteristically feel worthless and hopeless. Their lives may become an obsessive pursuit of hard drugs, alcohol, or both at the expense of jobs, family, friends, and health. They may try repeatedly to stop; every failure makes them feel yet more worthless and hopeless. Unless supported by family, extreme problem users lead a degrading, hand-to-mouth existence. They may survive by panhandling, scavenging, prostitution, odd jobs, petty theft, public assistance, or mooching from relatives and friends. Problem users of illegal drugs rarely deal; no distributor would trust them with drugs on consignment. Many are so-called polydrug abusers, consuming whatever intoxicants are available at the moment, often in combination. Though smallest in number, problem users account for the greatest volume of alcohol or drug consumption. They are also the most likely to suffer from disease due to contaminated needles or to die from overdoses.

Table 9.2 shows clearly that the harder the drug, the fewer the users and the smaller the percentage more frequent users make up of the total users. Assuming that the "Last Month" category includes all regular and problem users, then regular and problem users make up no more of the "Ever" category than 61 percent for alcohol, 15 percent for marijuana, 6 percent for cocaine, and 4.5 percent for heroin. There are no reliable estimates of what proportion of total consumption each group accounts for. However, in accordance with usual patterns of distribution, it's reasonable to assume that the top 20 percent of consumers account for some 80 percent of the consumption of each drug.

As suggested by the relatively small proportion of problem users, as well as by abundant sociological and psychological research (Peele 2004), drugs do not cause problem drug use. Rather, problem drug use is a symptom of the way people feel about themselves and their situation: that they are no good, unlovable, or incompetent ("worthless") and that they have no future and no control over their lives ("hopeless"). To ill-educated, poor people coming from abusive homes, or no homes, such feelings may seem to have powerful objective justification. Of course, the consequences of initial nonproblem drug use, such as rejection by family, expulsion from school, or imprisonment for drug possession, may exacerbate feelings of worthlessness and hopelessness, leading to full-blown problem drug use.

In 1995, the *New York Times* interviewed Dr. Jack Block, the director of a major ongoing longitudinal study of several hundred children in Oakland, California. Block reported,

> [W]hen the teenagers reached 18 . . . not all adolescent drug use boded a grim future. In this study, those teenagers who had experimented with drugs like marijuana during their teenage years—compared both to those who used them heavily and those who abstained—were the best adjusted. The teenagers who used drugs most frequently were the most alienated, had the poorest impulse control and the most emotional distress, while those who had never tried any drugs were the most anxious, emotionally constricted and socially inept. . . . Dr. Block's conclusion was that [problem] drug use is a symptom of maladjustment, not a cause, and that it can best be understood in the context of the larger course of life. (Goleman 1995a; Shedler and Block 1990)

Problem drug use is but one form of harmful behavior associated with feelings of hopelessness and worthlessness. Other forms include eating disorders like anorexia, compulsive gambling, and obsession with sex. These disorders respond to good counseling, often combined with antidepressant medication, to help people feel they can control their lives (Beck 1993; Peele 2004).

Drug Dealers

Legal dealers. Dealers of legal drugs, of course, are all respectable adults: liquor- and tobacco-industry members, shopkeepers, and bar and restaurant owners.

Illegal dealers. The greatest difference between legal and illegal dealers is volume. Retail alcohol and tobacco markets are supplied by relatively few, high-volume dealers. In the United States, the retail illegal drug markets are supplied by a guerrilla army of small dealers, most of them temporary, part-time, unsophisticated, and generally unprofessional in their business conduct. There are three major categories of small dealers: user-dealers, juvenile dealers, and "mules."

User-dealers. Most illegal dealers, from kingpins on down, are regular users. Retail user-dealers generally do not sell much beyond the amount necessary to pay for their own use. They sell drugs wherever they go or wherever they can: at work, at school, at parties. As a last resort, the poorest of them sell on the streets, exposed to arrest and violence from other dealers. A 1990 RAND study of drug economics in Washington, D.C., for 1985 to 1988, when the crack cocaine market was just beginning, estimated that one-sixth to one-third of young black men (ages eighteen to twenty-four) in Washington, D.C., or about twenty-four thousand men, sold drugs at the street level part-time or full-time. Two-thirds of these men also held low-paying jobs, averaging $7 an hour. They sold drugs primarily on evenings or weekends, when the market was active. The study found that few of these men made much money at this activity; they simply covered the cost of their own use and often spent some of their earned money in addition (Reuter, MacCoun, and Murphy 1990).

Juvenile dealers. In the United States at least, there is another important category of low-level dealer besides the user-dealers: nonusing juveniles, teenagers and preteenagers, mostly boys, recruited to the drug trade by older siblings, relatives, friends, or neighborhood gangs. Some of these youngsters are coerced into the business; others are attracted by what seems like easy money. In addition, as juveniles, they face relatively low penalties if arrested. Most of these juvenile dealers will eventually become users.

Mules. Mules are ordinary persons not regularly in the drug trade, who are occasionally recruited to transport large quantities of drugs precisely because they do not appear suspicious. Despite their peripheral involvement, mules face the heaviest sentences when caught since penalties depend on the weight of drugs and mules have little or no information to use in bargaining with prosecutors.

Drugs and Crime

The War on Drugs is often justified as a crime-control measure. In fact, the war may generate more crime than it controls. The relationship between drugs and crime is well reviewed by David Rasmussen and Bruce Benson in their book *The Economic Anatomy of a Drug War* (1994) and their report *Illicit Drugs and Crime* (1996). In brief:

Illicit drug use and crime. A large majority of those who commit violent and property crimes are also illicit drug users and small dealers. However, the converse does not hold. Most illicit drug users do not commit violent or property crimes. This is also clear from table 9.2: some 108 million people, 46 percent of the American adult population, admit to using illicit drugs at some time; 19.5 million admit using in the last month.

Drugs and violent crime. Alcohol is the only drug consistently associated with violent behavior performed "under the influence." Most "drug-related" violence arises in turf battles between rival dealers (Goldstein 1989).

Drugs and property crime. Both proponents and many opponents of drug prohibition agree that drug addicts must steal to get drug money. Proponents and opponents of prohibition draw opposite policy conclusions. Proponents advocate stricter and more punitive enforcement of drug laws on the grounds that making drugs unavailable and locking away addicts will lower property crime. Opponents argue that ending prohibition will bring down hard-drug prices so that addicts would not need to steal.

If drugs do not "cause" property crime, then both policy prescriptions will fail.

First, as noted, most drug users do not steal. They buy drugs with their own money. Consequently, a general war on drug users diverts scarce criminal justice resources from the pursuit and imprisonment of property and violent offenders. Rasmussen and Benson present statistics from Florida showing how the drug war in Florida from 1984 to 1989 resulted in the early release of non-drug offenders from overcrowded prisons and an increase in property and violent crime as police shifted their efforts toward the apprehension of drug offenders (Rasmussen and Benson 1994, 2003). An economic analysis of crime and drug statistics in New York City reached essentially the same conclusion, namely, that "increased law enforcement is a more effective method of crime prevention in comparison to efforts targeted at drug use." (Corman and Mocan 2000).

Second, sociological evidence indicates that most individuals first engage in criminal activities, including theft, as juveniles, *a year or two before they become drug users* (Reuter, MacCoun, and Murphy 1990). Often, of course, these are the same juveniles who are recruited as lookouts and runners for the illegal drug trade. Through the drug trade, they come into regular contact with older, confirmed property criminals. Thus, to the extent that the War on Drugs creates enticing criminal opportunities for juveniles, it may draw them into lives of nondrug crime.

Finally, down-and-out hard drug addicts steal as part of the degraded lifestyle of problem users. Too disturbed to be employable, they steal to survive and get high to make a miserable life briefly more bearable. A more punitive approach will not deter them. It will more likely confirm their degraded status. Nor will a fall in drug prices deter them. On the contrary, lower drug prices may make theft more rewarding by allowing them to purchase more drugs for their money!

Drugs, Personal Preferences, and Social Norms

Defenders of current drug prohibition argue that the fall in drug prices following legalization or even after some slackening of enforcement would lead to a large increase in drug "abuse." This claim rests on the standard prohibitionist assumption that all use is abuse and the further assumption that price is a major consideration for most users or would-be users. Prohibition defenders also argue that the drug war, besides punishing users and dealers, sends a message condemning drug use. By "sends a message," they presumably mean that it affects individual views, or "personal preferences," and shared group views, or "social norms."

I believe that the evidence shows that, as with most consumption, personal preferences and social norms influence most people more than the price of drugs. (As I show later, price *is* important to down-and-out problem users.) As for the "message" claim, the antidrug message may well have had a powerful impact on social norms—the norms of people who have little knowledge of or contact with drugs and therefore support the drug war. The message does not appear to have reached actual drug users. As many advertisers discover to their dismay, preferences cannot be manipulated at will, and norms have a way of taking off into unexpected fads and fashions. Moreover, norms are often specific to small groups in special circumstances, hard to influence from the outside.

Here are some examples of the power of personal preferences and social norms in determining drug use.

Alcohol has always been far more popular than other intoxicants in Western culture. This was true in the early twentieth century before Prohibition, when opiates and cocaine were legal and widely available. In several European countries and in Australia, actual, or de facto, decriminalization of possession has not produced any significant increase in drug use; alcohol remains king. Jeffrey Miron and Jeffrey Zwiebel (1991) estimate that while total alcohol consumption fell to 30 percent of prior levels at the beginning of Prohibition, it soon rose again to 60 or 70 percent, then remained stable through the end of Prohibition and for ten years afterward, rising again in the 1940s. (The failure of consumption levels to rise immediately may be due to the Depression.) In any case, serious alcohol drinkers quickly found their way around Prohibition.

Thousands of GIs became addicted to high-grade opium while serving in Vietnam. Despite fears of an explosion in opiate addiction, most quickly and easily kicked the habit on returning to the United States (Robins 1973). Why? It may have been acceptable to get stoned while sweltering in a bug-infested jungle camp, waiting for an invisible enemy, but the social norms of the communities to which the GIs returned did not tolerate opiate use, and the GIs themselves had better things to do.

According to a July 1995 *New York Times* series (Verhovek 1995), illegal drugs are easily and cheaply available in U.S. prisons, smuggled in by prisoners' relatives and corrupt guards. At one prison, drugs are so cheap that prisoners actually export them for sale outside. Imprisonment does not stop people who want drugs badly enough, and imprisonment without treatment does not deter problem drug users. If anything, it makes them feel more hopeless and more prone to drug use.

The Center on Addiction and Substance Abuse (CASA) at Columbia University issued the *National Survey of American Attitudes on Substance Abuse* (CASA 1995, 88). Among other findings, 30 percent of sixth through twelfth graders surveyed stated that it was easy to obtain cocaine or heroin; yet, 82 percent reported that none of their circle of friends used hard drugs, and another 13 percent reported that "less than half" used them, leaving only 5 percent reporting "more than half." The CASA survey does not distinguish between regular use and occasional experimentation, so even the 5 percent greatly overstates hard-drug use.

Problem substance users take intoxicants to escape feelings of worthlessness and hopelessness. Changes in the price of those intoxicants may affect the quantity and combination consumed but not the underlying feelings. Effective drug treatment relies on changing problem users' attitudes: convincing them that they have worth and dignity as individuals, that their situation is not hopeless, and that they can in fact control drug use that threatens their health, their jobs, their families, or other valuable parts of their lives (Beck 1993).

To summarize: Most people choose not to use illicit drugs even when they have cheap and easy access to them. Enforcement can have some effect on light users; regular and problem users will get their drugs even in prison. Drug treatment and changes in social norms have far more influence on drug use than enforcement because they affect individuals' attitudes.

ECONOMIC IMPLICATIONS OF DRUG POLICY CHANGES

In addition to their assumptions about drugs, prohibition supporters make two crucial assumptions about policy; critics make alternative assumptions (see table 9.3).

The following are seven possible options for change in drug policy:

1. We can give up foreign drug eradication and interdiction efforts, primarily in Latin America, which studies by the RAND Institute and others indicate have a negligible impact on domestic prices and the availability of illicit drugs.
2. We can scale back and restructure domestic enforcement to concentrate efforts on major traffickers and violent dealers, ignoring small user-dealers and ordinary users as long as they remain discreet and nonviolent. This is generally the practice in Europe, Canada, Australia, and some U.S. localities, notably San Francisco, California.

Table 9.3.   Prohibitionist Assumptions about Policy versus Alternative Assumptions

Prohibitionist Assumptions	*Alternative Assumptions*
A drug-free America is a realistic political objective to be pursued by a strategy of zero tolerance for drugs and drug users.	Aiming for a drug-free America is not just unrealistic but cuts off sophisticated consideration of alternative objectives and trade-offs among those objectives. A zero-tolerance policy in practice fosters ineffective deployment of resources, notably going first for the easy targets: small street-level dealers or marijuana smokers.
We have only two choices of policy: prohibition or legalization.	In reality, we can choose among a huge range of policy options along many dimensions. Policy options include not only actual laws but enforcement strategies and—a crucial reality often ignored by noneconomists—the allocation of limited resources among those strategies.

3. We can reduce penalties for drug possession or dealing, in particular the long, mandatory-minimum prison sentences that a 1997 RAND study has shown to be both costly and ineffective in deterring drug dealers (Caulkins et al. 1997). We can reduce or eliminate penalties for possession and shift from prison sentences to fines. We can eliminate property forfeitures.

4. We can provide treatment to problem users who seek it, including easy access to methadone for opiate addicts. We can provide clean needles and other health care to those who do not seek treatment.

5. We can provide better educational opportunities and counseling, including "big brother" and "big sister" programs, to disadvantaged children who are most at risk of becoming problem users or dealers.

6. We can replace drug "education" designed to frighten children and their parents with drug education that conveys accurate information about the characteristics and risks of different legal and illegal drugs.

7. We can follow some of the European decriminalization, legalization, and medicalization experiments or design our own. Many Western countries, including Great Britain, Germany, and Italy, treat possession of small quantities of drugs as a minor offense or no offense at all. For over twenty-five years, the Dutch have allowed adults to purchase small quantities of cannabis in "coffee shops."

The first three changes amount to a retreat from aggressive, indiscriminate prohibition enforcement. In practice, these changes would mean a return toward earlier U.S. policies, before President Nixon declared war on drugs in the late 1960s. I call such a change "downsizing the drug war" to indicate not only a smaller but a more cost-effective endeavor.

The second three changes—improved treatment, prevention, and education—simply expand on programs already sporadically implemented in some localities. A 1994 RAND study, financed by the U.S. Army (!), estimated that additional spending on treatment would reduce cocaine consumption by seven times as much as additional spending on domestic enforcement (Rydell and Everingham 1994b).

Only the last change—experimenting with extensive decriminalization, legalization, or medicalization—goes beyond policies with which we have direct experience in the United States. I refer to these as "experimental policies," to indicate that they are not well tested and encompass a wide range of possibilities.

In the discussion that follows, I focus on the consequences of downsizing the drug war for two reasons. First, it is hard to imagine the implementation of experimental policies in the United States without prior changes in criminal justice, health care, and education. Second, when prohibition defenders predict the consequences of legalization, they seem actually to describe—inaccurately, I believe—the consequences of a large, poorly controlled black market. Prohibition critics hope that the experimental policies they advocate will shrink and control the black market.

All else being equal, downsizing the drug war would accelerate the long-term trend of falling black market prices and increasing purity and availability of illicit drugs. However, we cannot simply assume, as prohibition defenders do, that such downsizing would automatically produce an explosion in drug abuse. As suggested above, for most people under most circumstances, the price and availability of illicit drugs are at best a minor consideration. The consequences of downsizing are complex and not obvious—and can be affected strongly by simultaneous changes in other policies.

In the rest of this section, I apply basic economic principles to suggest the consequences of downsizing the drug war. In the final section, I briefly address experimental policies.

Impact of Downsizing on Dangerousness of Drugs

Downsizing the drug war will shift consumption to less potent and dangerous drugs. The combination of two useful economic principles explains why.

1. *High transportation and transaction costs screen out low-value goods.* Only the best California artichokes get shipped to New York. It does not pay to ship average- or low-quality ones. During Prohibition (1920–1933), beer and wine were not worth smuggling. Bootleggers concentrated on hard liquor, including 120 proof liquor, which had a high ratio of value to transportation cost. Only the finest wines made it to the tables of the rich. After Prohibition, beer and wine soon dominated the alcohol market again, and high-proof hard liquor disappeared. Today, the cost and risk of drug smuggling shift the mix of available drugs toward highly concentrated heroin and cocaine, or designer drugs, and away from less-potent drugs, especially from bulky, odorous marijuana. Put another way, while drug prohibition raises the cost of all illegal drugs, it disproportionately raises the cost of milder drugs, especially marijuana. *Downsizing the drug war will lower the cost of marijuana more than that of hard drugs.*

2. *People constantly make trade-offs.* All else being equal, people who want to get high will do so in ways that offer the fewest dangers and side effects. Most drinkers choose beer and wine over hard liquor. Intravenous drug users choose clean needles if they can get them (Goleman 1995b). Opiate users sniff heroin or even eat opium if it's available. Cocaine users sniff powder rather than smoke crack. Most drug takers choose marijuana over heroin or cocaine. In fact, given the opportunity, many choose marijuana over alcohol. Combining the preference for safer highs with a fall in drug prices, especially the price of marijuana relative to hard drugs and alcohol, we get a clear economic prediction: *downsizing the drug war will shift consumption to less-potent, safer drugs, increase the use of marijuana in proportion to hard drugs and alcohol, and shift hard-drug users toward safer practices, for example, sniffing instead of injecting heroin.*

Impact of Downsizing on Casual, Regular, and Problem Users

Downsizing the drug war will affect casual, regular, and problem drug users quite differently. The number of casual and regular users may increase. Regular users may consume about the same amount but deal less. The number of problem users may remain stationary, but they may substantially increase per capita consumption.

Two other useful economic principles underlie these predictions.

1. *The market price of a good often poorly measures its cost, which includes time, risk, inconvenience, side effects, and any number of other*

considerations. Out-of-season asparagus is cheap for a greengrocer, who knows the produce market and buys wholesale. For me, asparagus not only costs ten dollars a pound, but I must also spend time searching for a store that carries it. Similarly, user-dealers pay far less than black market street prices of illegal drugs, while poorly connected users pay far more.

2. *The effect of cost on the buyer of a good depends heavily on how important the good is in his overall budget; the larger the budget share, the greater the effect.* I do not watch the cost of copy paper; an office manager does. The effect of cost on drug buyers depends on the proportion of their income they spend on drugs.

From these two principles we can derived the following conclusions:

Casual users. Convenience and risk matter more than price to casual users and potential experimenters. Casual users include teenagers sampling illegal drugs for the first time. Virtually all regular and problem users start use as teenagers. To a casual drug user, a high street price (say $100 per gram of cocaine) is barely relevant because drugs are so small a part of his budget. Even a fourteen-year-old can easily come up with $10 or $20 dollars from time to time. Casual users are strongly affected by convenience and risk. For an unconnected, would-be, adult drug buyer, the cost is the street price plus the time, inconvenience, and risk of cruising around to locate a dealer, as well as the risk of obtaining drugs of uncertain concentration that may be cut with some toxic chemical. In short, for the casual buyer, the cost is far higher than the street price. Whether a would-be experimenter buys at all depends on the availability of trusted dealers. For children too young or timid to go to town, drugs become accessible and attractive only if their circle of friends and acquaintances includes user-dealers. Downsizing the drug war may make illegal drugs more easily and safely available to casual users. (Marijuana is now more easily available to children than alcohol.) Since marijuana appears to be coming back into fashion—in the teeth of aggressive prohibition—downsizing might facilitate a substantial increase in casual marijuana use.

Regular user-dealers. Regular user-dealers obtain drugs at very low effective cost, making them insensitive to market price. Regular users include both adults and teenagers. These individuals may consume large dollar quantities of illegal drugs. Some may be addicted to heroin or cocaine but not to the extent that they cannot function. Most hold jobs or attend school. Unless they earn very high incomes or inherit money, regular users also sell drugs to cover the cost of their own use. That is, they buy drugs from a familiar wholesaler, sometimes on consignment, sell part retail and use the rest. (Even very rich users often give drugs to friends, which is still dealing in the eyes of the law.) For user-dealers with little earning power and low aversion to risk—true of most teenagers and many low-wage workers—a few hours a week selling drugs to pay for their own use may seem a negligible cost. Regular users prove particularly hard to discourage from taking drugs. Like regular or moderately heavy drinkers, they have enough control over use that they do not consider themselves to have a problem. Since they get their drugs virtually for free, a decline in drug prices will not increase their personal use of drugs. However, a decline in prices may lead some of them to spend less time dealing or to stop dealing altogether. Unfortunately, the ones least likely to be discouraged from dealing by a decline in drug prices are those with the lowest earning power: poorly educated teenagers. These are precisely the dealers it is most important to eliminate as they are the ones who recruit new users and dealers from their peers.

Problem users. Down-and-out problem users are strongly affected by the street price of drugs. They are too unreliable or emotionally disturbed to deal drugs to support their habit. No drug wholesaler would trust them with a consignment. Drugs constitute a major part of problem users' meager budgets. Although relatively few in number, they provide much of the demand that fuels the drug market. They pay the high street price and spend their lives in search of drugs and cash to purchase drugs. Their drug consumption is severely limited by the amount of cash they can beg, steal, scrounge, or earn by turning tricks. Fluctuations in the street price and availability of drugs make their lives an endless roller-coaster. Unlike experimenters and regular users, problem users will consume substantially more drugs if prices decline from current market prices. Only when the price has fallen so low that problem users can afford quantities near their physiological limit will further declines in price not lead to more consumption. The characterization of down-and-out problem users as extremely sensitive to price runs directly counter to the assumption of many prohibition supporters and critics alike: that addicts must get their daily fix and, if need be, will steal whatever it takes. From this assumption flows the—I think vain—hope that if drug prices fall, addicts will steal less.

Evidence from the RAND study of cocaine and user behavior. The 1994 RAND study of cocaine markets supports this predicted behavior of users. The study divides users into two groups: "light" and "heavy." The heavy users correspond roughly to combined regular and problem users. According to RAND's estimates, based on the 1990 National Household Survey of Drug Abuse, the 22 percent of users classified as "heavy" consumed 70 percent of cocaine (Rydell and Everingham 1994b).

Figure 9.1, taken from the RAND study, shows heavy and light users for 1972 through 1992, a period of steady drug war escalation. The number of light users peaks in about 1982, declines steadily until about 1990, then

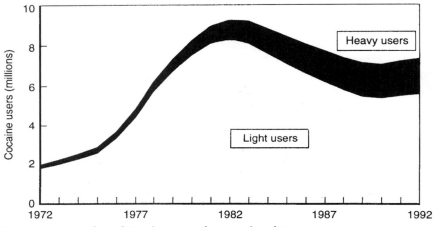

Figure 9.1. Number of Cocaine Users, by Intensity of Use

starts to rise again. The number of heavy users increases only slightly over the 1982–1992 period. Figure 9.2 for the same period shows consumption by light users first rising, then falling, while use by heavy users increases dramatically, especially after 1980. Figure 9.3 shows expenditure on cocaine for the period. While expenditure by light users rises and falls, expenditure by heavy users remains remarkably constant. Figure 9.4 shows a dramatic decline in real cocaine prices from 1977 to 1992, from about $750 per pure gram to a bit over $100 per pure gram (Rydell and Everingham 1994a, 2–4).

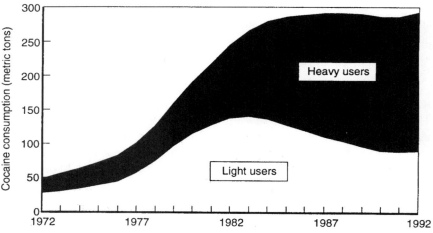

Figure 9.2. Cocaine Consumption, by Type of User

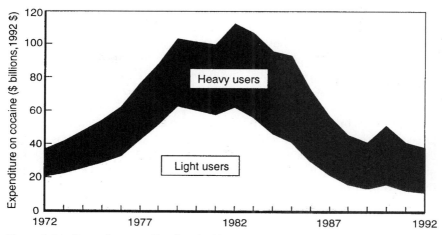

Figure 9.3.   Expenditure on Cocaine, by Users

These data support the following interpretation: Light and heavy users of cocaine increase in number during the 1970s as cocaine becomes fashionable and prices fall. In the 1980s, light users drop out (or never start) as the drug war makes casual use increasingly risky and inconvenient. Heavy users maintain an almost constant dollar volume of consumption over the period. During the second half of the period, the number of heavy users increases only slightly, so *per capita expenditure by heavy users remains nearly constant in the face of sharply declining prices.* This suggests, in turn, that a large proportion of heavy users spend everything they can get

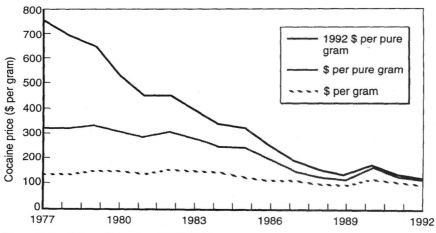

Figure 9.4.   Price of Cocaine: 1977–1992

on cocaine. Price times volume remains constant; the lower the price, the more they spend. Clearly, down-and-out problem users dominate the heavy-use category. They cannot scrounge enough money to consume anywhere close to the physiological limit (3g to 5g a day). Consequently, as prices fall, their per capita consumption increases in proportion. If prices fell from $100 per gram to $50 per gram, their consumption might double.

In this very limited sense, prohibition defenders are correct: a fall in the price of cocaine or heroin will indeed produce a dramatic increase in per capita consumption by down-and-out problem users. But booming illicit drug markets may eventually bring prices so low that junkies, like winos, can easily afford their physiological limit.

Impact of Downsizing on Drug Markets

Downsizing the drug war will shift the illicit drug market into the hands of fewer, older, less violent sellers. Illicit drug markets in the United States are notorious for the presence of large numbers of ill-educated, violent juveniles. This is not the case in European or Australian illicit drug markets, where drug dealing is not prosecuted with anything like U.S. zeal (Zimring and Hawkins 1992). The principle of comparative advantage suggests why.

People find the occupation not that they are absolutely the best at but that they are relatively the best at, even though they may be absolutely terrible at this occupation. The textbook example of comparative advantage is the lawyer and her secretary: the lawyer types much faster than her secretary, but it still pays for her to go to court, leaving the secretary at the word processor. An example closer to hand: most common criminals are astoundingly incompetent at crime and make at best a miserable living before they are (usually quickly) caught. The explanation: if these hapless individuals were more competent at anything else, they would not be criminals.

In any well-functioning, competitive market, buyers and sellers develop long-term personal relationships. Sellers try to retain their customers by providing quality goods and services. Customers seek out and stick with reliable sellers. Long-term relationships are even more important in "normal" illegal markets, like numbers or escort services or supplying drugs to the well-to-do—where trust and discretion are at a premium. Illegal sellers work out turf arrangements quietly and without violence, lest they frighten the customers or attract the police.

Low-end drug markets in the United States are another story. Police routinely conduct drug sweeps of poor urban neighborhoods, arresting and searching all the occupants of a building or all the pedestrians on a block. Persons caught with drugs are offered a deal by prosecutors: they will be charged with lesser offenses, carrying lighter mandatory sentences, if they cooperate by turning in or entrapping other drug sellers, buyers, or even potential buyers. (A tape recording of someone agreeing to buy drugs is enough to convict, even without any evidence that the person actually could or would buy the drugs [Adler 2004].)

Such "search-and-destroy" drug enforcement drives out any marginally decent or competent sellers. It pushes drug markets from one neighborhood to the next, giving an edge to sellers who can quickly establish new turf before the next sweep. It creates an atmosphere of suspicion and fear in which sellers and customers do not know each other and do not want to (Zimmer 1990). Who sells drugs in such a dangerous market? Low-income user-dealers who need to pay for their habits and young, ill-educated, violent teenagers, kids who will trade their very limited futures, even their lives, for a few hundred dollars.

Many prohibition critics and supporters alike share the assumption that retail drug dealing is immensely profitable. On the contrary, low-end illicit drug markets are the employment opportunity of last resort. As the RAND study of dealers in Washington, D.C., showed, most small dealers at best merely pay for their own use (Reuter, MacCoun, and Murphy 1990). Young teens may briefly make a few hundred dollars a day. Before long, however, they will be arrested or shot or become regular user-dealers, consuming their profits. Eventually, many will become problem users. Joey Tranchina, who operates the AIDS Prevention and Action Network in San Mateo County, California, conducted an unscientific survey of drug-treatment centers in four San Francisco Bay Area counties. He asked, "What percentage of your adolescent self-described drug addicts were dealers before they were regular users of drugs?" The answer was 70 to 80 percent (Tranchina 1997)!

Nicholas Pastore (1996), former police chief of New Haven, Connecticut, pursued a strategy of targeting violent drug gangs while ignoring discreet and nonviolent small dealers. Comparative advantage suggests that even with no change in drug laws, such an approach allows drug markets to be reclaimed by more businesslike adults, who care about serving long-term customers. A return of the markets to nonviolent adults in turn reduces opportunities for teenage dealers and, therefore, teenagers' access to drugs.

POLICY IMPLICATIONS: PROTECTING CHILDREN AND HELPING PROBLEM USERS

If a "drug-free" nation is an impossible dream, then we must settle for lesser objectives, set priorities, and accept trade-offs. I propose that we select two primary objectives: protecting children and helping problem users. Protecting children means both restricting their access to drugs as much as feasible and reducing the likelihood and seriousness of problems. (This is equivalent to discouraging children from early sex but still providing condoms.) Helping problem users means not only getting them into treatment but addressing their underlying problems, including depression, disease, and lack of education. To the extent that helping problem users shrinks the black market, it also furthers the goal of protecting children.

Downsizing the drug war contributes to the goal of protecting children. It shifts the market toward marijuana and away from hard drugs, it makes the markets less violent, and it reduces incentives for children to deal. On the other hand, downsizing the drug war permits a larger (although safer) black market with easier access for casual users, including nondealing children. Downsizing should not much affect the number of problem users, whose drug use arises not from drug availability but from emotional problems; however, *downsizing will enable problem users to consume more*, possibly much more.

Can experimental policies of legalization or medicalization retain the benefits of downsizing while controlling the disadvantages? According to the analysis above, here's how the illicit drug market works: Regular user-dealers sell to casual users on the one hand, and to problem users on the other. In addition, some retail dealers are nonusers, particularly young teenage recruits to the inner-city drug business. Casual users, who include teen experimenters, are not sensitive to price but are very sensitive to risk and convenience. Down-and-out problem users are very sensitive to price. Regular users are not very sensitive to either price or risk. Problem users account for the bulk of drug consumption. Can we design policies to take advantage of these characteristics?

Since children are casual users, to keep them out of the black market, we must make the market inconvenient; that is, we must make it hard for children to find sellers. The first step is to reduce or eliminate the primary sellers to children: other children. The second step is to shrink the black market itself; the smaller the market, the harder it becomes for casual users or would-be users to connect with dealers.

Marijuana

The above logic underlies the Dutch legalization experiment. For twenty-five years, the Dutch have allowed the sale of small quantities of cannabis (marijuana or hashish) to adults in "coffee shops," while keeping hard drugs illegal. By making the least dangerous and most popular illegal drug legal in this fashion, the Dutch have sought simultaneously to shrink the black market and shift consumption further away from hard drugs and toward cannabis. By making cannabis available only to adults under carefully supervised circumstances, they also hope to minimize black market access by children. After twenty-five years of coffee-shop legalization, estimated Dutch marijuana consumption per capita remains well below that of the United States—again suggesting that culture is more important than price and availability. The Dutch are satisfied that the policy works; the only serious complaints have come from prohibitionist neighbors, notably France.

The Dutch approach to marijuana—a limited number of outlets selling small amounts to adults only—resembles a restrictive version of U.S. alcohol control as practiced in most localities. What might it accomplish in the United States? I think we could expect a virtual elimination of black market marijuana dealers, including juvenile dealers. However, there would probably not be a great reduction in underage access.

Absent a black market, underage marijuana control depends on the questionable cooperation of otherwise law-abiding adults—as does alcohol control. There is no significant black market in alcohol. There are no teenage alcohol dealers in the schools. Yet, drinking is rampant among underage high school and college students, especially binge drinking on the weekends. Why? Because adults tolerate or facilitate it. Liquor sellers fail to check IDs. Kids newly turned twenty-one supply younger siblings and friends. Parents do not control access to their liquor cabinet. Parents permit their children to party without proper supervision. Colleges allow fraternities to serve liquor to underage students. Why do adults wink at underage drinking? Because they also drank as teenagers! (At my high school graduation party, not only were many of my classmates drunk, but so were three sets of parent chaperones!) Nonetheless, I maintain that parents who seriously want to keep their children from drinking can usually do so until the children leave home. Elimination of black market marijuana might give parents similar control over access.

Dutch-style legalization of marijuana of course "sends a message" of greater tolerance for marijuana. Norms already seem to be shifting toward greater tolerance. Prohibition defenders have a realistic concern that a change in laws may accelerate the shift.

Heroin

Heroin lies at the opposite end of the illicit drug spectrum from marijuana. Users are few compared to users of cocaine or marijuana but include a large number of problem users, many seriously ill. If we can just get the problem users out of the market, the market will shrink drastically.

We can, of course, get many problem users out of the market by expanding drug-free treatment—a proposal with which no one disagrees. We can get even more out by expanding methadone maintenance programs for heroin addicts unable to go drug free and lifting the restrictions that make these programs so ineffective (Rettig and Yarmolinsky 1995). In 2002, the Food and Drug Administration approved a promising new opiate substitute, buprenorphine, which lasts longer than methadone. As programs in the United States and Europe have demonstrated, many addicts can take opiate substitutes or even heroin indefinitely and still lead reasonably normal lives.

Cocaine

Unlike heroin, cocaine is psychologically but not physiologically addictive. A stimulant, it gives users a powerful feeling of well-being and alertness but does not cause withdrawal symptoms. Problem users tend to binge, staying awake for two or three days and then sleeping it off. This pattern seems to preclude maintenance programs like those for opiates.

Suppose cocaine were cheaply dispensed in small amounts to adult users by prescription? The prescription requirement might pose a substantial barrier of inconvenience to would-be casual users, although obviously adults with a prescription might share with friends, including underage friends. More important, a prescription approach for adults could eliminate teenage dealers, many of whom are at risk of becoming problem users.

What about Dr. Kleber's frightening predictions, quoted above, of an explosion in cocaine "abuse" consequent with legalization? His predictions are, of course, a guess, possible but exceedingly unlikely. Legalization by prescription might increase the overall number of users (whom Dr. Kleber conflates with abusers), but it might simultaneously decrease the number of problem users by eliminating teenage dealers.

The only way to find out for sure what would happen with legalization in any form is to experiment cautiously.

CONCLUSION

Downsizing the U.S. drug war to more modest and cost-effective levels of enforcement offers substantial benefits. There must always be some policing of illegal drug markets, just as with bootleg liquor markets. But the drug war makes the black markets very dangerous, therefore attractive to troubled young people with limited opportunities and a high risk of becoming problem users of hard drugs. The drug war does not cause the family and social problems that put young people at risk, but it does divert resources and attention from education and treatment programs that could help them.

However, some consequences of downsizing may surprise even opponents of the drug war. There will, of course, be a drop in prices and increased use of illicit drugs, combined with a shift to less dangerous drugs, notably marijuana. The number of small, part-time dealers will decline. Drug dealing will shift away from teenagers to more stable, less violent adults. The number of hard-core problem drug users will not increase and may even decline if treatment replaces imprisonment. Contrary to the popular impression, however, such hard-core users are extremely sensitive to cost because drugs form so large a part of their meager budgets. Thus, as prices fall, these problem users will proportionately increase their consumption.

REFERENCES

Adler, Charles, personal communication, 2004.
Beck, Aaron T., Fred D. Wright, Cory F. Newman, and Bruce S. Liese. 1993. *Cognitive therapy of substance abuse*. New York: Guilford Press.
CASA. 1995. *CASA national survey of American attitudes on substance abuse*. New York: Center on Addiction and Substance Abuse, Columbia University, July.
Caulkins, Jonathan P., C. Peter Rydell, William L. Schwabe, and James Chiesa. 1997. *Mandatory minimum sentences: Throwing away the key or the taxpayers' money?* Santa Monica, Calif.: Drug Policy Research Center, RAND.
Corman, Hope, and H. Naci Mocan. 2000. A time-series analysis of crime, deterrence and drug abuse in New York City. *American Economic Review* 90(3) (June):584–604.
Cotton, Paul. 1994. Smoking cigarettes may do developing fetus more harm than ingesting cocaine, experts say. *JAMA* 271(8) (February 23): 576–77.
Goldstein, Paul J. 1989. Drugs and violent crime. In *Pathways to criminal violence*. Edited by Neil A. Weiner and Marvin E. Wolfgang. Newbury Park, Calif.: Sage.
Goleman, Daniel. 1995a. 75 years later, study still tracking geniuses. *New York Times*, March 7, C1.
———. 1995b. Researcher kills a myth of syringe sharing. *New York Times,* September 20, B10.
Kleber, Herbert. 1994. Our current approach to drug abuse—progress, problems, proposals. *New England Journal of Medicine* 330(5) (February 3).
Miron, Jeffrey A., and Jeffrey Zwiebel. 1991. Alcohol consumption during Prohibition. *American Economic Review* 81(2):242–47.
Pastore, Nicholas. 1996. Personal communication.
Peele, Stanton. 2004. *7 tools to beat addiction*. New York: Three Rivers Press (Random House).

Rasmussen, David, and Bruce Benson. 1994. *The economic anatomy of a drug war.* Lanham, Md.: Rowman & Littlefield.

——. 1996. *Illicit Drugs and Crime.* Oakland Calif.: The Independent Institute.

——. 2003. Rationalizing drug policy under federalism. *Florida State University Law Review* 30:679.

Rettig, Richard, and Adam Yarmolinsky, eds. 1995. *Federal regulation of methadone treatment.* Washington, D.C.: Institute of Medicine, National Academy Press.

Reuter, Peter, Robert MacCoun, and Patrick Murphy. 1990. *Money from crime: A study of the economics of drug dealing in Washington D.C.* Washington, D.C.: RAND.

Robins, Lee N. 1973. *The Viet Nam veteran returns.* Washington, D.C.: U.S. Government Printing Office.

Rydell, C. Peter, and Susan S. Everingham. 1994a. *Controlling cocaine: Supply versus demand programs.* Washington, D.C.: Drug Policy Research Center, RAND. Data from U.S. Department of Health and Human Services, National Household Survey on Drug Abuse, Rockville, Md., 1994.

——. 1994b. *Modeling the demand for cocaine.* Washington, D.C.: Drug Policy Research Center, RAND. Data from U.S. Department of Health and Human Services, National Household Survey on Drug Abuse, Rockville, Md., 1994.

Shedler, J., and J. Block. 1990. Adolescent drug use in psychological health, a longitudinal inquiry. *American Psychologist* 46: 612–30.

Tranchina, Joey. 1997. Personal communication.

U.S. Department of Health and Human Services, Substance Abuse and Mental Health Services Administration. 2003. *National survey on drug use and health: Population estimates 2002*, available at www.oas.samhsa.gov/nhsda.htm (accessed March 8, 2005).

Verhovek, Sam Howe. 1995. Warehouse of addiction. *New York Times,* July 2–4, 1.

Zimmer, Lynn. 1990. Proactive policing against street-level drug trafficking in New York City. *Am. J. Police* 9:43–74.

Zimring, Franklin E., and Gordon Hawkins. 1992. *The search for rational drug control.* Cambridge, Mass.: Cambridge University Press.

Appendix 9A: Use, "Abuse," Adverse Health Effects, and Addiction

Mary M. Cleveland

Not only is "drug abuse" often defined as all illegal-substance use, but it is also commonly equated with both adverse health effects and addiction.

In reality, patterns of use vary enormously, from drug to drug and from person to person. I distinguish "occasional," "regular," and "problem" use in chapter 9 and avoid the term "abuse." Adverse health effects and addiction are separate issues.

Adverse health effects. The adverse health effects of drugs fall into three categories: (1) adverse effects of the drugs themselves, b) adverse effects of the mode of ingestion, and c) adverse effects of the degraded lifestyle of problem users.

1. *Adverse effects of the drugs themselves:* Prolonged heavy doses of alcohol cause liver damage and eventually brain damage, as well as mental retardation of children exposed in utero. Cocaine and amphetamines can cause heart problems and even heart failure in a small minority of susceptible individuals; otherwise, these stimulants have little scientifically documented ill effect on health. South American natives chew coca leaves all their lives to no ill effect. Cocaine is the local anesthetic of choice for nasal surgery—in doses higher than those taken by recreational users. Nicotine causes loss of peripheral circulation and even gangrene in susceptible individuals; women who smoke heavily during pregnancy also tend to have low-birth-weight babies. Caffeine causes a variety of ill-defined problems for susceptible individuals. Opiates cause constipation but no scientifically documented lasting injury to health; however, overdoses can be fatal. The active ingredient of marijuana, cannabinol, may cause some short-term memory loss after recent

heavy use, but no scientifically documented lasting injury to health, and there are no recorded deaths from overdose.

2. *Adverse effects of the mode of ingestion:* Nicotine and cannabinols are ingested by smoking, causing lung damage. Injection users of opiates, cocaine, or amphetamines risk sepsis, hepatitis, and AIDS from contaminated needles.

3. *Adverse effects of the degraded lifestyle of problem users:* Poverty, an unhygienic lifestyle, and desperation make problem users particularly liable to infection and disease from contaminated needles, as well as poisoning by adulterants to and accidental overdose of street heroin. In 1989, a "crack baby" scare erupted, attributing low-birth-weight babies to the smoking of crack (smokeable cocaine) by poor, inner-city mothers. Further investigation traced the cause not to crack per se but to the heavy-drinking, heavy-cigarette-smoking, malnourished lifestyle of problem users (Cotton 1994).

Addiction. Addiction is a slippery concept. The Latin root means "being led to." Addictive behavior belongs on a continuum that includes normal behavior like eating when hungry or falling in love. The most important component of addiction may be psychological: addicts feel a powerful urge to take some pleasurable action—to light up a cigarette, drink a scotch, eat a box of chocolates, gamble, go jogging, go shopping, make love, or snort cocaine! The urge is generally triggered by certain events or situations; for example, a smoker feels the urge to light up at the end of a meal. Some drugs, including alcohol, nicotine, caffeine, and opiates, are physiologically as well as psychologically addictive for some heavy users in that they produce withdrawal symptoms—adding a stick of physical discomfort to the pleasurable carrot encouraging repetitive use.

Addiction and problem use. The relationship between problem use and addiction is complex and depends on the substance, on the individual, and on the individual's culture and situation. As a rough generalization, most but not all problem users are addicted to alcohol, hard drugs (opiates or stimulants), or both. But the converse does not hold. While most alcohol addicts are problem users, many hard-drug addicts are not problem users. Nicotine and caffeine addicts are rarely problem users either. The difference between non-problem and problem addicts lies in the extent to which the addicts control or yield to urges with immediate adverse consequences.

1. *Nicotine:* Nicotine is by far the most physiologically addictive drug. Most people who try cigarettes quickly get hooked, and most smokers cannot go even a few hours without experiencing a "nic fit." Although

they may incur future health effects, nicotine addicts lead normal lives. They do not suffer the feelings of worthlessness, hopelessness, and drug obsession characteristic of problem users. (This might not always be the case were cigarettes illegal and expensive. I once read an essay by a woman who marooned herself in a country house without cigarettes in an effort to quit. Within a day she found herself walking along a highway collecting butts tossed from cars.)

2. *Alcohol:* Obviously, most alcohol drinkers are neither addicts nor problem users. Those who drink heavily and regularly enough to become physiologically addicted are also thereby impaired enough to count as problem users. Some nonphysiologically addicted binge drinkers probably qualify as problem users because of their degraded lifestyle.

3. *Cocaine and amphetamines:* Cocaine and amphetamines are not physiologically addictive, but they are psychologically addictive to some users, especially people with a poor self-image. These stimulants produce a sense of alertness, confidence, and well-being that such users feel a strong urge to repeat. Heavy users may binge for days, then sleep it off. Many regular cocaine or amphetamine users still lead relatively normal lives, keeping their daily intake at a level that does not seriously impede their productivity or bingeing only on weekends. My bar-hopping friends tell me this is the cocaine use pattern of many young Wall Street traders.

4. *Heroin, morphine, methadone, and other opiates:* First, most users do not become addicts, and even addicts often voluntarily stop use for days or weeks. (Opiate withdrawal symptoms are less severe than those for nicotine.) Nonaddicts include occasional smokers of heroin, so-called chippers. Pain patients may take regular, large doses of opiates without becoming psychologically addicted, although they do experience withdrawal symptoms. Second, unlike alcohol addiction, opiate addiction does not necessarily impair normal functioning. This is obviously true of methadone, which suppresses withdrawal effects without giving a "rush." It is also true for heroin and morphine. For example, Great Britain allows physicians to prescribe heroin. While few actually do so, there are nonetheless several hundred registered heroin addicts who have received prescribed heroin for as long as forty years while leading otherwise ordinary lives. It is one of the dirty little secrets of medicine that some practicing physicians and nurses are opiate (mostly Demerol) addicts—often with little apparent detriment to themselves or their patients.

5. *Marijuana:* Marijuana is not physiologically addictive and does not appear to hook users psychologically as does cocaine. Nonetheless, some

perpetual "pot heads" may rate as problem users to the extent that they neglect the concerns of their normal lives and try to escape feelings of worthlessness and hopelessness in a cloud of smoke.

Relative Drug Ratings. In 1994, two doctors compared heroin, cocaine, and marijuana with three legal drugs—alcohol, nicotine, and caffeine—as shown in table 9A.1.

Table 9A.1.   Two Doctors[1] Compare the Seriousness of Six Well-known Drugs

1. Henningfield Ratings (1 worst; 6 least serious)

Substance	Withdrawal	Reinforcement	Tolerance	Dependence	Intoxication	Total
Heroin	2	2	1	2	2	9
Alcohol	1	3	3	4	1	12
Cocaine	4	1	4	3	3	15
Nicotine	3	4	2	1	5	15
Marijuana	6	5	6	6	4	27
Caffeine	5	6	5	5	6	27

2. Benowitz Ratings (1 worst; 6 least serious)

Substance	Withdrawal	Reinforcement	Tolerance	Dependence	Intoxication	Total
Heroin	2	2	2	2	2	10
Cocaine	3	1	1	3	3	11
Alcohol	1	3	4	4	1	13
Nicotine	3	4	4	1	6	18
Caffeine	4	5	3	5	5	22
Marijuana	5	6	5	6	4	26

Source: Steven C. Markoff in consultation with Drs. Henningfield, Benowitz, and Perrine, 1994.

[1] Jack E. Henningfield (Ph.D. in psychopharmacology), formerly of the National Institute on Drug Abuse, and Neal L. Benowitz, M.D., of the University of San Francisco, rank six common substances in five problem areas.

10

Issues in Legalization

Steven B. Duke and Albert C. Gross

No sensible drug-legalization proposal contemplates an unregulated market in psychoactive drugs. There is some regulation of all markets for all commodities. At a minimum, those who sell or transfer any product have an obligation to reveal hidden dangers and not to defraud their customers. Hence, any coherent legalization proposal must answer questions about the nature and degree of regulation and who will administer the regulations. The following important questions should be dealt with:

1. Which drugs will be legalized?
2. Where will drug use be permitted?
3. What will we do about juvenile access?
4. How will the drug market be regulated?
5. What form will licensing and distribution take?
6. What will become of our pure-food-and-drug regulations?
7. Will drug advertising be permitted or restricted?
8. How will we cope with drug abuse in the workplace?

WHICH DRUGS TO LEGALIZE

One option would be to legalize selectively. We might sate the public appetite for intoxicants by legalizing some illicit drugs while we attempt to hold the line on more dangerous drugs. We might distinguish between marijuana, which is relatively benign, and cocaine, which is more hazardous. It seems likely that when legalization arrives, it will do so incrementally, and marijuana will almost certainly be the first important recreational drug to be converted from contraband to legal status.[1] But legalizing marijuana will not remove the evils of prohibition or even greatly ameliorate them. Because marijuana is so easily home grown, its price per dose can never rise very high for very long, and the profits from it cannot support major black market organizations.

The chief evils of prohibition are currently related to cocaine and heroin. We should legalize those drugs as well, in either the first or the second stage of legalization. Should we stop there? Some argue that we should not legalize drugs whose prohibition does not create serious social problems. Thus, since there appears to be no huge problem associated with the consumption of and trafficking in PCP, LSD, amphetamines, or methadone, we should perhaps not legalize them, even though we can expect a significant black market to continue for those drugs, as with tranquilizers, barbiturates, codeine, other opiates, and numerous designer drugs.

Such a halfway move toward legalization would not be advisable, other than as a cautionary step in the legalization process. The line remaining between legal and illegal drugs under such a scheme would make no more sense than the present dichotomy. There is little basis for distinguishing legally between amphetamines and cocaine, for example, other than the current consumer preference for cocaine, a preference that is almost certainly transitory. And it would be ludicrous to legalize the most potent, addictive, and dangerous natural opiate, heroin, while continuing to criminalize trafficking in all the lesser opiates. Since one of the advantages of legalization is removal of the black market incentives toward more powerful forms of drugs, thus encouraging drug consumers to use less potent, safer, less addictive forms, we should legalize all opiates and virtually all stimulants. We should certainly legalize coca when, if not before, we legalize cocaine.

It might be tempting to draw the legal line at crack and "ice" (smokeable methamphetamine) because these drugs seem to be so addictive. This temptation should be resisted. Crack is easily manufactured by anyone who possesses cocaine, and ice can be manufactured in the basement or garage of anyone with elementary chemistry knowledge who can read a recipe book.[2] If there is a strong market for these drugs, prohibiting them is certain to fail. Market forces, however, are likely to take care of the problem. If the price of cocaine were greatly reduced, as it would be under legalization, the incentives for manufacturing and using crack or ice would also be greatly reduced. If crack is more addictive than cocaine in powder form, then consumers will eventually become aware of that (if they are not already) and opt for the less addictive form of the drug. According to University of California, Davis, neuroscientist Michael S. Gazzaniga,

This is so because if cocaine were reduced to the same price as crack, the abuser, acknowledging the higher rate of addiction, might forgo the more intensive high of crack, opting for the slower high of cocaine. . . . [O]n another front—we know that 120-proof alcohol doesn't sell as readily as the 86 proof, not by a long shot, even though the higher the proof, the faster the psychological effect that alcohol users are seeking.[3]

Thus, market forces under legalization should largely eliminate crack and ice. It is arguable that some psychoactive drugs should remain in the controlled category. Some synthetic opiates, for example, are so powerful and dangerous that they are analogous to grenades or other highly dangerous weapons that are effectively prohibited. If the most popular plant drugs are legalized, it is doubtful that a serious, lucrative market is likely to develop for a synthetic drug, like fentanyl, that can be so deadly to its users.[4] Hence, we would recommend that such drugs remain controlled at least until it is demonstrated that their prohibition creates worse problems than it prevents.

Many other drugs would remain available only by prescription and only through pharmacies. Any proprietary drug manufactured by a pharmaceutical company that maintains a patent or other legal protection of its proprietary rights in the drug would not lose its privilege and responsibility for controlling the distribution of the drug. Such patent protection is a quid pro quo for holding the manufacturers of such drugs liable for the damage they inflict on users. We cannot hold the manufacturer of a drug liable for birth defects, sterility, or other serious damage unless we permit the manufacturer to retain substantial control over the distribution of the drug. We also have to protect the proprietary rights of the drug manufacturer in order to provide an incentive for the research and development of new drugs.

Some black market activity will persist regarding any psychoactive drug that is available only by prescription. But such activities, which are rampant now, will be greatly diminished when many other psychoactive drugs are available on the open market. Minor black markets are manageable costs of the necessary protection of the consumer and the manufacturer.

WHERE DRUG USE SHOULD BE PERMITTED

Between 1987 and 1992, Zurich, Switzerland, explicitly tolerated the unrestrained use of heroin and other drugs in Platzspitz Park.[5] Meanwhile, the possession and sale of drugs were ferociously suppressed elsewhere in Switzerland and throughout much of Europe. When the Zurich experiment began, the park served as an open-air shooting gallery for just a few hundred regular habitués. However, the park's drug clientele eventually swelled to twenty thousand junkies, one-fourth of whom came from countries other than Switzerland. Once a beautiful family park, Platzspitz became dangerous, unhealthful, and unsightly. By 1992, the disorder, the nonstop toxic-drug reactions, the crime, the discarded syringes and other litter strewn about, the use of the grounds as a public toilet, and the general degeneracy that characterized Platzspitz Park led the Zurich City Council to rescind its permissive policy. The experiment's physical impact on the park was so severe that more than a year's labor was necessary to restore the property to normal park uses.

Drug regulations after legalization should avoid restricting use to a few outdoor venues. The regulations should permit use in the privacy of one's own home. However, public use should either be forbidden or allowed in a sufficient number of locations to prevent problems of concentrated impact. Otherwise, the problems of drug immigration that destroyed Platzspitz Park will recur.

Drug consumption should be prohibited in those places where alcohol cannot now be lawfully consumed (generally, in motor vehicles and in public places). Arguably, that should be extended to semipublic places as well. There should be no "drug saloons" or the modern equivalents of opium dens. We see little reason why the consumption of newly legalized drugs should be permitted in restaurants, in public transportation facilities, or in other public facilities. Denying public uses would discourage consumption of pleasure drugs without paying the exorbitant costs of general prohibition.

Drug use in the workplace presents special problems. There is much to be said for prohibiting drug use in the workplace, especially if the work is hazardous. But much work is not hazardous to anyone, and drug use would not actually injure coworkers as cigarette smoke does. Opiate addicts, moreover, cannot be expected to go all day without a drug dose. To prohibit heroin addicts from taking heroin anywhere but in their own homes is to require them to work at home or not at all. Perhaps the matter would best be decided by agreement between employer and employees with employers allowed to designate semiprivate places where drugs, in addition to tobacco, can be consumed during break times.

An alternative is to prohibit conventional drug use in the workplace but to permit heroin addicts or other drug addicts to take their drugs through transdermal patches. The delivery of heroin through such a patch may be practicable. (If not, synthetic opiates can be, and are, delivered by patches.[6]) Delivery of heroin through a patch would eliminate or reduce the "rush" produced by intravenous injection and would probably provide even less "kick" than would the snorting of heroin powder. Transdermal delivery, therefore, may be an inferior means of delivery for many addicts. If necessary to keep a good job, most addicts would probably be willing to accept the inferior form of delivery, especially since it is far safer than the others.

Restrictions on the places where drugs can be consumed are enforceable, as we have seen with alcohol- and tobacco-use regulations. Violations of place restrictions, unlike the acquisition and private consumption of drugs, have witnesses and victims who are willing to complain and to pressure officials to prosecute. Many Americans are repulsed by the public consumption of marijuana, cocaine, or heroin, just as many of us are repulsed by public sexual activities. A society can legitimately protect us against such aesthetic assaults, and we think that it should do so. More important, those who are trying to quit using drugs, or trying to resist using them, are shielded from temptation if such consumption does not occur in public or semipublic places. The government should provide such a shield.

Such regulations of newly legalized drug use—essentially confining it to the home or semiprivate places—would involve substantial enforcement costs and would also be inconsistent with our more permissive stances on the consumption of tobacco and alcohol. While America is becoming much more restrictive on the places where tobacco can be smoked and somewhat more restrictive about alcohol consumption, we are not close to confining the use of those drugs to the home. Such a policy with respect to those drugs would be neither feasible nor just. With fifty million of our residents addicted to cigarettes, it would be impossible to prohibit them from smoking on the street. It imposes suffering on cigarette addicts to prohibit their smoking in the workplace, and that can only be justified on the ground that smoking physically harms coworkers or others.

The consumption of alcohol has been so accepted by our culture for so long that to prohibit drinking in restaurants or in bars, where customers gather to watch sporting events and otherwise to socialize, would be both politically impossible and inadvisable. Our culture even proselytizes against "solitary drinking" and thus encourages "social drinking" as more healthy and less problematic. As long as such attitudes prevail, we must move slowly in restricting the places where alcohol can be consumed.

But more restrictive regulations of newly legalized drugs is another matter. Users of such drugs are already accustomed to consuming their drugs in private to avoid arrest. There would be nothing revolutionary in a system that required them to continue to so confine their consumption. The semipublic use of tobacco and alcohol is the norm in American society, whereas such use of marijuana, cocaine, and heroin is the exception. We should try to keep it so, at least until our inability to do is clearly established.

MINIMIZING JUVENILE ACCESS

Most proponents of drug legalization propose to limit juvenile access to drugs severely. As things are now, children have varying degrees of access to each of the legal and illegal drugs. Unfortunately, some of our youngsters probably always will be initiated into drug use before they are mature enough to handle the attendant risks.

If they do not obtain it directly from their parents or siblings, children can obtain alcohol by raiding the home liquor cabinet, by coaxing an older friend to purchase it for them, or occasionally by purchasing alcohol directly from retailers. However, a retailer risks loss of a lucrative license by selling alcohol to a minor. Alcohol licensing regulations, if enforced, could represent a powerful model for restricting access to drugs by children. Recent experiments demonstrating the ease with which underage minors can purchase alcohol from retailers are one of many recent steps to pressure officials to enforce the laws against the sale of alcohol to minors.[7] Lax enforcement reflects, among other things, our preoccupation with illicit drugs. Acquiescence in underage drinking also reflects an implicit preference for one kind of illegal activity—underage drinking—over another one—illicit drug use. Law enforcement officers, parents, and other interested citizens feel ambivalent about enforcing the alcohol-control laws because of their fear of even worse temptations. The licensing laws, however, are a potent tool, which could be effective if all recreational drugs were treated equally.

Access to cigarettes by children is virtually unlimited, in spite of laws that prohibit sales to minors. Law enforcement agencies—in part because they are overwhelmed by drug-prohibition duties and ideology—usually ignore the statutes against selling tobacco to children.[8]

A serious trend toward prevention of early smoking is underway, financed by a huge settlement obtained by the states in a 1997 lawsuit, and if this effort accelerates, it could attain a level of effectiveness at least as great as the partially enforced ban on drinking by children. Cigarette vending machines have been outlawed by approximately twenty-two states.[9] Because children also buy or shoplift tobacco products from live retailers, some areas even require stores to limit their stocks to closely guarded cigarettes at the cashier's counter.[10]

Until they agreed to stop as part of the 1997 settlement,[11] the tobacco industry aggressively recruited juvenile smokers. The future of the nicotine business in America is absolutely dependent on finding children to replace adult Americans who defect from the ranks of smokers or die from the habit.[12] Of all new American smokers, 90 percent are in their teens or younger.[13] Aware of the public-relations implications of pandering lethal drugs to children, R. J. Reynolds cynically publishes materials that purport to fight against teen smoking. Meanwhile, Reynolds' "Joe Camel" advertising campaign radically improved the juvenile market share of Camel cigarettes—previously a largely adult brand. In the first three years of the Joe Camel campaign, the proportion of smokers under eighteen who chose Camel cigarettes zoomed from 0.5 percent to 32.8 percent. The illegal sale of Camels to minors increased the earnings of R. J. Reynolds from that source nearly eighty times, from $6 million to $476 million,[14] as a consequence of the omnipresent posters, billboards, and adolescent promotions, which depict the urbane, "smooth character" Joe Camel, an anthropomorphic caricature of a dromedary.[15] The *Journal of the American Medical Association (JAMA)* has published several studies on the Joe Camel campaign,[16] which cumulatively suggest that R. J. Reynolds is intentionally recruiting toddlers as customers. In addition to many other disturbing findings in the *JAMA* articles, one of the studies indicated that 91.3 percent of six-year-olds could identify the cigarette's cartoon logo.[17] The study presented symbols of twelve miscellaneous products, including both "adult" and "children's" brands, and only Mickey Mouse—the logo for the Disney Channel—achieved recognition comparable to that of Joe Camel (Joe Camel was forced to retire in 1997).

Under a comprehensive program of drug legalization, the government could effectively reduce the access by children to all drugs. The program could maintain the present bans on alcohol sales to minors and stiffen penalties for others who provide alcohol to children. Drug legalization could incorporate major improvements over the present situation by doing the following:

1. Banning the sale of cigarettes and all other drugs through vending machines
2. Enforcing existing bans on the sale or transfer of cigarettes to children
3. Genuinely banning the sale of presently illegal drugs to children

The sale of cigarettes, alcohol, and newly legalized drugs to children could be made a serious felony. We would not stop at punishing the willful distribution of tobacco, alcohol, and other drugs to children. We would encourage courts to impose civil and criminal liability for negligently providing children access to such drugs. The liquor cabinet and the drug cabinet, if there is one, should be locked if there are small children in the house. Since such drugs are dangerous to young children's lives and health, it would not be a great stretch of legal principle to hold the possessors of such drugs to a duty to prevent children from obtaining them.

Many states presently exempt parents from prohibitions against giving or selling alcohol to minors, especially if it is consumed at home in the presence of the parents.[18] This exemption not only accommodates religious use of alcohol by minors, but it also allows parents to introduce their children to the responsible use of alcohol rather than delegating that training to the uncertainties and excesses of illicit use by teenage peers. We can think of no reason why this approach should be retained for alcohol but not extended to other drugs. Responsible, recreational use of any drug is preferable to illicit, irresponsible use. If parents believe they should train their children in how to use marijuana, they should not be made felons for doing so. If they allow their children to overdose on any drug and become emergency room cases or permit them to operate machinery under the influence, however, legal sanctions should be imposed.

MODES OF REGULATION

Because the repeal of the alcohol prohibition amendment to the Constitution restored most of the control over alcohol regulation to the states, we have many different models for drug regulation. We should examine these models in our search for the best way to repeal drug prohibition.

Let us first consider the proposal of Daniel Benjamin and Roger Miller. In *Undoing Drugs: Beyond Legalization*,[19] they recommend that federal drug-prohibition statutes be repealed, leaving each state free to decide how it wants to deal with drugs: free availability, stringent prohibition, or somewhere between those extremes. There are two major advantages to this proposal. First, since it does not itself result in either legalization or prohibition but simply gives each voter in each state a greater voice in the drug policy that immediately concerns that voter, it may be politically feasible. The proposal permits each state to have the kind of drug laws that it wants. It permits us to try many different approaches to the illicit drug problem, to experiment, to discover and evaluate new ways of dealing with drugs. We already know much about how to deal with drugs since we have experimented endlessly with alcohol regulation, but there are differences among drugs, and there is always more to be learned. A single federal approach to the problem cuts off experimentation and creative competition in fashioning reactions to problems.

There is, however, a major problem with this approach. As we learned with alcohol drinking-age disparities, major differences between states concerning the legal availability of drugs create ugly state-line industries that cater to persons coming to buy and consume the drugs from states in which they are not legally available. Such differences encourage interstate travel under the influence of the sought-after drug. This dangerous condition, as it applies to drinking ages, was changed by federal legislation that effectively raised the minimum drinking age in all states to twenty-one.

Highway-safety considerations that warranted the change of drinking ages would almost certainly be less powerful considerations where other drugs were concerned. None of the three major illicit drugs is likely to impair driving capacity as greatly as does alcohol.[20] Alcohol is also a far more popular recreational drug among teenagers than all the illicit drugs combined—by far. It is all but inconceivable that this basic order of consumer preference would be reversed under legalization. Thus, the problem of state-line drug industries and impaired driving home from source states would almost certainly be less substantial than it was with respect to alcohol.

The likely outcome of the Benjamin and Miller scheme would be the gradual adoption of legalization, state by state. A few states would try it, if only for the revenue. Adjoining states would find their prohibition laws even less enforceable than they are now and, lustful for the loot, would align themselves with their more prescient neighbors. As the states who legalized experienced not only revenue enhancement but less crime, safer streets, increased property values, and general improvements in the quality of life, the remaining states would fall in line like dominoes. Arguably, the federal government should skip that step and not only legalize most of the drugs it now treats as "controlled" but at the same time deny the states the power to prohibit them. Some room could still be left for state regulations, as is now the case with most products, where the federal government and the states share regulatory responsibilities.

LICENSING PRODUCTION?

Should we try to license the production of plant-based drugs? It is possible to produce not only marijuana but coca and its derivatives and opium and its derivatives in the territorial confines of the United States. If we were to ban the importation of such drugs, we could give a boost to domestic farmers and exclude the Columbian *narcotrafficantes* at the same time. That does not seem feasible, at least in the short run. Subtropical climates have natural advantages in the growing of coca and opium, and our farmers lack experience producing either crop. The harvesting of coca and especially opium is also very labor intensive. It is unlikely that American farmers could compete effectively with South American coca producers or with Indian, Pakistani, or Southeast Asian opium producers, at least in the short to intermediate term. We would still have smuggling and still have major black markets if we tried to close our drug markets to importation.

More feasible is the licensing of later stages of drug production, say from the coca or opium stages to refined production of cocaine or opium derivatives. While we could not effectively prevent the importation of coca, opium, and all their derivatives from abroad, we might try to confine some refining activities to licensed American manufacturers. We could thus hope to control the purity of the drugs better and to reduce the risk of contaminated products. Health and safety could thus be promoted. We do not do this with other drugs or food products, however, and it is hard to see why we should treat pleasure drugs differently. If foreign pharmaceutical companies can produce cheaper drugs than our manufacturers and can satisfy customs and the Food and Drug Administration (FDA) that they have produced uncontaminated drugs, we see no reason—other than economic protectionism—why they should be prohibited from doing so.

REGULATION OF DOMESTIC DISTRIBUTION

The domestic distribution of pleasure drugs, like the distribution of pharmaceuticals, foods, alcohol, tobacco, and every other product, should be subject to regulation by American law. The question is what kind of regulation. Several options are available.

Government as sole distributor. One possible distribution system might be an exclusive federal-government dispensary system. By having the dispensaries run by the federal government, as opposed to the state governments, the problems of competition between neighboring states would be avoided. There would be one price-and-distribution system across the United States, and no interstate travel induced by the drug business. The effort to keep drugs out of the hands of juveniles would be greatly facilitated. Advertising could also be eliminated without any First Amendment problems. While private organizations may have the constitutional right to advertise their products, nothing *requires* the government to advertise.

There are, however, major disadvantages to government drug dispensaries. As we have learned from the Eastern Bloc countries, when government is the sole legal distributor of a commodity, competition and self-interest are not available to promote the efficient workings of the market. Thus, the Soviet Union and Eastern Europe experienced shortages, hoarding, and black market distribution, which greatly contributed to the collapse of their economies and ultimately their governments. The temptation of government to increase profits by raising prices on a controversial product would also exacerbate the problems. The black markets that legalization was designed to prevent would develop in parallel with the government drug-distribution system, just as illegal gambling organizations compete with state-run lotteries.

When the government has a financial interest in promoting vice, as it does in those states that have lotteries, states frequently engage in shameless promotions, even fraud, to induce their citizens to part with their money.[21] While there is little of this in state-controlled alcohol dispensary systems, the lottery example is another reason to worry about turning the drug business over to government-run monopolies.

A prescription system. Another option for distribution would be a "medical system," in which prescriptions would be filled at pharmacies. This could provide a modicum of state regulation and some protection against consumption by minors and drug abusers, but it would have black market consequences and far more regulation and cost than is desirable. People who can afford to pay doctor's fees can already get a potpourri of drugs from unethical physicians, who at present represent a gray market distribution system that competes with black marketeers. Legalizing the gray market would not solve prohibition's problems; it would merely make drug dealers out of our health professionals. Drug distribution as an adjunct to medical treatment or to maintain addicts as a stage of rehabilitation can be legitimate medical practice, but retailing recreational drugs manifestly is not. To impose that function on the medical profession would place intolerable pressures on it.

Licensed suppliers. A third possible distribution system would be to license and regulate distributors and retailers, who would sell psychoactive drugs as commercial products. The late New York state senator Joseph L. Galiber's proposed legalization bill would have implemented essentially this system, while funding treatment and education programs from taxes on retail sales.[22]

Alcohol distribution, which is already licensed, and tobacco trade, which is largely unfettered, could be brought under this regulatory umbrella, too.

The main advantage of this system of distribution is that it would be far more likely than government dispensaries or a prescription system to destroy the black market. A troubling disadvantage is that it would undermine a system in which psychotropic prescription drugs are distributed only by licensed pharmacists on written authorization of a medical doctor. But people who are reluctant to experiment or self-medicate with over-the-counter drugs will—if they can afford it—still seek the advice and guidance of a physician so that the prescription system, although weakened, would not be destroyed. Doctors today prescribe medication that can be bought without prescription. They would continue to do so under a legalized drug regime. Also, as noted earlier, there would, in any event, be a large number of psychoactive proprietary drugs that could legally be bought only by prescription. Nor would the legalization of psychoactives be inconsistent with the prescription-only system for medicinal drugs such as antibiotics. Many of these are proprietary drugs, and there is no significant black market problem.

Distribution licenses could be contingent on good character and proof of financial responsibility. Since a substantial benefit of legalization is that it would permit us to require drug distributors to sell uncontaminated and properly labeled products, distributors would have to establish their financial responsibility and ability to meet their obligations. This would be a major function of a licensing system. No monopolies or oligopolies should be created. Any person or organization meeting minimum requirements should get a license.

A commercial licensing system should also include mandatory warning labels, generic packaging (no brand names, slogans, or touting), and detailed description of contents and purities. It might also be advisable to limit the quantities of drugs that any individual could purchase, to require records of sales, and to forbid quantity-price discounts. If those regulations—and others dealing with purity, potency, and so forth—are complied with, the manufacturers and distributors of the drugs should receive immunity for the damage done by their drug. Alcohol and tobacco distributors now have the same immunity for the damage done by their products.[23] Otherwise, the price of drugs would have to reflect very uncertain liability risks and would therefore be very high relative to production costs. A powerful black market would result.

A practical choice. Given drug prohibition's counterproductivity and the drawbacks of the other options we have described, the most practical alternative would be commercial licensing. While government regulation is not risk free, there is ample, successful precedent for regulating dangerous products and services. The government would regulate the drug market in the public interest just as it regulates power companies, telecommunications companies, liquor sales, and gambling.

THE ROLE OF THE FOOD AND DRUG ADMINISTRATION

For the most part, the food and drug regulatory system accomplishes the goals that were set for it when it was first enacted in 1906. Prior to that, quackery was far more common than it is today, and the purveyors of patent medicines foisted on an unwary public myriad potions for ailments real and imagined. Often these remedies did more harm than the diseases they purported to treat. At best, many were harmless but ineffective.

Presently, a new drug must go through years of testing—often ten years or more—before it is approved for sale to the public. The FDA supervises testing to determine that the proposed drug product is both efficacious and safe, that it will do what it claims to do and will do no unacceptable harm to the patient if used as directed.

In recent years, the medical and pharmaceutical communities' authorized monopoly over medicinal drugs has been controversial. The FDA also has come under attack. During the 1960s and 1970s, the alleged cancer cure, laetrile, acquired a cult of advocates who warred against the FDA's refusal to approve that drug. In the late 1980s, there was controversy over scandals regarding the testing and regulation of generic drugs as substitutes for brand-name drugs. More recently the drug L-tryptophan was restricted, and advocates of its use claim the restrictions were unwarranted. Advocates for AIDS victims also frequently complain about FDA delays in approving AIDS drugs. Nonetheless, the FDA does much good by protecting the public from tainted food and unsafe drugs. It also provides powerful protection for desperate sufferers of medical fraud. It ensures that those with a disease for which there is effective treatment will not be sidetracked by worthless remedies.

No rational legalization proposal would subject well-established recreational drugs to the FDA's new drug approval process, for such drugs probably never could receive approval. Rather, the common recreational drugs that we would legalize should be "grandfathered" as were alcohol, tobacco, and aspirin, none of which was ever subjected to that process. Newly discovered plant drugs or synthetics, however, would be subject to FDA scrutiny, as they now are, before they could be sold. They, too, would receive a patent monopoly and could only be sold on terms fixed by the proprietor of the drug. This would reward the drug companies for the research and the lengthy process of testing necessary to get FDA approval.

The major difference between our scheme and the present scheme, insofar as newly discovered drugs are concerned, is that the FDA should approve drugs developed to provide intoxication, as well as those having "medicinal" value. This would provide substantial incentives to the pharmaceutical companies to develop safer and less addictive pleasure drugs than most of those now on the market. What should happen when the manufacturer's exclusive rights in such a drug expire? If the drug is a popular recreational drug, and no more dangerous than the drugs already available, it should enter the over-the-counter market.

The FDA could, of course, require sellers of recreational drugs to affix warnings on their packaging just as purveyors of tobacco and alcohol are now required to do.

BANNING ADVERTISING: A PESKY CONSTITUTIONAL QUESTION

Milton Friedman has expressed an important dilemma for drug-legalization advocates:

> With respect to restrictions on advertising, I feel uneasy about either position. I shudder at the thought of a TV ad with a pretty woman saying, "My brand will give you a high such as you've never experienced." On the other hand, I have

always been very hesitant about restrictions of freedom of advertising for general free speech reasons. But whatever my own hesitations, I have very little doubt that legalization would be impossible without substantial restrictions on advertising.[24]

A ban on all drug advertising, including cigarette and alcohol advertising, might be a worthwhile trade-off for the benefits of drug legalization. We already have a ban on broadcast advertising of cigarettes, the American Medical Association has endorsed extending that ban to print advertising,[25] and American distillers voluntarily keep their hard-liquor advertising off the air.[26] Certainly, the alcohol and tobacco lobbies would fight legislation that would produce such radical restrictions on their advertising. Those lobbies would be joined by some civil liberties organizations as well. Whether the bans, if enacted, would then be upheld by courts is unclear. Despite earlier Supreme Court decisions suggesting that "purely commercial advertising" is not protected by the First Amendment,[27] the Court has several times rejected that theory. Plain and simple, advertising is protected by the First Amendment.

Drug advertising should perhaps be an exception, and there is precedent for that position. As recently as 1986, the Supreme Court held that Puerto Rico, although it permitted gambling, could forbid advertising of gambling aimed at Puerto Ricans. Said Justice Rehnquist for a five-justice majority, "The greater power to completely ban casino gambling necessarily includes the lesser power to ban advertising of casino gambling."[28] He added that it would be "a strange constitutional doctrine which would concede to the legislature the authority to totally ban a product or activity, but deny to the legislature the authority to forbid the stimulation of demand for the product or activity through advertising on behalf of those who would profit from such increased demand."[29] The Court also suggested that all advertising of cigarettes and alcoholic beverages could be banned in all media on the same theory.[30]

The Puerto Rico case was an aberration, and the Court has repudiated the greater-includes-the-lesser theory of the First Amendment. In *Virginia Board of Pharmacy v. Virginia Consumer Council*,[31] for example, the Court held that a licensed pharmacist had a First Amendment right to advertise truthfully the prices of prescription drugs. Bans on truthful advertising of liquor have been struck down.[32] The Court has also invalidated restrictions on lawyer advertising[33] and on the posting of "for sale" signs on property.[34]

We are troubled by the free speech implications of a ban on drug advertising. Even if the Court were to uphold such a ban, we would oppose it, especially if it did not include tobacco and alcohol, and probably even if it did.

It is important under any drug regime—a legalized one as we propose or a dichotomous one as we have now—that there be free and open debate not only of the merits of legalization or prohibition but of the merits, risks, and evils of drugs themselves, either on their own footing or in comparison to other drugs. No one should worry about legal repercussions for advocating the use or nonuse of any drug. People should be encouraged to discuss, debate, and explain the safe use of drugs, the dangers of combining particular drugs, and the joys or evils of the same. An all-media prohibition on drug advertising would have a chilling effect on such debate because the line between advertising and advocacy is murky.

The reasons we have had little difficulty to date in distinguishing between advertising and advocacy is that in television and radio, where we have discouraged or banned alcohol and tobacco advertising, the costs of advertising are so high that it seldom makes sense for anyone to advertise who is not hawking a particular brand name in a thirty-second spot. In such an expensive medium, there is little doubt about what is and is not advertising. Very little private benefit accrues for advocating generic drugs.

Nonetheless, enterprising tobacco and liquor companies find ways of encouraging the audience to use tobacco and alcohol that escape bans on advertising. For example, much "public service" advertising urges television, radio, and print audiences to avoid "drugs" but rarely includes in its crusade references to tobacco or alcohol. The reason: tobacco and alcohol companies are major financial contributors to the campaign.[35] They realize that presently illegal drugs are in competition with their own products and it is beneficial to them that a clear line be drawn between those products and theirs. Hence, ironically, our largest drug manufacturers support campaigns against "drugs." We also see messages on public television, which eschews "advertising," that are difficult to distinguish from advertising. Programs are "sponsored" or "underwritten" by oil companies or other giant manufacturers or distributors of products, and the viewers are so informed. This is apparently public relations, not advertising.

If there is a lot of money to be made from advertising, a ban on advertising will encourage the creation of forms and modes of communication that come as close in function to advertising as is legally possible. The way to eliminate or greatly curb advertising is not to ban it but to make it unprofitable. If we prohibit the use of brand names on packaging or any other claims about the desirable effects of using a drug, confining descriptions to generic, chemical contents and explicit warnings about adverse consequences, we will eliminate most of the commercial incentive for advertising or its functional equivalent. Withholding trademark protection from newly legalized drugs would be the near equivalent of such a prohibition, and such a move is surely constitutional.

Manufacturers or distributors of marijuana might pool their resources and try to persuade potential customers to switch to marijuana from alcohol, and they might use sexual or other imagery to conduct that persuasion, but that would make economic sense only if most of the producers of marijuana could be induced to make a pro rata contribution to the "public relations fund." Otherwise, free riders could enjoy the benefits of the campaign without sharing any of the costs. We have some such campaigns by the tobacco industry or the beer industry because a small group of producers account for a large share of the total market, a state of affairs produced largely by brand-name advertising. If we make sure that there are no oligopolies in the marijuana business, there will be little pooling of resources for advertising. In a market where competition is mainly based upon price, there is little incentive for advertising anything *but* price. We should so structure the drug market that there are no excess funds to be spent on advertising. An alternative way to assure that there is little commercially motivated advocacy of particular generic drugs would be to require that any such advocacy by or on behalf of a manufacturer, distributor, or retailer of a drug, or any organization of such persons, be accompanied by specified warnings. In print advertising, the warnings could be required to be in no smaller type than the largest type in the ad (or one-half of that size, if we want to be generous to the merchants). If the spoken word is the medium, the warnings would have to be repeated every thirty seconds, and so on. No one has a constitutional right to commit fraud or to purvey falsehood, and claims about the desirability of any product are arguably fraudulent if not offset by disclosure of effects, side effects, and risks.

It is reasonably clear that we can legally prohibit drug advertising on radio and television, which are by far the most powerful advertising media for influencing children. There may be no First Amendment right to advertise on the airways because they are owned by the public. Just as no one has the right to advertise wares in the Supreme Court Building, neither does anyone have such rights on the public airways. That is not an entirely persuasive theory, but it appears to be well established in the courts.[36]

COPING WITH DRUG ABUSE IN THE WORKPLACE

Patricia Saiki, former administrator of the Small Business Administration, reported that substance abuse costs the economy "more than $100 billion annually in lost productivity and wages."[37] Estimates of the cost to American business of drug and alcohol abuse vary, but some measures support Saiki's claim, also putting the amount in the range of $100 billion dollars per year.[38] Consequently, during the late 1970s and early 1980s, federal-government experts on workplace substance abuse developed a comprehensive system, called the employee assistance program (EAP), that employers can use to deal with employee drug and alcohol problems if they affect an individual's job performance.

Many EAPs concentrate only on substance-abuse problems, while other so-called broad-brush EAPs also tackle other off-duty difficulties, such as compulsive gambling, family or marital strife, the stress of life, and mismanagement of personal finances.

At its optimum, an EAP is a resource that an employee can tap for confidential help when substance abuse or other problems have gotten out of hand. Ideally, the employee makes a self-referral to the program, although supervisors generally also can refer a "problem" employee to the program. In return for self-referral or cooperation after a supervisor's referral, the EAP is supposed to give the employee a measure of job protection. That is, so long as the employee carries out the program's reasonable recommendations for obtaining professional help and therapy, the employee usually will be able to retain his or her job. Such programs do not operate as a means for identifying and firing a problem person but as a positive means to use the employee's drive for job survival to encourage that person to come to grips with important problems, including drug-abuse problems.

When EAPs operate properly, they are humane, legally defensible, and fair. Employers like the programs because they protect legitimate interests of the employer, such as workplace safety and worker efficiency. Employees and unions like properly operating EAPs because they respect the workers' right to be left alone regarding off-the-job behavior as long as it does not affect on-the-job performance or safety. Under EAPs, law enforcement is left to the state rather than usurped by corporations.

EAPs encourage troubled workers to get outside help in a relatively nonpaternalistic manner that involves no more coercion than is justified by the employer's legitimate interests. Under an EAP, loss of a job is not punishment; it is an inevitable consequence of an employee's uncorrected performance deficits.

Professor Dale A. Masi of the University of Maryland was a pioneer in the development of such programs. From 1979 to 1984, he directed the model federal EAP for the U.S. Department of Health and Human Resources. Masi testified to the 1988 congressional committee hearings on drug legalization that "a majority of drug abusers [of both legal and illicit drugs] are in the workplace."[39] EAPs therefore could help reduce drug abuse by focusing attention where drug abusers are most likely to be found: on the job. EAPs succeed because holding on to productive and meaningful employment is a powerful incentive for a person troubled by substance abuse to become and remain sober.

According to general principles of behavioral psychology, the inevitable prospect of losing a good job as a result of a return to drug abuse is likely to

promote sober behavior, while threat of punishment would probably only promote guile in continuing the drug-abusing behavior. If they are nothing else,
successful EAPs are evidence that positive incentives can promote sobriety
even though the entire coercive apparatus of the state has failed to keep contraband drugs off the market.

EAPs are likely to be more effective in a system in which acknowledging
drug use—or abuse—is not a confession of crime, and one can seek help without accepting the stigma of criminality. The goal in a legalized system will also
be more reasonable and realistic: promoting not merely abstinence but the alternative of responsible use, thereby reducing drug abuse, not drug use.

Under a legalized regime, we would be compelled to rethink our present attitudes toward compulsory drug testing, both within and outside the workplace. Much of the support for routine testing today rests on the assumption
that users of illicit drugs are criminals, likely to steal or otherwise engage in
illegal behavior. When drug use is lawful, justifications for drug testing will
have to be closely tailored to specific job-performance requirements.

PUTTING DRUG-CONTROL MONEY
WHERE IT WOULD DO SOME GOOD

An American merchant seaman who visited Calcutta in the 1930s was as-
tonished to observe people sleeping on the streets in that city. In that respect, Calcutta of the 1930s is America of the 2000s. We have people sleeping on the streets, in subways, and in parks, and it no longer shocks us. The
gap between the wealthiest and the poorest in this country is growing, partly
because middle-class blue-collar workers have lost jobs to foreign competition, partly because minority participation in the middle class has declined
as a result of cutbacks in government employment and resistance to affirmative action, and partly because our educational systems have failed in
their mission.

The surest way to deal with drug abuse in this country is to do something
about the hopelessness felt by large portions of the American population. Instead of wasting our resources on futile drug prohibition, America needs to
invest in the economic development of its urban communities and in rebuild-
ing its educational infrastructure. Every dime spent on Head Start is worth ten
dollars spent on drug prohibition. Any young person who sees hope for ad-
vancement and for a rewarding and useful life will have something better to
do than obsessively pursue intoxication. One of the most important steps in a
comprehensive drug-control program under legalization is to reestablish opportunities for America's underclass.

NOTES

1. Great strides have been made in the last decade to legalize medical marijuana. See Eric Schlosser, "Make Peace with Pot," *New York Times*, April 26, 2004. It is not clear whether acceptance of medical marijuana use will help or hurt efforts to legalize recreational use of marijuana. While there will always be some recreational use of marijuana that is available ostensibly only for medical purposes, the legitimation of medical marijuana removes the most potent rhetorical weapon available to the legalizers: the cruel idiocy of prohibition as it applies to the medically needy.

2. See, for example, Uncle Fester, *Secrets of Methamphetamine Manufacture*, 2d ed. (Port Townsend, Wash.: Loompanics Unlimited, 1989, 1991); Michael V. Smith, *Psychedelic Chemistry* (Port Townsend, Wash.: Loompanics Unlimited, 1981).

3. Michael S. Gazzaniga, "Opium of the People," *National Review* (February 5, 1990): 34.

4. See Steven B. Duke and Albert C. Gross, *America's Longest War: Rethinking Our Tragic Crusade against Drugs* (New York: Putnam's Sons, 1993), 220–21.

5. Roger Cohen, "Amid Growing Crime, Zurich Closes a Park It Reserved for Drug Addicts," *New York Times*, February 11, 1991.

6. See, generally, on transdermal patches, www.duragesic.com and www.managedcaremag.com/archives/0404/0404.biotech.html (both accessed March 14, 2005). See also "Drug Dispensers," *Converter Magazines* (October 2003); "Getting a Dose of Salvation, 1 Day at a Time," *Seattle Times*, February 18, 2004.

7. Michele L. Norris, "D.C. the Most Lax on Issue, Study Says: Washington College One of the Few Places Where Youths Can Legally Buy Alcohol," *Washington Post*, March 3, 1993.

8. For some notable exceptions, see "State Suit Alleges Safeway Sold Tobacco to Kids," *Los Angeles Times*, June 17, 2004.

9. See www.healthpolicycoach.org.asp?id=3151 and Lungaction.org/reports/keyfindings 403.html (accessed July 29, 2004).

10. Kevin Duchschere, "Chanhassen Orders Cigarettes Be Sold from Behind Counter," *Star Tribune*, October 17, 1991.

11. See "Tobacco's Last Stands . . . ," *USA Today*, December 28, 1998.

12. See Joseph R. DiFranza, J. W. Richards, P. M. Paulman et al., "RJR Nabisco's Cartoon Camel Promotes Cigarettes to Children," *JAMA* 266 (December 11, 1991), 3149–53.

13. DiFranza, Richards, Paulman, et al., "RJR Nabisco's Cartoon Camel," 3149–53.

14. DiFranza, Richards, Paulman, et al., "RJR Nabisco's Cartoon Camel," 3151.

15. DiFranza, Richards, Paulman, et al., "RJR Nabisco's Cartoon Camel," 3149–53; Geoffrey Cowley, "I'd Toddle a Mile for a Camel: New Studies Suggest Cigarette Ads Target Children," *Newsweek* (December 23, 1991): 70.

16. Paul M. Fisher et al., "Brand Logo Recognition by Children Aged 3 to 6 Years; Mickey Mouse and Old Joe the Camel," *JAMA* 266 (December 11, 1991): 3145–48; DiFranza, Richards, Paulman, et al., "RJR Nabisco's Cartoon Camel," 3149–53; and

John P. Pierce et al., "Does Tobacco Advertising Target Young People to Start Smoking? Evidence from California," *JAMA* 266 (December 11, 1991): 3154–58. See also Henry Waxman, "Tobacco Marketing; Profiteering from Children," *JAMA* 266 (December 11, 1991): 3185–86.

17. Fisher et al., "Brand Logo Recognition by Children," 3145–48.

18. See 45 Am. Jur. 2d 274 (1995); 48A C.J.S. 259; *Bell v. Alpha Tan Omega Fraternity*, 98 Nev. 109, 642 P.2d 161 (1982); *Craves v. Inman*, 223 Ill. App. 3d 1059, 586 N.E.2d 367 (1991).

19. Daniel K. Benjamin and Roger Leroy Miller, *Undoing Drugs: Beyond Legalization* (New York: Basic Books, 1991).

20. See Duke and Gross, *America's Longest War*, ch. 4.

21. See Valerie C. Lorenz, "It's Time to Take Action to Halt Addiction That Knows No Bounds," *USA Today*, March 26, 1991.

22. Introduced as New York State Senate Bill S-1918, February 6, 1989. Reintroduced as New York State Senate Bill 4094-A, March 21, 1991.

23. They may, of course, be liable for fraudulent advertising. See *Cipollone v. Liggett Group, Inc.*, 60 U.S.L.W. 4703 (June 24, 1992).

24. Milton Friedman, "America after Prohibition," in *Reason*, October 1988.

25. "Media Advertising for Tobacco Products. Board of Trustees Reports," *JAMA* 255 (February 28, 1986): 1033.

26. See Peter Grier, "Coalition Asks FTC to Prohibit Liquor Ads Aimed at Young People," *Christian Science Monitor*, November 23, 1983, 27; *Valentine v. Chrestensen*, 316 U.S. 52 (1942).

28. *Posadas de Puerto Rico Associates v. Tourism Company*, 478 U.S. 328, 345–46 (1986).

29. 478 U.S. 346.

30. 478 U.S. 346.

31. 425 U.S. 748 (1976).

32. See *Liquormart, Inc. v. Rhode Island*, 64 U.S.L.W. 4313 (1996).

33. *Bates v. State Bar of Arizona*, 429 U.S. 813 (1976).

34. *Linmark Associates, Inc. v. Willingboro*, 431 U.S. 85 (1977).

35. Cynthia Cotts, "Condoning the Legal Stuff: Hard Sell in the Drug War," *Nation* (March 9, 1992): 300.

36. See *Capital Broadcasting Co. v. Mitchell*, 333 F. Supp. 582 (D.C. 1971), affd. sub nom. *Capital Broadcasting Co. v. Acting Attorney General Kleindienst*, 405 U.S. 1000 (1972).

37. PR Newswire Association, "U.S. Small Business Administration Named As Member of Federal Drug-Fighting Team," *PR Newswire*, January 29, 1992.

38. The United States Chamber of Commerce claims that drugs cost American business $160 billion per year (Eric Reguly, "Drug Abuse Still a Problem for U.S. Firms," *Financial Post*, October 25, 1991). A University of California, San Francisco, study commissioned by the National Institute on Drug Abuse estimates that in 1988 drug and alcohol abuse cost the U.S. economy a total of $144.1 billion, including medical expenses and other costs in addition to business-productivity losses [Dorothy

P. Rice, Sander Kelman, Leonard S. Miller, and Sarah Dunmeyer, *The Economic Costs of Alcohol and Drug Abuse and Mental Illness, 1985*. Report submitted to the Office of Financing and Coverage Policy of the Alcohol, Drug Abuse, and Mental Health Administration, U.S. Department of Health and Human Services (San Francisco: Institute for Health and Aging, University of California, 1990), 2].

39. Dale A. Masi, Testimony before the House Select Committee on Narcotics and Drug Control, September 29, 1989.

Index

About the Contributors

Mary M. Cleveland, Ph.D., an economist, is a past president of the Robert Schalkenbach Foundation and former director of research at the Partnership for Responsible Drug Information in New York City.

Steven B. Duke, LL.M., teaches criminal law and holds the chair of the law of science and technology at Yale Law School in New Haven, Connecticut.

Richard M. Evans, J.D., is a former executive director of the Voluntary Committee of Lawyers and practices law in Northampton, Massachusetts.

Jefferson M. Fish, Ph.D., is a professor, former chair of the Department of Psychology, and former director of clinical psychology at St. John's University, as well as adjunct coordinator of the Committee on Drugs and the Law of the Association of the Bar of the City of New York.

Robert S. Gable, J.D., Ph.D., now residing in Berkeley, California, is a professor of psychology (emeritus) at the Claremont Graduate University, where he previously served as director of the Institute for Applied Social and Policy Research.

Albert C. Gross, J.D., practices family law in San Diego County, California.

Douglas Husak, J.D., Ph.D., is a professor of philosophy and law at Rutgers University in New Brunswick, New Jersey.

Gary E. Johnson is the former governor of New Mexico.

Harry G. Levine, Ph.D., is a professor in the Department of Sociology at Queens College and the Graduate Center of the City University of New York and director of the Drug Research Group at the Michael Harrington Center for Democratic Values and Social Change at Queens College.

Jerry Mandel, Ph.D., is a sociologist in Berkeley, California.

Douglas A. McVay is the editor of *Drug War Facts*, compiled and maintained by Common Sense for Drug Policy, at www.drugwarfacts.org.

Stanley Neustadter, LL.B., a private practitioner in New York City concentrating in criminal appeals, is an adjunct professor of law at both Brooklyn Law School and the Cardozo School of Law; he is also on the board of managers of the Voluntary Committee of Lawyers.

Craig Reinarman, Ph.D., is a professor in and chair of the Department of Sociology of the University of California, Santa Cruz.